FORTUNE'S TURMOIL

D G Baulch

Paperback ISBN-13: 9798627125817
1st Edition: May 2020

Cover design by Milan Jovanovic

Dedicated to my Great-Grandfather,
Sergeant Charles Holly Phippen,
#14742, B Company, 8th Somerset Light Infantry,
Died of Wounds 26th September 1915, aged 38

Contents

Acknowledgements

This work would not have been possible without the inspiration gained from the lives and sacrifice of real soldiers of the First World War, researched over the last seven years. Men with stories so varied, from different backgrounds, social class, regions, age, education and fortune; all of which becoming heroes to me, elevated in my mind far beyond the reach of my earth-bound achievements or capabilities. The list presented here is by no means exhaustive, these few act as special homage to those who served and sacrificed. A full list of mentions would require a tome of its own.

Sergeant Charles Holly Phippen, 14742,
8th Somerset Light Infantry, Died of Wounds 26th September 1915

Driver Fortunatus Smith, T2/071445,
Army Service Corps, Died 13th December 1916

Private Thomas Pocock, 20057,
Royal Fusiliers, ex Royal Navy, Stoker (HMS Orwell), thought to have fought renowned boxer Bombardier Billy Wells.

Private Albert Jeffrey Cartwright, 1567,
2nd Welsh Regiment, Died of wounds 26th September 1915

Private Fred Breslin, 541,
13th Cheshire Regiment, Killed in action 13th May 1916

Able Seaman Harry Robert Hamblin,
Royal Navy Volunteer Reserve, Killed 25th August 1917

Private Thomas Jenkin Jones, 2020,
Welsh Guards, Killed in action 10th September 1916

Driver Albert Breedon, T2388, Royal Engineers

Private James Henry Trevis, 42103,
6th York and Lancaster Regiment, Died 22nd July 1918

Sergeant Walter Mappin, 12507,
9th York and Lancaster Regiment, Killed in action 1st July 1916

I would like to thank Jon Gliddon, friend and author, who on a drive back to Bristol inspired me to start my book, in March of 2016. Jon, having completed his first novel, Break in Communication, filled me with excitement, a yearning for what could be achieved from the comfort of my home office, imparting valuable knowledge from his own journey into self-publishing. Jon's feedback on my first draft opened my eyes to how readers perceive the narrative, leading to substantial changes, morphing the book into what I present to you today. Jon's constant and unwavering support has been instrumental in achieving my first publication.

Completing the novel while working full time, as a parent to teenage girls, has been a roller-coaster ride, in so much as most of the four years have been spent waiting for the ride to start. Varying degrees of inactivity, distraction and frustration were occasionally punctuated with furtive productivity. Having the time to commit to such an undertaking would not have been possible without the incredible support of my wife, Vicky. Taking the children away on weekends to give me the space to write, her valuable feedback from a reader unfamiliar with this genre, encouragement and positive affirmation as I explore my dream of becoming a published author and for the week staying at the wonderful Le Clos du Clocher, Gueudecourt, at the heart of the Somme battlefield, where my final draft took shape.

Huge thanks to my proof-readers, Jon Gliddon and Vicky already mentioned, my mother Val, sister Sophie and Craig Greenwood.

For the German and French translations which appear in the novel, thanks go to Carolyn Hutchison, Sophie Baulch and Julie Salviac.

Thanks also to Steve Lakeland, who listened attentively to the synopsis of my novel while walking the Somme battlefield at The Nab, in 2016.

Special mention must be given for the stunning cover design by Milan Jovanovic, bringing my concept to life through his amazing artwork.

Finally, none of this work would be possible without Mum and Dad's input over 45 years ago, thank you.

Introduction

The First World War is for many people an event of great fascination, especially during the centenary years throughout which public interest swelled the ranks of armchair historians and professionals alike. It is a multi-faceted and complex subject which boasts historical sources of such diversity and detail never before seen for a British conflict. For not only are there a myriad of history books describing the progress and execution of the war, but there also exists a vast collection of personal accounts in the form of diaries, paintings, sketches and spoken word recordings, describing the personal experiences of veterans in great detail.

It is therefore possible, with minimal research through on-line resources, to understand where and when events unfolded, at Army, Division, Brigade, Battalion and sometimes Company or Platoon level. Armed with a regimental diary and a set of contemporary military maps one can determine the exact route taken by a group of soldiers across the battlefield. For the first time aerial reconnaissance was employed to construct extremely accurate cartography of the front-line, maps which can still be used to this day to navigate the terrain of the Somme or Ypres Salient battlefields.

In the United Kingdom our landscape is decorated by historical buildings from a distant time, churches, town halls, the remains of city walls, castles and canals. But the passage of time has brought with it development, expansion, rejuvenation and consequently the world in which we carry out our everyday lives bears little resemblance to the period of the Great War, only one hundred years previous.

On the old battlefield of the Somme, however, the hills, roads and woods are as they were and where they were, before the war began. Villages and roads have been reconstructed on their original layout and the trees of old woods, dashed into splinter by years of shelling, stand tall once more observing the same boundaries to the fields which surrounded them.

Coupled with a lack of new residential development the Somme battlefield has not changed drastically at all.

A battlefield tourist can walk the frontlines, identify the topographical relics of the war and begin to appreciate the tangled web of events which was the Battle of the Somme. Evidence of the titanic struggle is still very evident on those hallowed fields. Unexploded shells are uncovered by farmers with frightening regularity, often seen piled at the side of the road awaiting collection by the authorities. Barbed wire, pottery, service buttons, spent bullets and hand grenades are not uncommon finds. One-hundred years on, the soil is densely packed with shell shards and shrapnel balls. Holding a green tarnished bullet, last handled by a British soldier a century ago, one can connect physically with a conflict which has captivated us all.

There is another aspect of the Great War which should be considered. Everyone who lived through the turbulent times was touched by the war in some way. The men and women that served in the armed forces, the nurses and surgeons, administration, munitions manufacture, farming, industry and mining and the families of the home front all played their part for the war effort. By 1916 conscription touched every family; the Total War being waged left no one without obligation to their country. These men, women and children are our close ancestors, our great grandparents, uncles and aunts. Details concerning those that had a role to play in the Napoleonic wars a century before the Great War are difficult to find, whereas the contribution of our family members in the 14-18 war can be ascertained with minimal effort online.

As a researcher I am often told by my clients that their family probably did not take part in the war. This is a common misconception. Over ten million men served in the British armed forces, teenagers and octogenarians and every age between. It is, therefore, unlikely that there is not a link to someone who served in every family. Consider also that families were larger in Edwardian times, with many siblings born at the tail end of the nineteenth century, thus increasing the chances of finding an ancestor in uniform. With surviving service records, pension records, medal rolls and contemporary newspapers it is possible to find these men and put a story to their name.

The last surviving soldier known to have served in the trenches of the First World War, Harry Patch, passed away at the age of one hundred and eleven in 2009. The generation who suffered so much for the freedom of Europe and the World have now only just passed into living memory.

And so now to the crux of the lengthy introduction. Writing a novel set in the First World War, one must truly appreciate all I have described above. With so many sources of historical information, from the mundane to the extraordinary, a work of fiction of this kind must insert itself with precision into the actual events of the war. It is well documented where each unit was stationed, on what day, what the weather was like and to some degree what they experienced. Entwining a fictional story and characters into this complex web of fact has many challenges. Firstly, literary freedom is stifled, constrained by actual events. Secondly, the names of those who served, certainly the names of commanding officers and key individuals are generally known. This leaves the author with the uncomfortable decision of whether it is acceptable to put words into the mouths of real people, assign deeds and personality to soldiers who have no ability to object to the actions prescribed to them within the novel.

Therefore, with the greatest of respect for all of those who took part in the events of the 14-18 war and the descendants of those brave men and women, the author has chosen to avoid any disrespect to the actual regiments and men of the British army, but rather to create a fictional unit, the 2nd line 8th Somerset Light Infantry, 2nd/8th for short, ensuring all the men who wear its cap badge within this work are purely fictional.

The 2nd/8th Somerset Light Infantry are attached to a real Brigade and Division who saw action during the Battle of the Somme. The experiences, conditions, equipment, timeline and indeed even the weather conditions are all historically accurate where possible. The characters within are in no way representative of actual people and any similarities with veterans of the Great War are purely coincidental.

The story within the narrative is revealed chronologically and the reader would benefit having a basic understanding of the sequence of events leading up to the Battle of the Somme on 1st July 1916. There are three distinct time periods covered in the novel which are briefly described here for those not familiar with the subject matter.

1915 and the Battle of Loos

By the summer of 1915, the British army was rapidly growing its fighting force through the training and disposition of the volunteers who had flocked to the recruitment offices in late 1914 and early 1915. So many men had applied to join that the armed forces that the government and military were struggling to accommodate their large numbers. Many recruits were not provided with a uniform let alone a weapon until the manufacturing industries of Britain could be brought to bear. The height restrictions on applicants were altered several times to either stem the number of recruits or increase them. There was a severe shortage of experienced soldiers who could be set aside from the fighting already going on in France and Belgium in order to train the civilian army and as a result older men who had served in the Army before the war, now reservists, were called upon to become Non Commissioned Officers, corporals and sergeants, to take charge of the new battalions. Many of the officers called upon to lead these new battalions had no combat experience at all.

The war was essentially a Franco-German affair and the British, upholding a treaty with Belgium, had stepped in to assist. At the start of hostilities in 1914 the British army consisted of a quarter of a million men, stationed throughout the British Empire, employed in a peace keeping role. They were, without doubt, the most modern of fighting forces at the time. Lessons learnt from the South African war had heavily influenced doctrine, training and equipment. In contrast, the German and French armies boasted a staggering size; both nations fielding forces of around 4 million men apiece. When the German army ploughed through Belgium and met the British Expeditionary Force the British were heavily outnumbered. The Germans attacked at Mons with more than 160,000 troops and 600 guns. A million more were following close on their heels. The British force, consisting of experienced and hardened soldiers threw 70,000 men into the fray.

While the British fought a gallant retreat, covering 250 miles on foot in two weeks, finally halting their fearful journey within a few miles of Paris, the constant rear guard actions and skirmishes had taken their toll. By the end of the Battle of the Marne in the tail end of 1914 the "old contemptible army" had been decimated. They would never be replaced in skill or experience. The narrative set in 1915 concerns the mobilisation of the new armies, the civilians in uniform. There was extreme pressure from the French government to press the attack in late 1915, even though the British would not be ready to deploy a significant force until the following year. With the French dictating how the war would be waged, a joint offensive was planned where the British would act as a decoy to the main French attack. The first British "big push" would occur around the small mining town of Loos en Gohelle on 25th and 26th September 1915.

It was perhaps no coincidence that the French pronounce Loos "Loss".

The build up to the Battle of the Somme

The Battle of the Somme, in 1916, was a monumental undertaking of planning and resource management. Moving hundreds of thousands of men, equipment, ammunition and artillery into place for such an assault was unprecedented. For many soldiers, with little or no experience of trench warfare, this would be their baptism of fire. Territorial forces, volunteers and regular army battalions would go into action side by side. Overall, trench life was dull and while it must be said the trenches were not entirely favourable places to live, an infantry battalion would only find itself in the front-line for a few days in every few weeks. Battalions were constantly rotated in and out of the trenches to ensure moral would not fade and to give the men time to rest. There was little rest behind the lines, the men providing labour for engineering work during the night. Trenches had to be dug, re-dug after bombardment, roads cleared, sandbags filled, supplies moved and delivered. This was back-breaking work under the cover of darkness. Often there was little let up during the day, the Army providing constant work for its manpower to keep the men distracted from their thoughts and worries and physically fit for when the time came to go over-the-top. For a few days in any rotation the men would be able to relax. The Army was keen to keep men occupied and sporting events or entertainment evenings were common. The soldiers would also be able to spend some time and money in the local French towns and establishments.

Before the Battle of the Somme some battalions had been in and out of the front-line many times, gaining experience of the conditions of trench warfare. In other cases, battalions had little experience of such things. Some old timers had been through it all before, at Loos or Festubert or Ypres. Great trench systems were dug behind the lines based on reconnaissance photographs into which thousands of soldiers practised their assault.

A myriad of shafts and tunnels were dug into the Somme chalk and clay. Striking out under no-man's-land the miners constructed large galleries beneath the German defences into which tens of thousands of pounds of explosive were prepared, ready and waiting to be detonated in the opening minutes of the huge attack.

Whereas the Second World War was a war of air power, the Great War was the conflict where artillery took centre stage. The infantry had but one purpose, to rush over and capture an area decimated by artillery, to occupy and defend after the gunners had done their dirty work. Platoon tactics and the strategies of combined arms would be developed in late 1917 and deployed en mass effectively in the final big push of 1918, but in 1916 infantry were deployed in great lines, reminiscent of the Napoleonic campaigns. Behind them batteries of guns would blaze away smashing the defences into which the men would advance. The generals had seen satisfying results with this tactic at Loos and Verdun, there was no reason to question the validity of this truly "modern" approach.

It is said the Great War fell at the wrong time, technologically. It is the only large conflict where commanders have lacked communication with their men and first-hand oversight over the battlefield. Army leadership in the 1800s had sat atop their horses surveying the field and issuing their orders, long after came reliable radio enabling communication down to the squad level. In 1916 the most effective means of communication with 100,000 men fighting in the battle was a handwritten message delivered by a runner. Carrier pigeons and messenger dogs were used by both sides, telegraph cables were laid across the countryside, into trenches and across no-man's-land to connect Brigades with Divisional HQ, Divisional HQ to Corps HQ and so on. Signallers ran about repairing cables after shelling had torn them up, often under fire these brave men might run into no-man's-land several times in a battle to ensure the telephone systems were maintained.

As a battle developed information on its progress struggled to get back to the commanders, their view of progress was skewed by the quality of intelligence reaching them. Sadly, it is too common to read about battalions making their assault as the order to call off the attack has failed to reach them in time.

The scale of the conflict is unlike anything that had ever come before. The Battle of the Somme took place between 1st July and 18th November 1916 and involved over 3 million men, over a million of them becoming casualties. In the run up to the infantry attack on 1st July the allied guns bombarded the German lines for 7 days firing over 1.5 million shells. It is said many of them failed to explode due to poor manufacturing practises in the fledgling factories swelling with unskilled labour. What is more the British employed shrapnel shells to break the barbed wire entanglements rather than high explosives. British munitions manufacturing had focused on shrapnel rather than high explosive, preparing for open warfare in rolling countryside rather than building a siege arsenal. The lead balls were no match for thick iron barbed wire. In the areas of wire which were disrupted by British shells the Germans would hastily repair them during the night.

The dawn of the attack was breaking and the manufacturing powers of Europe would throw their deadly new mass-produced machines and ordinance at each other on a dramatic scale. Into the maelstrom of steel and iron the brave civilian army of volunteers would walk proudly in their woollen uniforms and tin helmets.

The first day of battle

On the 1st July 1916, the British Army launched their infantry attack upon German defences along a fourteen-mile front, from Serre in the north to Maricourt in the south. Diversionary attacks were also pressed along the front-line, most notably at Gommecourt, two miles north of Serre. 140,000 soldiers were thrown into the assault throughout the first day of the offensive. For seven days the British artillery had pounded the German front-line and strong points. The infantry had been told nothing could survive, what was at the time, the largest bombardment in history; the barbed wire and machine gun posts would be pounded to dust.

When the first waves of attackers went over the top at 7:30am in the morning of the 1st July, it was very soon evident that the Germans had survived the bombardment and the barbed wire was not cut in many places. Within the opening phases of the assault the British Army was brutalised. Over 57,000 men had been killed, wounded or taken prisoner, many of these casualties sustained in the first two hours of the battle. In some places success was followed by failure, any gains made by the initial waves lacked the support and reinforcement to sustain them and what was left of the attacking battalions fell back.

Those that survived the hail of machine gun bullets and shell fire lay in holes, ditches and scratch trenches, waiting for help to come, night to fall, or death to relieve them. Thirsty, wounded and cut off from aid, many succumbed to their wounds under the hot July sun.

Part 1 - Anamnesis and Atonement

"The life of the dead is placed in the memories of the living."

-

Marcus Tullius Cicero

Chapter 1 - An old man remembers
Sheol Care Home

A passing lorry broke the tranquillity of the small room with a deep rumble, shaking the window and furniture from the street outside, forcing the old man to look up from his pondering. Suddenly reminded of the world beyond his recollections, his face was overcome with sorrow, the reality of his existence drifting back to him. The old man braced his forehead with a large wrinkled hand, drawing it down over his face, emerging from its shadow with flickering eyes adjusting to this world. He closed the photo album on the table before him, resting the palm of his hand firmly on its ageing cover, preventing a return to the memories held within.

Something heavy banged against the door to his room in sudden rhythmic frustration. The door swung open violently as Nancy the cleaner pushed forth with sweeping movements of her vacuum cleaner.

"Looking at your pictures again are we? Did you make it out today? No? They had some kids down from the school today, show and tell, not that they would want to see any of this I spose. My Gareth is into the war stuff you know. D-Day and all that. There was something on the telly about that the other night, the war. Did you see it? No? Don't care for it myself, I make myself scarce when he puts them on. No time for it. You know? Why look back at all that black and white stuff? Stuffy things, you know? Why look back? No sense in it, enough to worry about here and now I always say. Legs up please."

The old man strained to lift his tired limbs to one side. He longed for the strength to kick the vacuum cleaner from beneath him and stamp upon its plastic hood. But those days were long behind him. Instead he patiently allowed the annoying woman to go about her duties, her words muffled in his ears, indiscernible and unimportant. He pondered his small collection of possessions carefully, willing her to leave as he ignored her presence.

The few books he had been allowed to keep rested on the sideboard. A pocket-sized Classical Philosophers collection, the memoirs of Winston Churchill, a very decrepit copy of The Little Prince by Antoine de Saint-Exupéry and the Good News Bible. The final volume in the small collection was weary from its arduous journey through life, with a badly battered red cover and split spine, its title omitted from view by dirt, only the word "Courage" remaining.

Next to the books he had photos grouped in diverse, mismatched frames. A family group, colourful but now dated, from a wedding. Next a black and white photo of a man and woman, both in uniform; her hair worn high, his cap perching at a jaunty angle on his head. Two small photos of children faced each other; hinged at the centre and free standing. Finally, an old sepia group photo, of men in uniform sat on a waggon. Upon gazing at the final photo, the old man grasped at a distant memory, the recollections returned with full vigour and he smiled momentarily.

The cleaner bashed the sideboard without a care for the valuable items it proudly displayed. A dark framed display case, holding 3 medals and their dimly coloured ribbons clattered to the floor. The old man thrust himself forward, both arms outstretched, groaning in anger and resentment.

"Who put them there like that? That was silly wasn't it? Could do with a dust. Here, let's put them out of the way up here, less trouble that way," the woman cackled.

While maintaining her cleaning strokes she scooped up the frame and placed it face down on a shelf above the sideboard, pushing a pewter tankard to one side, thus obscuring its engraving from view. Rage reached its crescendo within the quiet man as he imagined what he would do to stop this scene from unfolding, given the strength to enact his punishment. Instead he sat, powerless and inanimate as the clumsy woman handled and belittled his objects of admiration. He remained silent, watching with an intense stare. The cleaner mumbled on to herself as she went about her chores, the old man's attention then drifted from her towards the photos he cherished so greatly.

His mind began to drift from the present scene of anguish, to a safer memory, recollecting a dinner dance in a dimly lit hall. A smell came to him, the scent of tobacco and Brylcreem. The old man smiled. Couples shuffled together locked in tight embrace while a band played its serenade to the young lovers in uniform. A large Union flag hung above the stage between two windows, their view to the world beyond blotted out by black paper and tape. A warden dressed in black with a steel helmet daubed with the letters "ARP" pushed through the dancing throng to reach the windows, where he stood for a short while inspecting the black-out preparations with the air of authority expected of a General inspecting his brigade.

The old man looked at the couples near him, scrutinising their faces. The expressions entrenched upon the lovers' faces told a bleak story. He had seen this before, a long time before. A woman staring up into the eyes of her lover, a smile firmly set upon her face but her eyes did not sparkle with joy, instead they quivered in the lamp light and at last a drawn out blink of her long-lashed eyelids dislodged a tear. Another woman, resting her head upon a soldier's shoulder, clutched at her darling's back with a talon like grip. As they slowly turned on their special spot the old man caught sight of shaking red lips and trails of mascara running over her pale cheeks. The men, on the other hand, displayed no such emotion.

The old man could feel their hidden excitement as he watched the soldiers catching glances of each other, sharing smiles and raised eyebrows. He too remembered this from a time long ago. These men longed for one thing, to be together once more, as a unit, with aspirations for heroic deeds on the battlefields of Europe; a secretive, exclusive faculty of comrades, experiencing life and adventure as no civilian could ever truly understand or rationalise. Many would spend the evening exploring the smooth lithe contents of stockings and frilled undergarments, but in truth their minds were transfixed on the day ahead of them. They would for this short while allow their partners to believe they were the soldier's muse. They were shipping out in the morning.

The old man briefly recalled a more distant memory, a troop train slowly puffing out of Taunton station many years before, the platform crammed with waving children, wives and sweethearts, obscured at once with a huge plume of white smoke from the engine. With family blotted out from the minds of the men on board they turned to each other, rejoining that sacred union of Army life which would stay in their hearts for the rest of their days.

Back in the dance hall a handsome young man, his dark hair swept tightly to the top of his head beneath an army cap, pushed his way through the crowd with a pint of mild in each hand and a cigarette clamped firmly between his lips. His right eye squinted to avoid the smoke which drifted upwards over his face.

"Here y'ar Dad," announced the Artillery corporal passing a thick handled glass to the old man.

"Thomas!" the old man exclaimed with a croak.

"Eh?" barked the cleaner, soon returning to her duties upon receiving no response.

"Let's sit, can we?" enquired the young soldier.

They made their way to some booths along one side of the hall where couples were enjoying a respite from the dancing. Finding a table, they sat,

Thomas throwing a packet of cigarettes and a lighter on the table. The old man stared.

"Still have that old thing then?" he asked.

"Of course," proclaimed Thomas proudly.

"All set then I spose," the old man announced in a sombre tone.

"First train tomorrow. Will take us down to Southampton, over by noon they say."

The old man did not respond. His son scoured his father's face but could not meet his downward gaze.

The old man took a large gulp of his drink and lurched for the packet of cigarettes without objection. Having retrieved a Lucky Strike he paused for a moment, looking down at the disk-shaped lighter. He reached into a pocket and withdrew his own. He took a long drag on the virgin cigarette. His shoulders sank back and he exhaled with an almost coital gasp of pleasure.

"You alright love?" asked the cleaner, pausing from her dusting.

"You've got those socks I gave you?"

"Yes Dad."

"And you'll make sure you tie your puttees like I showed you, not too tight at first cos when they get damp it will constrict your shins."

"I know Dad," Thomas smiled.

"Always a round in the breach as well as your ten in the clip, like I showed you, eleven is the magic number. Saved me many a time."

"I know Dad, it's all up here," Thomas tapped his head, "You've told me so many times. The stories, the tips you gave me, how could I forget any of it? It's half the reason I'm here today wearing this."

"Don't put this on me Tom," the old man's demeanour changed in an instant, "This is your choice, just like it was mine. Nobody else makes you, you do this for you, you hear me! I'd have you here with me, on the farm if it were up to me," the old man snapped.

"You'd deny me all of this and what's to come, for the farm? No, you wouldn't do that. It's in our blood Dad, in yours, in mine. You wouldn't stop me."

"I would this time," the old man shook his head.

"Poor old fool," muttered the cleaner.

"This was your life, the only thing that meant anything to you. She pleaded didn't she, she begged you not to leave again? But off you went and re-enlisted. You'd only been out for a few short years and yet, you couldn't ignore the call of the colours, could you? Get back to where you belonged. How did she react when you went? Did you feel anything that day, watching the crowds as the train pulled away? Me on the way and sis only, what three or four?" Thomas countered angrily.

"Don't bring her into it," the old man was cut short.

"Look," Thomas calmed himself, "Can we just try to, to put all this behind us, talk about something else, I'm sorry. I'm sorry you don't understand," Thomas drew another cigarette from the packet, the old man watched him as he used the old lighter once more.

"I understand son," the old man said softly.

"You don't, you should but you don't."

The two men sipped at their drinks for a while, looking everywhere but at each other, the old man finally breaking the silence.

"Lying out there, on the 1st of July 1916, in that damned shell hole, I had plenty of time to think, to properly think for the first time, about leaving them and what would have happened if I hadn't gone. Did I feel guilty, did I do the right thing? Given the chance again, would I do anything different, you know?"

"And?"

"No son. Plenty of regrets but that wasn't one of them. The Army was the only family I ever truly wanted or felt part of."

Thomas looked away, wrestling with his emotions as his father continued.

"But now, I know that I was wrong, misplaced see. I wasn't well. In here," the old man raised his eyes momentarily and looked to the ceiling, "And being in the Army, that illness was, well suppressed, no, managed. Son when you get home, the civvies they don't get any of it, they can't, how could they? You only find solitude with more of your own kind once you've been out there."

The old man stared at the burning cigarette, transfixed by the glowing embers and swirling smoke. He remembered this cigarette like it was yesterday, with such clarity, a moment in time fixed in place with a smell and a taste.

"Look out for your mates and they will look out for you," the old man composed himself and once more took up the mantle of instructor.

"Yes Dad, I know."

The old man thought for a moment.

"Helmet strap on your chin, not under here," he tapped his throat, "Pulled a young lad out of the dirt by his feet, after a shell had buried him."

"And the weight of the soil broke his neck, yes Dad, I remember."

"Fine then," the old man stubbed his cigarette out aggressively twisting it onto the tabletop.

"Don't be like that Dad, not on my last night," Thomas pleaded.

"This whole thing will be done and dusted by Christmas Dad, we'll have 'em beat soon, everyone is saying it. Then I'll be home."

The old man chuckled at the irony as a single tear ran down the right side of his face. Unblinking, his eyes swelled with moisture. He made no effort to wipe the display of grief, quite the opposite, he seemed to deny it was there.

"Dad don't, please. You went over, you did your bit, now let me," Thomas leaned forward, his brow furrowed, his voice stern.

"Oh Son," the old man sighed, "I couldn't stop you then and it's too late to stop you now. I'm proud of you son, always have been, more than you ever knew, don't think it's any other way, but it don't make it any easier every time I sit here."

"I'll write you, send when I can," Thomas reached over and cupped his dad's hand with his.

"I know. Five times, eight pages in all."

The old man turned his hand and grasped Thomas' tightly, "Eight pages is what I have of you now."

Suddenly, Nancy stood upright, adjusting her apron which had become sandwiched beneath her belly and her trousers. Tapping the vacuum cleaner off with her slippered toe she stood tall for the first time, hands on her hips. Without invite she began to talk at the window.

"It's murder, that's what it is I tell you. Honest to god, it's a crime. There's no excuse, it's not human," she moaned.

The old man's mind became sharp for a moment as he studied her words. They struck out at him with punishing clarity, ushering forth tormented images he had forced away from casual acknowledgement. What was she referring to? What did she know? He dared not ask.

"All those poor men. My Gareth is beside himself, you should hear him cursing at the telly of an evening. It's a crime see. First the miners now the newspapers. They should be ashamed of themselves. Replaced them with machines you see. Now there ain't no need for them. Those poor families, what will they do? Gareth says he might drive down on the weekend and join the picket. Silly man, he wouldn't cope without me of course, where would he get his dinner? And he has to sign on this Tuesday," she laughed suddenly with a shrill annoyance which startled the old man.

Having almost choked on her own expression of joy she launched headlong into another rant.

"Well I said you should stay out of it, it's no business of yours. He said it's principle, what's next? Nothing is safe. These bloody businessmen and politicians think they can play with people's lives, like we can be discarded. I mean how will they cope? All on the dole like our Gareth, can you imagine? Horrible times we live in, don't we? Dark days is what my Gareth says. Dark days."

With a sniff the cleaner whipped a duster out of a large pocket at the front of her apron and started to give the ornaments and surfaces a cursory going over. With every item she touched the old man felt more anguish and resentment. Her lack of respect for his important things was more tortuous than any of the draconian rules imposed on the inmates of the retirement home. The daily demeaning by the staff and the erosion of personal dignities were insignificant annoyances compared to the violation of his precious artefacts by this wicked woman.

"Where's Mary?" the old man enquired quietly.

"Mary? Who's Mary m'dear?" she responded.

"It's normally Mary that comes," he insisted.

The cleaner stopped and stood upright with both hands on her hips and scrutinised the old man properly for the first time. She paused for what seemed like an eternity, the inner ruminations of her mind made evident by the flickering of her eyes and turning of her lip. She moved to the door and pushed it closed, trapping the vacuum cleaner cable beneath it.

"Everything must be so confusing. Bless you. One day to the next, there's no difference between them, endless goings and comings out there yet nobody to see you."

"Mary comes."

The old man turned to look out the window.

"Why do they send these demons to torment me?" he pondered in frustration.

"You must have a terrible time..." she said, slowly opening the first drawer of the sideboard.

She waited to gauge his reaction at the indiscretion. The old man looked at her almost casually then restored his gaze to the outside world with tired capitulating eyes.

"...remembering where you put things. I bet you lose stuff, don't you? Poor thing. My Gareth says it doesn't matter if things go missing. You won't be long here and then it's no use to you anyways. You won't even know it's gone. Put it to better use where it's needed, he says. Not gathering dust, that's no good to anyone."

Moving to the second drawer her approach became more thorough, initial nervousness subsiding. Moving gloves aside and pulling a scarf from its dark containment she came across a leather wallet, softened by age, its rigid form a distant memory now malleable in her fingers. She stopped. Allowing the flap of the wallet to fall open she quickly peered within. Noticing the enticing disclosure of paper edges, she delved further.

"What's these?" she snapped, "No good to me, letters, are they? No good at all."

She shoved the wallet unceremoniously back from whence it came, eight old pages of notebook paper crumpled into their dark leather recess. Doing so she nudged something which had resided at the back of the drawer, unseen until now.

"Oh," she exclaimed, "Naughty old so and so aren't we? You know you can't have this in here. I'll be taking this away for you own safety. You'll be lucky if I don't tell the warden about this. Oh dear oh dear. There will be fall out over this you know."

In her stubby fingers she turned a brass disk-shaped object back and forth, admiring the embossed surface carefully. Her eyes widened as the circular brass lid flipped open to reveal a keepsake compartment. Within, a crudely cut sepia photo of a man in uniform had been wedged in place. The corners of her mouth turned downward as her attention diminished.

"Does it work?" her face became animated like that of a child opening a present.

With a flick of her fingers the flint of the lighter was engaged. She spun the small wheel once more and it grated on the flint within. A small spark lived its brief existence. Once more the lighter's wheel bit at the flint and this time a family of sparks dived and jumped in momentary ecstasy. A flame sprang forth, dancing triumphantly for its audience.

"Smoker then I'm guessing? Spose everyone was at it back then weren't they? No idea of the dangers. Can't imagine it these days, can you? My Gareth says we need something to keep our chin up in these dark days and if it's the cigs then so be it. With everything that's happening in the world, I mean the bombings and that, one minute it's a bar somewhere, next it's a plane, where will that end? Three million out of work here and strikes and that all the time. Scandals in the news whichever way you look. I'm surprised we all aren't smoking ourselves to an early grave with the worry of it. How shall we ever survive? Dear oh dear."

She turned to the old man and acknowledged his stern glare.

"It's not like the good old days is it?" she squeaked in a patronising tone fit for a child.

She was right of course; it was not like the old days and it had been this way for longer than he cared to remember. The stifling rules, the curfew, dreadful cafeteria food and almost total isolation, save for the occasional trip into the town, albeit with supervision. His treatment all amounted to an indefinite prison sentence. This one-dimensional banshee, was she just another tortuous tool employed by Sheol to break his resolve? Like so many others over time they would fail, he pondered, they underestimated him. Indeed, this lack of foresight on their part would be their undoing. Every petty attempt to unhinge him was bolstering his stubborn exterior armour.

The old man suppressed a smirk from within his frail shell; an involuntary reaction to a momentary thought which had presented itself in the limelight of his clouded mind. He eyed the drawer in which the wretched creature had discovered the lighter. Losing his precious item was a brief setback, a minor engagement in a war long fought. The real treasure lay undiscovered, he gloated internally. The small yellow pills they had attempted to trick him with every morning, safely stowed away in a brown envelope at the back of the drawer; they remained undiscovered. Acknowledging this minor victory, the room fell silent, he was alone. He would not be distracted from his memories any longer.

Murder she had said, a figure of speech surely? She could not know the truth, did they? There was murder, there were many. A long time ago, in a distant place where killing was a daily habitual pastime. The old man winced as the old memories began to invade his mind. A guilt struck out at him, tearing at his abeyant heart, forcing him to remember feelings which had been suppressed for so long.

"No," he raged, thumping the windowsill with a clenched fist, "Not like this! We'll start at the beginning, like we always do, in that damned hole."

Chapter 2 - Into the hole
No-Man's-Land

A weary soldier of the Somerset Light Infantry appeased his aching form on the muddy slope of a large shell hole, motionless save for the heaving of his chest and the sporadic blinking of his straining eyes. His gaze was cast far beyond the lone F.E.2b recon-plane which fumbled and droned its way slowly through the clear blue sky above him. What measure could be applied to the events of the day to assemble sense and order from the chaos and confusion? Wielding control over the dark thoughts which coursed through the man's mind seemed an unfathomable task; they were a dominating force, over-powering his rational consciousness, too violent and chaotic to be brought into check by his tired, stretched mind.

As they danced their macabre ceremony of pain and death before his eyes, he felt his rational mind recoiling further into the dark recesses of his being. The soldier grunted, a friendly voice in a cacophony of fear. The conscious man began to fight once more, the sudden realisation that he must win this inner struggle, or be forever lost, urging him to banish these twisted, foul scenes. With grim determination he sought to dash the troubling images from the forefront of his mind, desperately searching for reason and serenity in a disturbed whirlwind of recollections.

"Shut up, come on, shut up, shut up!" he cursed himself quietly, his anger growing steadily as he repeated his warning.

In frustration he pulled the steel helmet from his crown, allowing his head to tip back onto the soil. An exhausted grunt of appreciation and a laboured sigh of relief brought his frantic, exaggerated breathing to a slower pace. He fought overwhelming fatigue to bring his knees up the bank, planting his hobnail boots firmly on the earth beneath his buttocks thus anchoring himself in place.

"Shut up, shut up!"

His eyes remained fixated on the heavens while his bloodied right hand struggled to unbutton his service dress tunic pocket, the trembling of his fingers forcing the utmost concentration on the task. He eventually removed a crumpled packet of Capstan Full Strength cigarettes. With an upward sweep of the thumb a single cigarette rose from the packet. The soldier moistened his parched lips with the tip of his tongue before gripping the 'smoke' in the corner of his mouth. Carefully replacing the packet in his tunic pocket, the tremoring hand probed the interior for a means of lighting the cigarette. Momentarily a small brass disk was withdrawn from the pocket.

With another tired grunt the soldier brought his head upright and quickly flicked the flint wheel to spark the fuel. Inhaling deeply the cigarette was lit and immediately began its short-lived transformation to ash. His lungs tugged on the Capstan impatiently, the reward came quickly, his head sinking back to its original attitude. Still clutching the lighter at his side, he slowly traced the embossed design on its face with his grubby thumb. The brass was cold and familiar to him.

With every prolonged inhalation the Capstan burned brightly and then dwindled. Replacing the lighter alongside the cigarettes in his tunic pocket, he grasped the dying butt and flicked it into the bottom of the crater in which he lay. With a subconscious brush of his hand he cleared the ash from his filthy jacket. Only two of the general service buttons remained on the front of the tunic and the right sleeve was badly torn, up to the elbow. The sergeant's chevrons on his left upper arm hung loosely where they had been partly wrenched from the tunic. The seam of the jacket was soiled with grubby imprints; dried blood mingled with grime. However, the puttees which bound his lower legs, below the knee, were holding fast. Their robust state after such a day of activity was a testament to his familiarity with their use from his years of service.

A sudden and momentary awareness of his surroundings and a potential danger brought his senses to bear. The cigarette had bridged the gap between temporary insanity and the reality of his tenuous position. The soldier wearily scanned the shell hole, his heart gathering pace once more. The large muddy depression was some fifteen feet across, if not more; its massive expanse gouged into the earth was now the resting place of several soldiers, their motionless bodies doubled over in eternal slumber on the opposite side of the crater. The detritus of war littered the area; equipment, rifles, ammunition, bloody field dressings tangled with a soldier's webbing and a torn satchel all littered the small space around the three corpses. A wooden Mills bomb[1] crate had been unceremoniously dumped on its side, the deadly contents spilling onto the freshly gouged earth. A bundle of pickaxes and a spade, untarnished by use, lay

---

[1] William Mills, a hand grenade designer from Sunderland, patented, developed and manufactured the "Mills bomb" at the Mills Munition Factory in Birmingham, England, in 1915

abandoned beside the corpses; a tantalising irony in the midday sun, as if awaiting the undertakers return.

Further around the shell hole, lying with arms outstretched in anticipation of rescue was the body of an officer. His neck, chin and moustache were drenched in crimson from a deep gash in his throat, his once immaculate uniform torn asunder at the chest, exposing a bloodied shirt. One of his tall field boots had been half wrenched from him by some force, while the leather Sam Browne belt lay crumpled beside him, the pistol holster devoid of its charge. The dead officer and men shared their muddy grave in silent reverence.

Beyond the contents of the damp hole the lip of the crater was surrounded by knee high grass. It swayed majestically in the gentle breeze caressing the battlefield, which carried the shouts and cries of the wounded from their hidden deathbeds. The source of danger was then apparent; the poppies amongst the grass were shedding their petals like bursting fireworks. Like an invisible child scattering the flowers as they ran through the field, a German machine gunner was sweeping the scene once more from his distant vantage point on the ridge to the north. A cracking sound beat through the air like a lion-tamer's whip as Death frolicked triumphantly over the field above. A mortuary of suffering; the cornflowers and poppies an impromptu decoration for many sun bloating corpses.

Something else was moving, beyond the crater lip, the source of the distant killer's rattling attention. The soldier instinctively grabbed at his Lee Enfield rifle,[2] which was resting from the day's violent exuberance, patiently waiting to be called into action once more. Sitting upright the sergeant quickly grasped the bolt, pushed it up and then back to reveal the chamber. A .303 round was already loaded so he pushed the action back into place and the weapon was primed. He raised the rifle to take aim, resting its heavy wooden forestock on his left knee.

"Make yourself known!" he shouted with authority, eyeing the scattered Mills bombs on the opposite side of the shell hole.

"Don't shoot!" came the response, "I'm a Yorkshireman."

Emerging from the grass a young man, his face plastered in dirt save for his reddened eyes, crawled into view and tumbled down into the shell hole. Lying prostrate, panting, the terrified soldier began to sob.

"Where's your rifle boy?" the sergeant enquired angrily.

The young Yorkshireman looked back behind him as if expecting to find something in the grass.

"Back there, lost. I think. I mean I had it, then..."

---

[2] The Short Magazine Lee–Enfield is a bolt-action .303 calibre, magazine-fed, repeating rifle that served as the main firearm used by the military forces of the British Empire and Commonwealth during the first half of the 20th century.

"That's an offence, as you well know!"

"Don't shout at me! What I've witnessed this day is an offence!"

The venom and passion by which the young man's rebuff reached its crescendo took the old soldier by surprise.

"Alright lad, come now, rest. You've done your bit I'm sure."

"Done my bit, done my bit! And what part have I played in this terror? What instrument have I become, to be wielded by Godless men?"

The old soldier's stare intensified, scrutinising the young man's wild countenance. His initial reaction was to tightly shut his eyes, urging the final remnants of his fear-soaked thoughts to disperse. However, on examining his surroundings once more, the Yorkshireman was still there.

"I'm Percy, um Private Trevis, 8th York and Lancs."

He brushed his palm on his tunic several times then extended it in greeting. His counterpart placed his rifle beside him on the bank of soil and lay back, facing the sky once more. After a silence he replied.

"Fortunatus Henry Berriman, Somersets, but they call me Fortune," adding under his breath, "Only God knows why."

"One of the Seventy Disciples," Percy replied, composing himself and withdrawing his unanswered handshake.

"So I am told, yes. You know your scriptures then?"

This boy had been educated; his lack of a strong regional accent was soon explained.

"My father was the Anglican vicar at Woodkirk, do you know it? Reverend William James Trevis."

"Gather what you can from them, the day isn't over lad," Fortune instructed while gesticulating at the contorted bodies in the hole, "Fill your pockets with them Mills bombs."

"Right, yes, of course."

William Trevis, the name resonated for some reason, although Fortune could not think why. The fatigue he was experiencing drowned his conscious thought in muddy confusion. Percy took one last lingering look at his new companion, busying himself collecting anything of use from the three soldiers. He took up a Lee Enfield and attempted to clear the mud from the barrel.

"Check she's loaded, if it isn't then do so. Take as many charger clips[3] as you can from them. If they have water decant it."

Fortune spoke with a calm air of experience; Percy respected the stripes upon his arms and had no reason to question his instructions.

"What happened?" enquired Percy.

---

[3] Thin metal strip holding 5 rounds of ammunition together, ready for loading into a rifle.

"Same as happened to the rest of us today, they didn't have a chance poor sods, shell caught 'em while attending to this one's wounds," came Fortune's grim reply.

"No, I mean......what happened out there this morning?" Percy began to breathe deeply and closed his eyes once more.

"Not for us to be concerned with for now, a bloody shambles by no mistake but you and I have done enough. Can't go out there now, not while Fritz and his Maxim are on duty."

Fortune took another Capstan from his pocket and with a slight pause for his thoughts he lit the cigarette.

"Where were the 8th Yorks? They never came. We couldn't hold them forever, we just couldn't," Percy slumped onto his heels, descending into despair once more.

"Didn't leave their trenches lad, pinned down from up on the ridge. Would have been murder to let 'em cross to help us. It is what it is, no doubt we've done alright elsewhere," after a slight pause he added, "Do they have any iodide left?"

Before Percy could reply a loud explosion shook the earth to the north of the crater. Dust, soil, chalk and clumps of grassy earth began to rain down upon their small refuge. Fortune quickly snatched up his steel helmet and protected his head from further debris. Turning to his right he pulled his rifle into his body and lay face down with one hand on the rim of his helmet, securing it. Percy lay beside the three dead soldiers, pulling his knees up to his stomach, holding his helmet tightly just as Fortune had.

Another explosion rocked the field a little further off and was immediately followed by a cry of pain and screams of panic. There followed shouting between two men close by and in the periphery of his vision Fortune sensed movement. Someone was running. Almost immediately several rifle shots cracked over-head followed by the *tat, tat, tat* of a machine gun close by. The injured man continued his wailing, while the gunfire had ceased.

"Bastard," Fortune snorted under his breath; his Capstan had been put out on the soil.

"There are more, out there Fortune, like us? Trapped?" the young Percy enquired, knowing full well the answer to his questions.

"Scattered all along the front aye, waiting now, till darkness comes. The Hun are seeking us out. Don't dare bloody run boy, whatever happens, don't bloody run!" Fortune exclaimed with conviction.

"We're safe here, aren't we?" Percy hoped.

"None of us are safe, not till you're on that train heading back to Etaples with a cushy Blighty wound."

"Have you ever been wounded Fortune?" Percy probed as he turned out the pockets of one of the dead soldiers, "I keep thinking I will be brave, but how can one be sure you'll do the right thing, behave the right way?"

"Have they got any smokes? Check 'em. Yeah," he paused for thought, "I've taken one or two in my time, for Queen and country."

"Queen?" Percy stopped his foraging and sat up.

"North-West Frontier, with the 1st Somersets, long time ago mind you. Back in 97. A different world then of course. And a different enemy. We felt invincible as we marched out from Peshawar under Major-General Elles. We'd soon discover that was not the case. Caught a tribesman's musket ball up at the Bedmanai Pass," he prodded and poked at his left shoulder to show where his injury had been suffered.

"In Africa was in a tight spot, escorting a convoy we were, 19….01 I think, yes, 1901. Shot here and here."

There had been scrapes and scratches of course, too many to mention let alone recall. Percy was in awe and had so many questions to ask of the man crouching opposite him in the crowded hole. He thought better of it and allowed Fortune to continue. Removing a tobacco tin from one of the dead soldiers he tossed it across, landing short and rolling twice before resting on the earth.

"My father fought in Africa, well I say fought, he was a pastor, with a regiment," Percy explained adding, "Church of England."

"What was his name again lad?"

"William Trevis, Reverend William Trevis," the boy looked hopeful.

"Nope, thought I did but - nope," Fortune still pondered the name but thought it best to silence the line of questioning or suffer yet more unsolicited small talk from the boy.

"Broke my arm in camp on Salisbury Plain back in, oh I dunno when," Fortune smiled at the recollection, "That were my fault though."

"And in this war?" Percy felt the time was right to ask.

"We're all wounded now ain't we," Fortune delivered the line with a stern expression.

Percy observed the emotions revealing themselves on the veteran's face; a weathered face, deeply tanned and worn by a tough life exposed to the elements. The untold burden on this man's soul was evident in the frown which permanently tarnished his grim visage. His staring, strained eyes pierced all they surveyed with a cold, deliberate ferocity which unnerved Percy.

Fortune turned over, away from his interrogation and slowly edged up to the lip of the crater. Upon reaching the top of the slope he turned to face back across the dirty pit and beyond, towards friendly lines. To the north a barrage was coming down on a ridgeline in the distance, now obscured by smoke, which flashed and pulsed from deep within a swirling mass of white and grey. A machine gun rattled out across the valley, its location a mystery. The British trenches could not be seen from where he lay, obscured by the grass of the field and a smoky haze beyond it.

"How long have you been out here lad?" Fortune scurried back down into the shell hole and into perceived safety.

"21st April."

A breeze ran its invisible fingers once more through the grass surrounding the shell hole. Fortune continued his rest on the muddy incline, staring upward into the blue sky above. The sun warmed his face and for a fleeting moment all was calm. A lapwing fluttered rapidly over the battlefield, unmolested by the petty arguments of men. Its piercing song a reminder of life and freedom to the hundreds who lay concealed below.

The breeze brought with it sheets of note paper, which blew in and swooped around the shell hole like a flock of white birds coming home to roost. Countless pages, the letters from loved ones in a far-off land and the final messages home from anxious men, littered the field beyond; migrating effortlessly from the pockets of the fallen, caught in the final laboured breaths of the afternoon.

Percy was transfixed as the pages danced around the crater, coming to rest upon the bodies of the lifeless soldiers. Trapped from escaping on the wind, they floundered like dying butterflies. The young man, poised above one such fragment, plucked it from its death throws off the breast of a fallen countryman. Fortune sighed deeply and extracted yet another Capstan from his tunic pocket.

"Don't do it son. Leave their final thoughts to the ghosts, they ain't our business."

Percy began to read.

"*Dearest Mother.*"

Percy paused, his eyes filling with tears as he stared at the paper before him, held tightly in trembling hands. Even in his distressed state he did not appreciate the impact those first two words would have, their simple syllables forcing a knot upward in his dry throat. He could not continue without a shameful loss of stolid composure. At last he folded the papers in silence and tucked them into the tunic of the dead soldier beside him.

Fortune smiled grimly.

As Percy's grief deformed into anger, he recalled a text of his own to fill the void and bolster his resolve.

"*For if you will indeed obey this word, then there shall enter the gates of this house kings who sit on the throne of David, riding in chariots and on horses, they and their servants and their people. But if you will not obey these words, I swear by myself, declares the Lord, that this house shall become...*[4]"

---

[4] Jeremiah, Chapter 22, Verses 4-5, (ESV)

"...a desolation," Fortune interrupted.

With a troubled demeanour he watched the young lad struggling with his emotions once more. Forcing his eyelids shut, with a grimace of determination, Fortune willed himself to recall by gone times; anything to wipe from his focus the events of the day. With every memory which he forced to life, with every small detail and image recalled, his mind was distracted from the anguish which presented itself in this oppressive hole. He remembered happier times at the outbreak of the war; a warm yet stormy summer spent in Aldershot. Bicycles on tow paths. A young brunette woman and the dark privacy of a cinema during a Saturday matinee. Clean clothes. Cold beer. Soft linen caressing his feet in a comfortable bed. A warm deep bath. Running his fingers through his daughter's hair while she slept. Holding his new-born son beside the hearth. The compression blast of a shell forcing air from his lungs. Terror in the eyes of his comrades. The emotionless vacuum of killing at close range.

Torment had once again broiled to the surface of his mind, washing away his fragile constructs like blood from a surgeon's table. Vivid recollections of horror loomed dominantly before his mind's eye. A low stone wall. Screams. Men screaming. Shouting. Gun fire. Smoke. Explosions. Fragments of stone, kicked up by an unseen force, striking his face. Sweat pouring over his eyes. Blood fouling the ground at his feet. Kneeling. Curling tightly his whole body beneath the shadow of the wall. Hands tugging at his tunic. Then silence. Stillness. Lifeless bodies against a low stone wall in the searing heat. A stench, foul and relentless. A cry from afar, unanswered.

Chapter 3 - Home comforts
No-Man's-Land

"Sergeant! Sergeant wake up! Wake up! Fortune!" Percy's voice recalled him suddenly from his distant recollections.

Fortune jerked and sat up with a start, grabbing Percy around the throat instinctively, shaking him violently and pressing his thumbs firmly into his windpipe. As his clouded mind returned to the present, he realised his surroundings, releasing his grasp immediately. Percy slumped beside him coughing and gagging for air. Fortune could hear the explosions from his dream, muffled and distant at first, becoming more real, growing in intensity. He sat up, moved to all fours and made his way up to the grass line. He reached back and grabbed at Percy, frustrated at his incapacity.

"They're bombing up the line," he exclaimed excitedly, "If we make it to them lad, we'll be amongst friends at least."

Percy turned to face Fortune, his reddened eyes gleaming with moisture.

"Come on boy, you get the Number Fives,[5]" Fortune pointed to the overturned box of grenades. He slid back down to the base of the crater and snatched up his webbing which had been discarded near the body of the officer. Percy, slowly at first, began to gather his equipment. He filled a canvass bag with as many of the pineapple shaped bombs as he could. Meanwhile Fortune checked both rifles were fully loaded. Once satisfied he passed one to Percy. Then, withdrawing his blood-stained bayonet from its scabbard he rapidly affixed the blade to his rifle in one fluid movement. Percy followed suit, clumsily removing the 17 ½ inch bayonet from his own webbing. His hands trembled as he pinched the locking mechanism, struggling at first to find purchase with his clammy fingers. With a click, his rifle became a medieval pike.

---

[5] No. 5 Mk.1 Mills Bomb

Percy took a deep breath and crawled up the earthy bank to the grass line, to join Fortune who waited for him on the lip of the crater. He closed his eyes and muttered a short prayer, clutching something hidden about his neck as he did so.

"Spirit of Love and Truth,
Breathing in grosser clay,
The light and flame of youth,
Delight of men in the fray,
Wisdom in strength's decay;
From pain, strife, wrong, to be free.
This best gift I pray.
Take my spirit to Thee,[6]*"*

Fortune said his own words under his breath and kissed the brass knuckle duster which now furnished his right hand.

"There's a sap just beyond the wire, twenty yards or so. We'll dash and crawl. Keep your rifle up or she'll anchor in the ground. When we get into the sap, I want you to hand me bombs, no matter what is happening, keep them coming. Understand?"

"Yes."

Percy's face was pale, a stark contrast with the red of his eyes. His facial features were exaggerated by the dust and dirt about his cheeks and chin. His lips were cracked and his tongue darted from side to side within his open mouth. His wide, blood-shot, unblinking eyes stared into the abyss. Like the dead rising from their earthy graves, both men emerged from the crater and ran.

There was no time to take in the surroundings, both men devoid of reason, charging forward as an animal flees from a fire. Percy fell behind his mentor, not knowing where to run. The advance lasted for an eternity; all sounds ceased save for the straining of his lungs and the surging of his blood in his ears. He felt weightless. Disconnected from his body he observed Fortune, doubled over, striving forward with an expression of determination on his stern face. Percy heard his mother calling him. Softly at first, but somehow far away, her gentle voice subdued the scene of devastation before him, replacing the visceral intensity of the experience with a vivid memory from his childhood. He ran along the lane towards the vicarage. Still she called. Turning into the garden he could smell the meat pie steaming in the kitchen. Tossing his stick to one side he ran headlong into the open door.

Having sprinted several yards from the crater Fortune slammed himself down to the ground. A bullet cracked overhead as Percy passed him at speed, a broad smile playing across his dirty face. The young

---

[6] Prayer by Henry Charles Beeching (1859-1919)

Yorkshireman was laughing. Instinctively Fortune jabbed out the butt of his rifle to trip his companion, who, stumbling over his own feet landed roughly on his chest and chin.

Fortune began his military crawl; right arm forward, left leg diagonal at the knee. Left arm forward, right leg diagonal at the knee. All the while his body dragged along the ground. He soon reached Percy who was lying stunned in the grass. Fortune did not stop. In his limited vision he could see several bodies hanging over barbed wire entanglements ahead of him. The sap was just beyond to the right. He changed direction and moved diagonally in front of Percy who was now groaning into the dirt.

Passing between the broken corpses of two British soldiers he soon reached the wire. The thick mass of metal had been tossed and thrown and twisted in the days of bombardment which preceded the attack. In places it was so thick that no light could penetrate, other sections had been pulled apart revealing significant gaps. The sap, he remembered, was clear of wire. He could see timber, splintered and charred, lying about a long mound of chalk and dirt. Bullet casings littered the ground and a Brodie helmet sat up-turned on the summit of the soil heap, beside a disembodied outstretched hand, pleading for a donation to this church of suffering before he entered to seek his salvation. This was the sap, a trench dug perpendicular to the front-line, probing out into no-man's-land so its occupants might hear some indication of his enemy's activities after dark. Earlier that morning the British had poured out from their own saps into the incessant fire of German rifles and machine guns. There had been a strong resistance here that morning, Fortune remembered.

The sounds of fighting some distance to the right were growing in intensity. Indiscernible shouting and rifle fire were punctuated with the muffled bangs of exploding grenades. With a final glance back at Percy, who was now crawling forwards, Fortune picked himself up and flung himself over the soil heap into the trench.

What had been a sizable excavation was now no deeper than a few feet. Its sides had either collapsed or been blown outward and any uniformity was long since pulverised. The ditch was filled with body parts and corpses, discarded weapons and equipment; the refuse of war lay thickly in the shallow excavation. Soldiers, those who still resembled men, lay in agonised and contorted attitudes throughout the trench. Crouching, watching for danger, Fortune paused, motionless. The morning's battle had passed on by, like a famine ravaging a biblical land. Nothing was alive here.

Percy slithered into the sap, gasping for air. Without stopping to ascertain his condition, Fortune moved forward. With exaggerated steps he made his way through the mass grave. The sap was far from straight and offered cover to them now as they advanced slowly. As they progressed further, the number of dead men became less frequent. By the time they reached a kink in the ditch it was only one body deep in death.

Percy stopped at the macabre scene of two soldiers embracing. A German and a Tommy, lying with one another, arms wrapped tightly about each other's torsos. The nature of their wounds could not be determined. They were, as if asleep in the sun. Percy crossed himself instinctively at the terrible sight.

Fortune had stopped up ahead and Percy came to join him. Fortune raised a finger to his lips. Footfalls on wooden boards could be heard, close by. Suddenly the distinctive sound of German voices conversing softly made Percy's blood run cold. Fortune, focusing on the kink in the trench, held his open hand back towards Percy, who fumbled in his canvass bag for a Mills bomb.

Upon handing one to Fortune he was surprised Fortune had not taken it fully. Fortune turned to him sharply, a quick nod indicating Percy's folly. The vicar's son pulled the safety pin from the top of the grenade. Fortune held the deadly device tightly, his fingers holding the strike lever firmly in place. As soon as he released the bomb the lever's spring would spark the fuse into life.

The unseen Germans were talking once more in hushed exchanges beyond the muddy wall. It was time to act. Fortune edged forward ever so slightly, then with a surge of movement launched the grenade around the corner.

"*Grenate!*" a German shouted in terror as the metal egg bounced from one side of the trench into their midst.

There was a loud thud and the trench was instantly full of dust as debris belched out of the top of the muddy channel, falling all around Percy and Fortune as they moved around the kink to see their adversaries. Fortune dashed into what was once a square, timber lined area with wooden boarding as a floor. Seven days of British bombardment had reduced the well-engineered construction to a shamble of soil and splinters.

Two German soldiers lay crumpled against the far wall, fresh wounds issuing forth blood onto the dirty planks where they had died. Beside them a stretcher held another corpse. Bloody bandages smouldered beside a wooden first aid box containing smashed bottles. To the right a short platform allowed access to a covered vantage point, a machine gun post. Leading off from the area to the left was a more substantial trench. A similar exit could be seen to the right, beyond the platform.

Moving into the bloodied station Fortune nearly crashed into a German soldier who ran from the left-hand trench. Fortune's reactions saved him from a confrontation, shooting the soldier in the chest at point blank range. In an instant he reloaded his rifle by pulling back the bolt and pushing a new round into the breach. Another German clattered out of the opening and straight into Fortune, who without time to raise his rifle to meet the aggressor, smashed the rifle butt upwards into the face of the oncoming foe in a low arc. The German collapsed beside his comrade; his jaw obliterated by the force of the blow. Blood gushed from his head covering his dirty grey uniform within seconds.

Germans were shouting from further down the left-hand trench, their exultations were soon followed by a stick grenade, which twirled its way into the redoubt in a low arc. Fortune was well versed in the weapon's disadvantage, its long fuse. He snatched up the grenade by its haft and lobbed it back into the trench from whence it came. There was an instant bang, Fortune shielded his eyes as earth and debris billowed out of the opening.

Fortune's dry throat strained to make an audible sound, "Come on lad, we won't get through that way, have to go around!"

Percy looked on in shock as Fortune disappeared into the dusty opening, rifle cracking rapidly as he egressed. Suddenly alone in the carnage, Percy froze. The sap from which they had emerged clawed at him offering safety and concealment. The British bombing party could be heard fighting their way up the trench-line to the right. There were also Germans to the right, between him and their salvation and clearly Germans to the left where Fortune had advanced. Percy's fear was soon compounded by a noise to his immediate left. One of the Germans, who until a few moments before had sheltered here, was still alive. He began to cough and then moaned in pain.

Percy gathered up his rifle clumsily and started over slowly towards the injured man. He reloaded his rifle as he went, expending an unused round onto the dirt at his feet. Percy prodded the man with the tip of his bayonet, the injured man was too badly maimed to give any reaction. Glancing quickly at the two exits Percy placed his rifle against the muddy wall. Crouching by the German, ensuring no contact was made, he visually searched for something he could do to aid his enemy. Percy's concern turned to horror when he caught sight of the gold crucifix, hanging on a light chain, protruding from the German's shredded tunic. In disgust Percy backed away, snatching up his rifle and he headed quickly down the trench to catch up with Fortune.

The German front-line trench was littered with bodies, from both sides. What had once been a deep, timber-lined trench was now little more than a smashed gully in the chalk. Earth had collapsed into the wooden passage partially covering the bodies of many of the silent occupants. Limbs protruded from beneath the soil, arms outstretched with contorted fingers, poised to tear at Percy as he moved forward. Fresh corpses lay gasping upwards at the sky. A boot with its foot still residing within stood proudly on what remained of the fire step. There was no sign of Fortune.

Breathing deeply Percy continued. The front-line trench twisted and turned at regular intervals, every section enough to station a few men. Each traverse took the ditch at right angles to itself; behind each turn another small stretch of trench and yet another traverse. Fighting earlier in the day had been brutal and costly here. Once into the trench the attackers had been faced with its constantly changing direction and defensible corners. Each turn had witnessed a fierce battle, a fight with bombs and bayonet, every yard costing lives. British dead lay in their multitude here. Now disfigured and twisted in the afternoon sun, the sons of the Empire had been slaughtered, for several yards of a muddy ditch.

The world outside of the twisting trench was invisible to Percy as he sought his companion. Any sense of direction had long since eroded. At every traverse Percy listened for signs of life but there was none. The German army could have been yards away beyond his muddy passage and he would not have seen them. It was claustrophobic, the stench terrible. Navigating around a collapsed traverse Percy came upon a pile of bodies, resting against a barrier of wood and barbed wire which had been placed across the trench.

The trench had been plugged to stop further advance, a terrible conflict occurring here for its control. A confused Percy looked for Fortune in the chaotic collage of death which engorged the furrow. As he stood there panting, his mind raced considering fully his extremely dangerous position. Alone in a German trench with his mentor nowhere to be found, far from the British lines, he crouched and wept. All sense of time escaped Percy as he waited, his mind paralysed from rational thought. His fear of what lay beyond cemented him to his grotesque spot, exasperated and confused. Unable to decide on a course of action he remained for some time, hoping the whole damn war would pass him by.

Chapter 4 - Two sides to turmoil
Mittenwald

Fortune was enjoying a well-earned rest, slouched on a wire frame bed deep within an abandoned German dugout. He panted for breath between every large guzzle of Schnapps from its dusty green glass bottle. A bombardment was falling close by, each shell-burst reverberating through the earth. Crump, crump, a pause then another crump, they continued to fall. Dust and dirt, dislodged from the ceiling, fell like spits of summer rain. A short length of plank, nailed to a ceiling beam, bore the word "Mittenwald" in black capitalised characters before another shell, landing far above, scored an insignificant victory, bringing the crude sign crashing to the floor. Despite the cosmetic damage being inflicted, the dugout was deep and well-constructed. Thick timber and concrete thirty feet below ground was too great a target for the British 18-pounders[7] which fell on the surface above. Fortune sighed; he was stuck down here until the barrage lifted. Where was the boy?

Candlelight illuminated the enclave with its flickering yellow flame, bringing dancing shadows to life as the soft glow caressed the contents of the shelter. Fortune, with feet up on the bed and knees spread wide, quickly finished the bottle and tossed it to one side onto the bed to join the others who had eagerly given up their contents moments before. He lit a Capstan and enjoyed its relaxing vapours for a few moments, until his solitude was rudely interrupted by yet more shellfire above.

"I'd offer you one but - any more Kraut booze?" snorted Fortune wide eyed, "Well?" he snapped, "Got any more? Where is it? Hey...I'm talking to you!"

---

[7] The 18-pounder gun was the standard British Empire field gun of the First World War-era, firing a 18.5 pound projectile up to 6km

His voice raised to a shout as he reached for a Schnapps bottle and threw it across the dugout, smashing it above the shaking figure who rested against the far wall.

"*Ich verstehe nicht! Ich kann kein Englisch!*" came the response from a terrified German soldier, cowering on the floor opposite the bunk, his arms in front of his bloodied face to protect him from more brutality.

Fortune grunted in annoyance, dragging himself to his feet. Stumbling across the small room he started displacing items from a table and shelves. Tin plates and cutlery clattered to the floor, then Fortune turned his attention to a tired sideboard, propped against the timber wall. The sideboard had seen better days in a French farmhouse behind the lines, now a shadow of its former self, covered in dust and despoiled by months of uncaring use. Its contents were of no interest to Fortune in his hunt for alcohol. The futile search ended with an angry outburst as Fortune lashed out at a chair, smashing it under the force of a stomp and a kick from his hobnailed boots.

"Where's the fucking booze?" raged Fortune.

He grabbed another discarded bottle from the cot bed, marched over to the terrified German and forced it into his face, pointing at the drained vessel angrily.

"*Unterm Bett! Unterm Bett!!*" the soldier screamed, clasping his head in terror.

"The bed?" Fortune shouted, pointing behind him for confirmation.

"*Ja, Bett, Bett*" pleaded the desperate German.

Fortune tugged and thrashed at the cot bed like an enraged animal testing the bars of its cage. With the cot bed torn from its housing, a hollowed out recess in the wall of the dugout, Fortune shoved the ruined frame to one side, kicked the mattress out of his way and stood peering down at a shallow wooden crate with a hinged lid, flanked by short rope handles.

Fortune began to laugh, a broad smile and wide eyes replacing the grimace and frown which had tortured his dark face only moments before. He crouched above the box, his fingers poised, outstretched and flexing.

"Fortune no! Stop!" Percy exclaimed, his voice breaking as his dry throat strained.

The young soldier stood at the bottom of the stairway, his eyes flicking between the two men nervously.

"What's happening?" Percy raised his rifle momentarily with the German in his sights, then lowered it, then raised it once more.

"Bastards are hiding the booze from me boy," Fortune whispered, "Come help me."

"What? Don't touch the box Fortune, don't do it," Percy slowly swung the rifle to bear on Fortune, "Step away," Percy's voice broke, "Please."

Fortune turned to face Percy, rage pulsing through his very fibre. He stood slowly, fists clenched at his sides. He stared at the face of the young man. Percy was covered in dust and dirt, his eyes bloodshot and filling with moisture, his mouth quivering while a dry tongue flicked over his lips. Fortune's expression turned momentarily to that of confusion. His eyes darted around the floor in front of him as if searching desperately for an answer. Inhaling deeply his focus locked onto the young lad once more who stood before him. His frown returned and nostrils flared.

Fortune took a step towards Percy.

Percy edged back slightly but then stood his ground, reaffirming his aim at the frenzied Fortune.

"Don't touch the box Fortune. Even I know what it might be. What are you doing? We haven't come this far today of all days to be blown to bits in search of a drink? You've had plenty, it's clear to see, you don't need..."

"Don't ever presume to tell me I have had enough boy!" Fortune interrupted, "What do you know of it?"

"What are you doing? We're in a German dugout Fortune! We're trying to find the others, I thought. What have you done here?! Explain to me, educate me, I'm scared Fortune. We need to leave, now!"

Percy was clearly distressed. This Fortune was not one he recognised from above; this was unexpected and terrifying considering his current situation.

"What do you know of the pain a soldier carries with him every day?"

"I grew up in the shadow of my father's torment Fortune. A torment earned on the battlefields of South Africa, played out through destructive verses in the village of Woodkirk, behind closed doors. He suffered Fortune, for what he saw men do to each other, the great abyss open before him filled with man's destructive desires. God gave him his strength to survive. While his temper was short his faith was broad, firm. There was no drink in our home for we had Jesus in our hearts."

"You smelt it this morning, didn't you? How could you not have? That unforgettable aroma of rum and cordite, hanging over our lines like the wings of an angel; that's our protection boy. It shields us from the sin we must commit, from the sights we must behold and after our work is done, she numbs the guilt and revulsion so the lucky ones might sleep. So, don't ever tell me I have had enough, there is no such quantity to remove the stain which blights my soul. I've done my killing and now I need a drink."

"Now is not the time," Percy pleaded.

"There is always time," Fortune snapped.

Percy considered another approach.

"God is our salvation in such times of need; he listens to us, comforts us with the words of his Son Jesus Christ, and empowers us, the righteous, as we fight in his name. Drink you speak so highly of is not an angel Fortune, it is the devil, you have been deceived. Listen to me Fortune. I saw men staggering out of our trenches, hardly able to walk forward, blind to the peril that requires a man's wits to survive. The perverse stench of rum and blood, lives thrown away through blind drunkenness. Gather your senses, please. Focus. We are not safe here! I need your help!"

"Lives were thrown away regardless of sobriety boy. They were thrown away against machine gun and shellfire and barbed bloody wire. If a soldier cannot go to his early grave with a belly full of rum and a smile on his face, then this isn't the British bloody army."

Fortune stepped closer pointing randomly off to the ceiling, "Captain Morecombe, A-Company, two bottles of scotch of a morning just to feel 'straightened out'. He strode over no-man's-land like a true hero and didn't the boys know it. Our courage doesn't come from here," Fortune slapped his chest, "It's from the bottle. God has no place here, he does not quench my thirst or heal my pain or help me sleep. God left me years ago and he has left this place today for good."

"You are wrong Fortune, it doesn't have to be that way. Talk to God and he will listen. We have all witnessed things we will struggle to rationalise but unlike them," Percy waived his rifle at the German, "We are not animals, feral and violent by nature, reacting to these events in a primal manner. We do not seek to despoil all that is pure and natural in this world, we are here to protect it. The instincts of the Devil, the beast, are manifest in you because of this poison. Accept God on your right hand and we march into battle, sober, knowing we are protected. Those that have fallen have done so with honour and are at his side now."

"Percy, you are full of shit. There's no mistake. But your words distract me. There were many of your type in India; Temperance wives and padres, meddling in the affairs of poor old Tommy. Good whores and regular rum rations, that's the fuel for an army, that's the drum that beats the march for us. And the fight, I wouldn't miss the fight for anything, if it weren't for the nightmares that follow. Why should my soul be so plagued with guilt for something I enjoy? But the drink detaches me from this weakness of mind."

"You enjoy the bloodshed?" Percy was clearly horrified at the thought.

"Yes, yes I do. Not all mind, much of it is senseless, but I grew to like it. The good ones."

"You are drunk Fortune, you don't mean that, nobody can feel that way. It's a necessary evil to get this work done. A sin yes but to counter a greater sin, it can be absolved for the greater good."

"No boy, for you maybe, but for most they signed themselves up for a fight, to kill, to butcher, to maim," Fortune took another step forward.

"It's not true. We are good men. We are not animals Fortune. We answered the call to arms, to protect our nation, our people, from tyranny. These are normal hard-working people Fortune, from every walk of life. We are not butchers. We are not criminals. We were forced into this situation by Them. We stand up for what is right and proper in this world. That is the truth. This is our crusade."

"When that whistle blows, we become what we want to be, deep down. The beast, as you put it, comes forth. We fornicate, drink and kill, in the King's name."

"Stop it, your tongue is poisoned Fortune."

"Where else can a man feel truly alive? Unbound by the laws of our land, actively encouraged to take lives with brutality and without mercy,"

Fortune hunted in a pocket and brought forth a crumpled piece of paper reading from it once he had flattened the creases.

"The following red and blue establishments should be considered off limits in the city of Amiens. There's a big list of knocking shops here, followed by a bigger list of brothels which are clean. This isn't just turning a blind eye Percy, this is a helping hand. Have you seen the queues of Tommies scratching themselves into oblivion outside the MO's tent? Then there's the rum and wine and beer, spirits for the officers, in such huge numbers it makes your eyes water just thinking what an endeavour it is to get it here for us; what an undertaking to keep us drunk! We are armed, taught to kill, shown where to fuck and fuelled with alcohol. There is nothing civilised or Godly about this army Percy. It is an army of sin, built to sin, fuelled to sin. That's how we'll win."

"You are wrong, Fortune. Your words do not deter me from my clear conscience. I stood in line at the recruitment office, with my friends, colleagues, peers. We didn't lust for death and carnage; we were doing the right thing, for our country, for the world. The adventure was calling us, to see other countries and experience new things. Many of the lads hadn't eaten so well in all their lives. Some joined up to impress their sweethearts, others to escape the monotony of the factories, the deprivation of the city alleys and yes some were full of bravado for teaching the Hun a lesson. We'd all seen the pictures in the periodicals. We knew what we were facing, unrestrained evil and barbarism. But we had no desire to become the perpetrators. Duty above all other influences made us stand in line. There was no desire to kill in us that day, instead a calling, to do the right thing," Percy put all he was worth into his explanation, leaving him drained at the finale.

"Bollocks, in my day we joined up cos the law was after our hides, or our stomachs were tired of eating themselves while we slept. Why pay for your booze when the Army will provide it and a sovereign for your other needs? Crack some heads and get paid, better than the beatings for free that landed you in front of a magistrate."

"What made you this way Fortune? You are tormented. You were a pillar of strength up there," Percy pointed upwards with his rifle, "You were the centre of my world for a moment, my only escape, a saviour. That's the real you, I know it. A good man."

"A good man? Ha! If only you knew. It's but a distant memory," Fortune paused for some time leaving Percy to deal with the uncomfortable interlude.

Percy looked over at the German who had remained crouched, apprehensive but relieved that the focus of the heated engagement was not himself. The soldier could not have been older than he was. Percy quickly dismissed his curiosity and turned his attention to Fortune once more.

"Tell me then, while we wait for this barrage to lift. But please let's get out of here once it does," Percy lowered the rifle.

"Do you have family boy? People who care for you back home?"

"Yes."

"I figured as much."

"My Mother Anne. A sister, younger, Beatrice."

"A sweetheart?"

Percy blushed but his momentary exposure was hidden beneath the dirt on his face.

"Well, yes. We are on a promise," Percy confessed.

"I had all that once. Now there is nothing for me back there. A soldier doesn't need that. We are stronger without it you know. Nobody stressing. Nobody to disappoint," Fortune consoled himself and strengthened his resolve.

"I care Fortune, God cares," Percy suggested.

Fortune's mood shifted once more for the worst. Once again, his nostrils flared with two deep inhalations of the rank dusty air.

"August 1914, do you remember it? The call to arms. Reservists mobilised. Eager recruits clamouring to wear uniform."

"Yes, of course I do."

"Signed on again at Taunton, by mid-August I was in Aldershot. Stripes on my arm and boys to train up. The Major remembered me from the South African war. Wanted me to serve with him once more."

"Must have been exciting?"

"Aye was good to be in uniform again. I'd missed it. But I had family now. Not like back then, without attachments or responsibility. A wife, children. Leaving them behind to chase a memory of my youth. A happier place from a bygone age. The Army is your family, you see. And while those at home like to think they are the most important aspect of your life, it's not true. Your buddies, companions, fellows who will fight and die by your side, they are your true family. You'd think it would be hard to walk away from your home, your missus, your little girl, baby boy. But it's not. You know what's waiting for you at the other end. This way of life gets under your skin boy, in or out of the Army it's never forgotten. Always there.

It was a Sunday, my papers had arrived and the train would leave at noon. I'd packed two days before and been restless ever since. Drinking, yeah there was drinking. To pass the time, calm the nerves. We didn't part on good terms lad. Put it that way. Was the last time I saw them."

"I don't..." Percy had not time to formulate an adequate response before Fortune continued.

"Drowning. The newspaper said it was a drowning. Mabel had tried to go in and save her, got in trouble herself. They found them both at the ford near the schoolhouse. Didn't go to the funeral. Couldn't get away," Fortune's lip curled slightly at one side as the emotions churned within him.

"Fortune, I am so sorry. That's terrible, you must have been..."

"I've had to cope with many deaths. Some tragic, some deserved. But none with a sting such as theirs was. This war killed them, they would be alive today if I had been there."

"You can't possibly know that or blame yourself."

"Can't I? Who do I blame then? Who will carry that burden on their shoulders for me? This little shit here?" Fortune was incensed again.

Arm outstretched pointing at his captive he raged.

"These fuckers started all this shit. These fuckers made us come here!"

"Yes but," Percy needed a moment to construct his response.

"Every last fucking one of them will suffer for this, but until I'm satisfied they have paid their debt this yoke around my shoulders will not subside. Its weight is unbearable, yet I must bear it. Every bloody day. That's why I drink lad. I'd sleep soundly if it were not for the pain which tears me apart from within. None of this hell here can compare to the knife which twists in my guts every morning, when I wake up and realise I am still alive and helpless to save them."

Before Percy could respond Fortune took one more step forward, grabbed the fore stock of Percy's rifle in a blindingly fast movement and snatched it from the startled soldier's grasp. With his free hand he punched the young man directly in the chest sending him tumbling against the wall of the stairwell.

"So, don't ever fucking tell me I've had enough to drink!" Fortune bellowed.

Fortune turned to the German, who had been watching the scene unfold before him in terrified silence. The German edged himself further into the corner as Fortune's intense stare scrutinised him.

"Do you think he is any different to us?" Fortune pondered suddenly calm, "Is he any more deserving of a bullet than I?"

Taking up Percy's rifle Fortune pulled back the bolt to inspect the chamber. Confirming it was loaded he pushed the bolt back into place with a sharp movement and raised the weapon to take aim at the German soldier. The German reacted with panic, scampering with feet and hands moving himself backwards further into the corner of the dugout.

"*Nein, bitte , bitte nicht , nein! Ich habe eine Familie! Ich habe Kinder, kleine Kinder! Bitte! Bitte!*" the terrified soldier pleaded for mercy.

"Fortune don't! Please!"

Percy was barely able to speak, still reeling from the punch which had winded him so badly.

"Bestial you said, primal you said, and an enemy to the natural world, you said. They should be destroyed should they not? Give me one reason why I shouldn't end this one now."

"I know but, it's not the same, this is not right Fortune."

Percy tried to stand but slumped back to where he had fallen.

"Not the same?" Fortune paused, turned to Percy and waited for his response.

The German began to plead once more, his face showing utter desperation. His intent was clear even though neither of them could understand his words. Fortune pushed the tip of the rifle into the German's forehead sharply and shouted for him to be quiet. The German quivered and whimpered but said no more.

"You can't murder him, it's murder Fortune. He is unarmed, your prisoner. You mustn't."

"Murder? You've changed your tune boy, a minute ago they were the Devil. Now you are trying to save him. So, which is it?"

"You are twisting my words. You know it's not the same, war is war and this is murder. They are not the same thing."

Percy once more attempted to stand, using the wall to steady himself, he stood awkwardly. The young man staggered a few painful steps towards Fortune, stopping short by a few yards. On the wall above the cowering German soldier, a wooden crucifix and Christ hung on a nail. Percy was transfixed, reviled by the conflicting emotions which surged within him. He paused to watch Fortune standing over the defenceless German, rifle prodding relentlessly at his chest and head. A similar scene already emblazoned in Percy's mind from the illustrated family bible at home.

Fortune lowered the rifle.

"You see boy, this is exactly what war is. Me and him. Soldiers both. Our job is to kill each other. Your righteous ideals hide the grim truth of what is actually happening here; men killing each other because other men have told us to. Strip it down to its bare bones and what do you have left?

Me standing here with a rifle putting a bullet in his head. At least I have good reason to end him. Unarmed you say? You create rules to satisfy this idea you had that war is in some way governed by morals. I step outside of your lawful war making and become a criminal? Bollocks. We've shelled them for seven days and nights. How many do you think have perished in their trenches and dugouts, sheltering as best they can from the rain of death? Mass slaughter is justified somehow and yet I can't plug a bullet into this man's skull?"

"You can't Fortune, you shouldn't. A good man wouldn't. There is a line there, albeit an elusive and poorly defined one but there the line is, between human decency and depravity. Yes, you are right, it makes no sense here, you win, you've made your point for goodness sake but you know this is wrong."

Fortune grabbed the German by his collar and dragged him across the floor. The German fought against his strong grip to no avail and was soon dumped face down beside the wooden crate beside the remains of the cot.

"Open it," Fortune demanded, "Open it, O-PEN, O-PEN!"

He raised the rifle once more aiming at the German's face, slowly backing away towards the stairwell.

"O-PEN the fucking box!" Fortune shouted.

"*Nein, nein, bitte*," the German sobbed.

"Open the god dammed box."

Percy edged along the wall of the stairwell and peered up to the first landing. The shellfire above had intensified or become closer, it was hard to tell, the dugout shaking nervously following each explosion. More and more dust fell from the straining ceiling.

"Please Fortune, stop," Percy tugged gently on Fortune's tunic in childlike desperation for an adult's attention.

The German slowly sat himself up beside the wooden crate. He looked back at Fortune who shook the rifle at the wretched prisoner to proceed. The captive inspected the crate; the lid had not been nailed into place. Trembling fingers lightly grasped the container. Once more he looked back at Fortune.

"Do it!" Fortune shouted.

A tremendous crash directly above them was followed by a biblical thunder, shaking the room and its contents violently as the shell exploded. The ceiling splintered and groaned, dust falling throughout the chamber, snuffing the candles and plunging the dugout into darkness. Percy leaped at Fortune, grappling with all the strength he could muster.

Chapter 5 - Fortune's fable
No-Man's-Land

Percy awoke to find Fortune grinning gleefully at an array of items carefully laid out between his legs.

"At last," Fortune exclaimed, "Look at all this lot, cornucopia of wonder this is."

"Where are we?"

Percy pushed himself up on the muddy incline of the shell hole.

"Same place you started. Now - look see, I've three virtually unused packets of Capstans, a handful of Woodbines, Black Cat - not to be fussy but I doubt I'll have those, two tins of baccy, a bottle of beer and this monstrosity."

Fortune held up an ostentatious white pipe with a huge decorated bowl.

"German of course, they ain't got no taste, savages."

Percy did not respond to the inflammatory remark, thinking it best not to re-ignite the argument once more, even though the cross words in the dugout seemed very distant and dream like in its lack of clarity in his mind. Instead he took time to gauge his surroundings. He was indeed back at the shell hole. There the officer still lay, clawing at the sky while the three Tommies huddled in their muddy tomb.

"How - how did we get here?" Percy enquired sternly.

"How do you think?" Fortune snapped, all the while playing with his treasure and not once recognising Percy's glare, "Not so much as a thank you, honestly."

"Why have we come here?"

"Couldn't stay where we were. This is safety here, in surroundings we know."

Percy scrutinised the old sergeant as he rearranged his precious cigarettes repeatedly. He was purposely avoiding Percy's gaze, that much was clear. Then it struck him. He looked about his person, shifted his weight on the incline then patted nervously at his pockets.

Fortune raised his rifle from the dirt to face Percy, moving his left hand to sit resolutely over a neat stack of ammunition charger clips beside him. Percy slumped back, the tension dispersing from his shoulders.

"We're not quite back where we were, in some respects at least," Percy concluded.

"No in some respects not, we'll agree on that much. Come now lad, it's been a long day, we may have had our differences but that's well in the past now isn't it? All we have to do is sit it out until dark, then we might be able to move on, pass on, so to speak, to where we belong."

Fortune prolonged the selection of a cigarette brand with his meandering finger before deciding to take pleasure in a Woodbine. Having plucked a disorderly strand of tobacco from his lips he settled back on the muddy bank and blew smoke clouds into the sky.

"I have a son, had a son, your age. Went off to fight his own war. Much like you, he asked a lot of questions, thought he knew the answers. He didn't come home. His mother blamed me, was natural to I suppose. I was putting ideas into his head she said, at such a young age, how the Army would make a man of him. See the world I used to tell him. He sat there cross-legged with his tin soldiers at the hearth, staring up at me, waiting for one of my stories about the war. He would have gone anyways, they all went, they had to. They answered the call just like we did. Such excitement, do you remember? The thrill, the sheer adventure of it? Becoming a real man Percy."

Ignoring the now predictable rhetoric Percy decided to strike back.

"You told me your wife had died."

Fortune's penetrating stare lashed out at Percy from across the shell hole.

"You're smart, Percy, you think that makes us so very different, don't you? We're smart in different ways, I'm smart enough to have the gun, so where does that leave you?"

"I'm smart enough not to need one," Percy almost growled with his retort.

"There you are!" Fortune exclaimed, "There's your fire boy, keep that burning and the world will be a better place someday. That's what I like about you lad, you question it all, just like my boy did. Times are changing, boys like you questioning why the world is this way, that's dangerous; powerful. All the marching and fighting and killing, that never changed anything, it just kept things the way they always were. It maintains an order rather than fashioning a new one."

"You're starting to sound like me now Fortune. I'll not rise to an argument again on this subject. If I'm to be your captive, we'll need to derive a new talking point."

"I'm not arguing."

"We would have."

"No, we wouldn't. Besides, you aren't a captive of mine," Fortune shook his head.

"I'll have my rifle back."

Feigning considered thought for a short moment Fortune replied with "No, you won't."

Fortune lowered the weapon to the ground and focused his attention back to his precious cigarette. Percy eyed the soldier for a reaction as he began to inch his way backwards on his hands, slowly edging his way up the bank.

"You'll have to shoot me, I'm leaving," Percy's voice quivered as he made slow progress on his back.

Fortune flicked the remains of the Woodbine up and out of the hole, exhaling its final vapours from the corner of his mouth. With a sigh he reached towards his rifle. With a determined grasp he snatched up the Black Cat cigarette packet, extracted a cigarette, smelt its length under his up-turned nose and reluctantly started to smoke it.

"I figure it's going to be a long day, so the Black Cats can go first," he announced, ignoring Percy's escape.

Percy quickened his ascent, now scrabbling upward with more frantic movements. Upon reaching the lip he hauled himself onto his front and began to crawl into the long grass. Without as much as a glance back at the old soldier - he was gone.

"You can't leave. Goodness knows I've tried," Fortune confessed calmly.

Percy opened his eyes and sat up with a start to find himself back in the shell hole once more. Consumed with confusion the young man looked about him, desperately seeking answers that were not forthcoming. His initial panic drove him around the crater like a crab looking for the safety of a rock.

"What…what is this place Fortune?" Percy shrieked.

"No-man's land, in a shell hole."

"How long was I -"

"A while, it takes a while."

Fortune pulled a pocket watch from his tunic and popped open the lid, squinting at the clock face he shook his head. He held it to his ear for a moment after which he surrendered the time piece back to its pocket.

"Dial hasn't moved for a long time, still ticking though, it's had it I'd reckon. Putting in the effort but not getting anywhere."

Percy, his face pale with fright, scrambled up the side of the shell hole in a blind panic. Having slipped halfway, due to the flailing of his frantic uncoordinated limbs, he slowed enough to make the final few feet into the tall grass.

"We could spend all day at this, if needs be," Fortune bellowed, "It's a bloody good job I pilfered this lot ain't it!"

Percy opened his eyes and sat upright in a sudden, almost violent, spasm. Shaking his head in disbelief at his shell hole surroundings, he sat blinking rapidly for several minutes watching Fortune smoke. He'd elected to smoke in silence, allowing Percy time to gather his thoughts. The relaxed attitude of the sergeant only compounded the young soldier's bewilderment further. In time he stood, listening attentively for any audible trace of life beyond the hole. The battlefield seemed at peace, the cries and shouts for help were silent, the machine gunner now an apparition of a distant memory.

"It's quiet," he announced at last.

Fortune nodded slowly, maintaining his silence.

Percy's breathing had calmed somewhat, his movements less erratic, but the rapid blinking of his widened eyes eluded to a turmoil which broiled within. He clambered up the incline of the crater once more, this time as if he were approaching a dangerous animal, rather than fleeing one. At the lip he paused, building confidence in the security of his position the longer he remained there, at any moment expecting a sniper's bullet to find its mark. After several minutes he progressed further, standing to his full height and from his vantage point began to take in the enormity of his surroundings, a sudden disconcerting assault on his senses which had become so accustomed to earthen excavations with no field of view.

"You can see everything Fortune," he gasped, "The ridge, the wire, bodies, the wood."

"Keep looking lad. It's safe. What do you see?"

The breeze which had played through the grasses of the field had ceased, the sky devoid of birds or cloud.

"There's no shelling. No smoke. No movement. No fighting. It's all…"

"Dead."

Percy glanced back at Fortune, an acute frown silently punishing his choice of word. With a deep breath he advanced cautiously into the field and disappeared from view.

❖   ❖   ❖   ❖   ❖

"Want to go again?" Fortune enquired after he had finished a cigarette.

Percy opened his eyes and calmly sat upright.

"No. No need."

"Good. Progress lad. Good progress."

"What are we doing here Fortune? Is this - ", Percy's emotions brought a quiver to his speech and moisture to his reddened eyes.

"Now don't you jump to any of your smart, know it all, conclusions just yet," Fortune warned.

"*In my Father's house are many rooms,*[8]" Percy's stare fixated into space as he spoke slowly and softly.

"Alright - and that means?"

"Jesus reassured his disciples there would be rooms in the kingdom of heaven and a purpose for them. It's metaphorical as well as literal. Heaven, as a construct, is after all - "

"Alright, Jesus Christ, that's enough. This ain't no heaven. Does this look like heaven to you?"

"Well, no. Clearly not."

"Fine, we're agreed. I know why I am here and I know why you are here."

"Why?"

"Will you please listen me boy? Christ."

Percy winced at Fortune's flagrant blasphemy but politely allowed his companion to continue.

"You've shown you don't think the way I do, you are smart, educated, well-read, you know your scriptures, none of which I can admit to - to the same degree. That's why you are here lad, don't you see it? You need to hear my story, I need your counsel. You're rational, like my boy was. I know my strengths, you know them well enough by now I'm sure, but a mind bent on rational thought I don't possess."

"We're in agreement on this point, I concede."

Fortune grumbled under his breath.

"To get out of here I need to tell my story, start to end," Fortune explained excitedly.

"Is that why you have created this chimeric sophistry, for your own preservation?"

---

[8] John, Chapter 14, Verse 2, (ESV)

Fortune looked confused and agitated.

"If we confess our sins, he is faithful and just and will forgive us our sins and purify us from all unrighteousness,"[9] Percy preached unashamedly.

"Sins is a strong word, let's stick to stories."

Percy's countenance had now changed to one of exasperated acceptance. He wiped his eyes with a dirty sleeve and sat upright as if at school, albeit with a quivering bottom lip.

"How do I get to leave?" Percy enquired.

"When you help me, I suppose."

"How do you know that?"

"I reasoned it."

"If my role is one of counsel and cross examination then I'd request the reasoning is left to me."

"Fine."

"And if this does not provide you with your absolution?"

"My release you mean?"

"Indeed."

"Well then you've wasted your day listening to an old man talk rubbish in a shit hole," Fortune scoffed, "No different to how you lot spend your Sunday mornings."

There was no further reply from Percy. Fortune sat in silence smoking all the remaining Black Cat cigarettes while drinking the beer. His gasps and grunts betrayed enjoyment of the German beverage although he would never admit it to Percy.

Percy stood for a long period of time at the base of the crater, looking up at the sky, his hands in his pockets and neck strained backwards, gaining a full appraisal of the blue heaven above them. Occasionally he would wipe away a tear, periodically a nervous chuckle would betray the relentless monologue running through his mind.

"The sun has not moved this whole time Fortune, were you aware? The bayonet I placed in the ground has not changed the angle of its shadow in over an hour. Quite the spectacle," Percy announced cheerily, breaking the pause in conversation.

"Aye, spectacle," Fortune grumbled impatiently.

"No birds, planes, shouting, shells, machine guns, nothing. The creatures of the soil, worms, insects, all gone, I've dug in several places."

"No worms? You are thorough lad, there's no mistake. Thoroughly pissing me off!" Fortune growled.

Percy turned to face the old soldier with an excited grin.

"Very well Fortune, I'll do this for you. You were right I do have a part to play here, although not well defined at this juncture. I'll not deny to you

---

[9] John, Chapter 1, Verse 9, (NIV)

40

that I have the skills to provide aid to your cause. My father taught me to debate, to formulate counter arguments and to also appreciate the position and opinions held by others. He would lecture on the principles to follow in order to please in conversation,

The person to whom you speak is not to blame for the opinion he presents. Opinions are formed by circumstances. With the same environment, coaching and circumstances around us, we would have the same opinions ourselves.'

He also revealed to me the rules of avoidance for such debating,

Avoid impatience,

Do not argue,

Do not interrupt another when speaking,

Do not -"

"Well lad, your father was indeed wise, but this story of yours better have an ending soon or I'll need to be off to pilfer more smokes," Fortune chastised gleefully, "You've decided to hear me out, that's grand, when can we make a start?"

Percy's chin fell to his chest in mournful capitulation. With a sigh he edged over to the flattened dirt where he had been sitting, lowered himself down nimbly, finally sitting with his knees up within linked arms.

"I'm listening," Percy announced when ready, adding under his breath and directed upwards, "I am ready father, for this undertaking. *Do not show partiality in judging; hear both small and great alike. Do not be afraid of anyone, for judgement belongs to God. Bring me any case too hard for you, and I will hear it.*[10]"

"When you have quite dispensed with Deuteronomy can we begin?" Fortune huffed.

"Yes, please go ahead."

"What changed your mind?" Fortune asked.

"I'm injured, that much I am sure of, more than likely unconscious at a casualty clearing station somewhere, sleeping off the effects of a gas attack."

"You're dreaming? That's what you came up with after all this time?"

"Yes."

"Can you dream me up some more beer then?"

"If this is my dream there will be no more alcohol Fortune, your thirst only serves to prove my hypothesis, this is my construct not yours. I'm sorry."

"Apology not accepted," Fortune scathed.

"Please, begin your tale, I'll be waking up soon, those wonderful nurses reviving me with a pot of hot tea," Percy was smiling finally.

---

[10] Deuteronomy, Chapter 1, Verse 17 (NIV)

"Christ on a bike lad," Fortune shook his head in disbelief, "Do you remember your training lad? Those were happier times, weren't they? We'll begin in the summer of 1915, Aldershot military town."

Having pondered and meandered slowly through his first few words, Fortune soon gathered his thoughts, his voice becoming authoritative and invigorated once more.

"While the British Expeditionary Forces held the might of the Imperial German Army at bay on the Western Front and struggled desperately against the Ottoman Turks in the Dardanelles, a new army of volunteers was training in England."

Percy was fixated on Fortune, looking and listening for any clues which could be used in a counter argument. His companion had taken on a new demeanour, his face showing a warmth yet unseen. Fortune seemed relaxed, less agitated now his story had commenced. The opening statements had sounded like the preface to a book, rather than an improvised introduction. How many times had the old soldier practised his story?

"Go on, please."

"Tailors and teachers, clerks and shoemakers, farm hands and factory staff, shop floor and middle managers, postmen, gamekeepers, London bus conductors, butchers and bakers, miners and bank staff answered the call to arms; every trade and profession was represented. Men who had lived and worked together in the towns and villages of England, Wales, Ireland and Scotland had responded to the patriotic clamour for more soldiers. The far-flung colonies of the Empire were also surging to take part, to carve their names in the glorious lists of honour. And so here they were, in army camps throughout the country, men of all shapes and sizes, ages and ability, slowly being fashioned into a fighting force.

There I was bumped up through the ranks to sergeant on account of my experience, having to train the rabble as best we could. It was a time of high spirits and confident ignorance. But mark my words lad, a darkness was already brewing under that veil of innocence and I was in the thick of it."

Chapter 6 - An officer and an accent

16th August 1915
Aldershot Military Town
1100 hours

A warm day, dedicated to the rehearsal for an unknown war, waged against straw-stuffed sacks hanging defencelessly in a flat open field, had passed almost without incident; like countless before in the stormy summer of 1915. A sudden downpour of rain had saturated the ground, the tow path beside the Basingstoke canal was glistening in the sun as Fortune prepared his pipe. Needing the tobacco skilfully between thumb and finger he watched a lone punt making its way slowly towards Aldershot village. Three cyclists approached causing Fortune to step back from his peaceful contemplation.

"Sorry!" the scandalously trousered women hollered after she had passed by.

She was followed closely by another young woman, thankfully wearing more suitable attire. Fortune frowned. The World was turning upside down in more ways than one. Finally, a uniformed man raced by whom, attempting to salute, wobbled dangerously, aborting the action prematurely. Fortune glared at the boy as he went by, making no attempt to move aside.

"Sergeant!"

Fortune's attention was diverted to a Private hurrying down the tow path. The young man, out of breath, halted in front of Fortune and composed himself.

"The old man wants us moving out in thirty minutes Fortune," reported the red-faced boy.

"That would be Lieutenant-Colonel Bradbury to the likes of you lad and first name terms for N.C.Os is against regulation."

"Yes Fortune, sorry Fortune," puffed the soldier.

Fortune inhaled sharply through his nose. The men in his charge were quite a different breed to the regular soldiers he had served with for so many years before this war. Many struggled with the authoritarian doctrine of the Army, priding their free thinking and liberal attitudes. Others were plain stupid. Their offensive spirit under enemy fire had been called into question by the top-brass and politicians alike. For Fortune the concerns were more practical, could he rely on them, could they rely on each other, could he prepare them for what lay ahead? This lad could not be a day over seventeen, Fortune thought, lied about his age no doubt or the recruiting sergeant saw an easy shilling in his deceit.

"Sergeant Berriman, it's sergeant lad, remember it. Others won't be as lenient," he warned sternly.

"Yes sir, I'm sorry."

"Good God boy it's not sir, I'm not an officer," frustrated Fortune prodded the young man's chest with every syllable.

"Sorry sergeant."

"Name?"

"Private Arthur Leyland…sergeant, from Coventry"

"Right then Leyland, get back up to barracks and tell Sergeant Fitch I'm on my way back. He is to cover for me ahead of my return. Tell him I need to see a man about the milk. Will you remember this?" Fortune's eyes widened; his tone became patronising.

"Yes sergeant. Sergeant Fitch is to cover for you and you'll see about the milk."

The boy looked pleased and stood waiting for more instruction.

"Well piss off then!" Fortune bellowed into the poor boy's face with arm outstretched; finger pointing down the tow path.

Arthur turned on his heels and ran.

The camp at Aldershot had been in existence since 1854, starting from humble beginnings of canvas bell tents and dusty dirt tracks, the military town was now unrecognisable from those early days of red coated soldiers and plumed cavalry men. The Basingstoke canal separated the north camp from the south as it wound westerly between the two. The camps were arranged logically in square blocks containing red brick barracks, each one housing nearly seven hundred men. The sprawling establishment was maintained by a host of services all with a representation within the camp from quartermasters and their stores, farriers and black smiths, to doctors and their orderlies. The camp sported YMCA[11] huts and a church, a

---

[11] The Young Men's Christian Association (YMCA) turned its attention to providing support and wholesome pursuits for troops fighting for Britain and her empire. Activities included providing writing paper, film showings, libraries, religious services, concert parties, folk dancing and educational lectures.

gymnasium, a swimming baths, an athletics ground and even its own military police force and fire station.

The camp was, during the day at least, a bustling nest of soldiers and supporting civilians, hurrying along the criss-crossing roads fulfilling their duties to the hive. Bugles sounded, horses whinnied, while drill sergeants screamed and spat their orders. Thousands of boots drummed the earth and metalled paths. Everyone had a purpose and it was often a noisy one. This environment was home, safety, family. Fortune strode along at a good pace and upon reaching Queen's Avenue, the long road which dissected and linked the camps together, he quickly diverted south away from the battalion barracks. He too had a purpose.

Moving quickly past the Headquarters offices and military police barracks, Fortune made his way beyond Gibraltar barracks. Each barrack in the Stanhope Lines of the south camp was named after famous battles of the Napoleonic wars. Continuing west now he soon found what he was searching for, outside the Barrosa barracks on Hope Grant's road. A group of soldiers were lifting milk churns from the back of a Poulsom's Dairy waggon. A corporal, supervising the lifting, turned to face Fortune as he approached.

"Carry on," Fortune insisted with a hint of annoyance.

He progressed, without stopping, to the front of the waggon and clambered up to the footplate. An ageing man with wild grey curly hair, wearing a loose-fitting off-white shirt and grey waistcoat, sat hunched over at the reins.

"Bugger me, you gave me half a fright!" exclaimed the driver.

"The plan has changed, we're off somewhere tonight, dunno where, till I get back. We don't have any time to load the churns."

"But they'll be waitin," the driver half turned to face the sergeant, clearly anxious at the news.

"Then they'll bloody well wait. Nothing to do until we're back!" fumed Fortune.

The driver calmed and leaned in to speak softly.

"Keep your voice down for pity sake. There must be a way? How about I take it on while you are off soldiering?"

"Not bloody likely, we ride with you or it doesn't leave here," Fortune removed his dress cap, mopping his brow with the back of his hand.

"No skin off my nose, maybe I'll speak to these chaps 'ere?"

The driver stood and looked over the back of the waggon. Most of the churns had now been unloaded.

"Alright, alright! I'll spare someone, let me work it through," Fortune relented after some thought.

Fortune hurried back towards the North Camp keeping a close eye on the time with his pocket watch. He encountered two companies of soldiers marching along Queen's Avenue and onto the Queen's Parade with full kit. Officers were mounted on horseback accompanying the throng of men and several 18-pounder field guns were following on behind, towed along by four horses a piece. To one side of the road a team of artillery drivers were practising on balance horses; wooden contraptions emulating the movement of a mount, not dissimilar to a child's rocking horse toy. Fortune had no time to stop and deride the surreal scene before him, his Battalion would be mustered by now. There was not much time.

On reaching the Mandora barracks, where the 2nd/8th Somerset Light Infantry were already lined up ready for inspection, Fortune headed straight into one of the rear entrances, through the mess hall. Turning down a long corridor he caught up with a private, moving slowly under the weight of his rifle and equipment which hung from his left shoulder precariously. Fortune waited until he was right up behind the unsuspecting soldier.
"What's this then? What a bloody shambles!"
The soldier, startled, nearly dropped his pack.
"Well volunteered boy," he added gleefully with a pat on the back.

Fortune emerged from the building and onto the drill square; in a few short moments he had fetched his helmet, Lee Enfield rifle, webbing and pack from his quarters. The Battalion was arranged in the square by companies. His company was to the front right. Making his way quickly around the back of the lines he darted forward at the double to join his platoon. The Lieutenant-Colonel, sitting atop his faithful gelding, began his address of the men. He was an old soldier, into his sixtieth year, anyone doubting his soldiering ability was quickly reminded of his achievements. He had fought the Zulus at Isandlwana in 1879, escaping the massacre across the Tugela river. He has been part of the garrison besieged at Chitral in 1895 on the North West Frontier. His horse had been shot out from under him in the Eastern Transvaal during the Second Boer War in 1901. This was a decorated and experienced officer. Fortune had served with many of his ilk; career soldiers, who fought the righteous fight against the enemies of the Empire, bringing vengeance and domination through the superior firepower of the British Army. This war was not like those others, Fortune thought; all the old man's experience was obsolete. He had never had to rush a machine gun over open ground. Eight hundred and fifty men stood silent. The Lieutenant-Colonel spoke with a slight, low-land, Scottish accent.

"Your commanding officers will distribute my orders shortly. We shall be conducting an exercise simulating an assault on a fortified village. A and B companies will play the part of the Hun and occupy the village of Cove. C and D companies will prepare and execute the assault in accordance with their orders. A and B companies will move out now. C and D will begin their march at 1300 hours. One final note, 2nd Lieutenant Richardson joins us from the first-line 8th Somersets today, temporarily replacing 2nd Lieutenant McGregor of C-Company who has been invalided on account of his broken leg. That is all. Carry on Major."

Lieutenant-Colonel Bradbury turned his horse to the right and began to exit the square, followed closely by his Headquarters staff. Major Findley gave a quick nod to the commanding officers of A and B Companies. Orders were soon flowing down the chain of command and the sergeants and corporals began to move their sections of men from the square in organised columns.

A firm hand grasped Fortune's shoulder from behind.

"Down by canal again?", enquired Sergeant John Fitch in a deep west country accent.

John Fitch was broad in the shoulder and short in the leg but what he lacked in height he made up for in tenacity and drinking prowess. A farm labourer and renowned brawler before the war, he was well known to the magistrates of Axbridge in Somerset. The Army had given him the perfect opportunity to hone his violent tendencies and had discovered a good leader in the bargain.

"Yeah."

Fortune's lip turned up at the corner for a momentary snarl, as much emotion as he cared to display today.

"I got the message John. Change of plan. Old Smithy will collect the churns while we have gone. Private Leake from 1-Section will accompany him to make sure there's no monkeying."

"Leake? Who's Leake?", Fitch tightened his grip on Fortune's shoulder.

Before he could answer the company was brought to attention by the sergeant major. Captain Wilmslow was showing the new 2nd Lieutenant to the men. Standing at the edge of the platoon Fortune could get a good look at the new officer. 2nd Lieutenant Richardson was tall and wiry. His service cap sat slightly off centre on the very top of his head. He had very thick eyebrows which nearly met above his slight curved nose. An immaculate moustache complimented his otherwise thin and featureless mouth. His eyes were dark, Fortune observed him staring at the individuals who the sergeant major was presenting to him. He did not seem to blink. His attire was faultless, his brass buttons and badges gleaming in the sun light and the leather of his Sam Browne webbing appeared new and buff.

Captain Wilmslow departed shortly and the sergeant major accompanied Richardson down the line. With eyes facing front Fortune could feel the men approaching. Something willed his gaze to shift and focus once more on Richardson, but he resisted. The small party moved quickly past, but as they did Richardson stopped suddenly, turned back and raised his cane sharply to Fortune's chest, resting its tip on the medal ribbons which adorned his tunic.

"South Africa?" the officer enquired with an accent Fortune had not heard since that very conflict.

"Yessir."

Richardson lowered the cane and scrutinised the sergeant. His dark intrusive eyes clawed at Fortune, who remained composed, staring ahead throughout. Finally, Richardson continued down the line.

"Prepare the men, we don't have long to get there," Richardson ordered softly.

"Very good sir!" the sergeant major replied enthusiastically.

As Richardson walked away, the sergeant major turned on the spot, his chest puffed out like a pigeon and strode down the line in the opposite direction; swagger stick tightly gripped in his armpit, the peak of his cap barely revealing his glinting eyes.

"Stand to attention!" he barked.

"Heels touching!" he spat at a private to his right.

"Look up!" his swagger stick swiped rapidly from its rest to the forehead of another soldier.

"Hoy, you! Neck at the back of the collar. Stop standing there like a question mark!"

"Stand perfectly still, now!"

He was only inches away from another private's face, bellowing at the top of his voice.

"Company is abysmal!!!"

Within the hour the remaining companies began their march out of the camp towards the village of Cove. Fortune was the platoon sergeant for 1 Platoon, C-Company, of the 2nd/8th Somerset Light Infantry.[12] 1 Platoon joined the line of troops plodding their way out onto Farnborough Common. The path was well trodden by the time they found it, the standing water from the showers throughout the day had created mud under foot and any vegetation they brushed against moistened their

---

[12] The battalion was divided into four companies, A, B, C and D. Each company was commanded by a Major or Captain. Within each company were four platoons. The platoon command was given to a subaltern, either a Lieutenant or 2nd Lieutenant who beneath them had two sergeants, four corporals and over forty privates. Each platoon was subdivided into four sections, each of around twelve men under a non-commissioned officer, either a lance-corporal or corporal.

uniforms. The sky, for now, was clear save for a few white clouds, the sun warming the men's faces. Numerous birds darted overhead alerting their brethren to the approach of the Somersets. The pleasant summer afternoon was the last thing on Sergeant Fitch's mind. The burley soldier steamed along the path to catch up with Fortune, spinning him on the spot as he caught him by the arm.

"Who's Leake? What are you up to?" he scorned.

"Carry on Corporal, I'll catch you up."

"Yes sergeant."

Fortune pulled at John's grip unsuccessfully, reluctantly settling for a sidestep from the path.

"Now look John, I had no choice but to think on my feet. I've got Private Leake down as invalid on account of his broken finger, so he's back at the barracks now waiting for Smithy's waggon. He will help load the churns and sit with them out of the camp. We'll have to try to meet up with him as soon as we can later, after all this."

"Some bloody good he will do with a broken finger," Fitch grumbled.

"It's not broken yet and I'm sure will turn out to be a nasty sprain once an orderly looks at it."

Sergeant Fitch released his grip with a wry smile on his face.

"Can he be trusted?" he probed.

"Oh aye. He thinks it's part of the exercise. He will follow my instructions. Has no reason not to," Fortune insisted with confidence.

"You'd better be right," Fitch warned and stomped off down the line to his platoon.

Chapter 7 - A lesson in lying
16th August 1915
Aldershot, Village of Cove
1500 hours

The village of Cove lay on the northern edge of Farnborough common, a small settlement of farms and thatched houses; its northern boundary the embankment of the London and South-Western railway, carving its way through fields and towns alike, connecting agricultural settlements to the big city. The attacking companies had taken too long getting into position for the assault, their tardiness the product of both poor map reading and confusion as to the correct jumping off point, described within the typed orders held by the commanding officers. Several riders had made the short gallop from the outskirts of the village to ascertain what the hold-up was and by 1451 hours the leading wave had finally set off down into the marshy wetland that meandered along the north side of Farnborough common.

D-Company had advanced first, in open formation, while C-Company and Fortune's platoon watched from the top of the rise. The remaining men sat around smoking their pipes and cigarettes in the afternoon sun, watching the spectacle unfold before them. The air was thick with the aroma of tobacco. The village of Cove could be seen at the top of a shallow rise on the other side of the marshland. Cattle grazed nonchalantly in a field through which the Somersets would advance. A farmer, resting on a gate, watched in fascination as heavily laden soldiers splashed through the sodden pools and up into his field. As D-Company emerged from the marsh their formation had become loose, groups of men helping each other through the reeds, their NCOs[13] trying desperately to reshape the line at the frustrated beckoning of the junior officers.

A lone horseman cantered from behind one of the farm buildings at the edge of the village and raced down towards the first wave. Stopping by an officer, there was a brief exchange after which the line of D-Company began to fragment. Soldiers dashed about, widening the gap between them. Some dived to the ground and began to crawl while others pulled each other forward, at a quickening pace. The horseman galloped back to the village; the imaginary artillery bombardment had begun.

Dashing up the slope small sections of men could be seen seeking cover however they could. NCOs continued to direct the line although their main obstacle was not the unseen artillery but the distressed cows who had decided to mount their own panic-stricken charge.

"Bloody hell, the British army scattered by Friesians, would you believe it hey chaps?" called out a private sat near to where Fortune was observing.

The men laughed heartily. A hip flask was being passed around. A few of the men had brought food wrapped in brown paper and were eagerly feasting as the battle unfolded.

Fortune stood, keeping a watchful eye out for the officers who, upon the advance of the leading company, were further down the slope discussing their next move. 1st Platoon was out of sight in their elevated position, nevertheless it would not take long for the officers to reach them. Finding the men in this state would certainly lead to disciplinary action but they were nimble and knew Fortune was not going to let anything spoil the warm afternoon matinee. C-Company was spread out along a thousand-yard frontage at the edge of the common. The undulating nature of the surroundings and, in some places, the dense vegetation, offered Fortune and his sections a good deal of concealment. From where Fortune stood guard, he could see the other platoons further along the line, adopting similar postures. Wispy trails of smoke rose from where hidden soldiers nursed their pipes in hollows and behind bushes. Lookouts stood on tiptoe surveying the valley and the village beyond. Further along, an officer could be seen making his way from section to section, each unit standing in preparation just in time for his arrival. The lookouts were doing a good job.

The crackle of rifle fire caught everyone's attention, soldiers' heads bobbing up into view like startled animals. The attacking force had entered the outskirts of the village, the gentle afternoon breeze bringing with it shouts and sharp cracks and bangs.

---

[13] A non-commissioned officer (NCO) is a military officer who has not earned a commission. Non-commissioned officers usually obtain their position of authority by promotion through the enlisted ranks, I.e. corporals and sergeants

"Won't be long now boys, be ready," called Fortune.

3-Section started to equip themselves. Fortune watched as his men helped each other don their heavy packs. Private Charlie Pocock was stood between two new recruits, Privates Cartwright and Breslin, securing their 1908 pattern webbing.[14] A soldier who was used to wearing the webbing could ditch his heavy load quickly and set off just as fast. However, to new recruits its use was an alien one and many struggled to coordinate themselves at first, flapping and grunting as the unwieldy piece of attire flopped and contorted like an octopus out of water. Whereas Cartwright and Breslin had been with the battalion for less than a month, Pocock was in comparison, experienced.

Charlie Pocock had joined the Royal Navy when he was just twelve years old. The story he chose to share had him flee an abusive father and alcoholic mother, seeking refuge and security in the armed forces. Charlie had enlisted in 1903, shore bound until his 18th birthday, he joined the crew of the Town-class light cruiser HMS Gloucester. By 1912 he was a stoker in the bowels of the vessel earning two shillings a day. He had, by that time, made quite a name for himself as a boxer. He often claimed, when under the influence of rum, to have fought Bombardier Billy Wells in Bombay. Charlie had deserted the Navy in 1913, although his motivation to take flight was never discussed openly. Enlisting once more in September of 1914 he failed to disclose his prior military service and slipped into the ranks of infantrymen clamouring to defend the realm once more.

He was a thin, wiry man of incredible strength and stamina, with a gaunt, almost sickly appearance which mislead any scrutiny completely. He had lost most of his hair before his 20th birthday save for an isolated island of short blond hair just above his forehead. Another one of Charlie's tall stories from his Navy days attributed his hair loss to a vigorous prostitute on the island of Malta. Both his forearms were heavily tattooed, easily as wide as his biceps in girth. With cauliflower ears which protruded from his head like handles on a teacup and several missing teeth, it always astonished the other men how lucky he was with the opposite sex. Appearance and tall stories aside, he was a well-respected and valued member of the platoon. He was certainly NCO material,

---

[14] The webbing was simple in design but extremely effective. A thick and sturdy belt, worn just beneath the chest, supported two long shoulder straps which crossed at the back and reattached at the rear of the belt. From this framework a multitude of bags and containers could be connected to hold the soldier's equipment and ammunition in place. The weight of the entire ensemble was distributed efficiently through the shoulders and did not require a fastening at the front if the soldier was on a hot march and wanted to air his shirt. When fully assembled the webbing formed a single piece which could be put on or taken off like a jacket.

however, he had turned down the stripes on two occasions in favour of remaining a private, arguing he would lose them within a week for brawling or drunkenness, so there was little point pursuing it. The recruits feared and yet admired him. Everyone felt invincible with Charlie Pocock nearby. This made him a valuable asset for Fortune and the Battalion.

The platoon had mustered quickly and now stood with rifles slung on their shoulders watching the village. Men could be seen dashing about between buildings, the adjudicators of the battle galloping forward and back, shouting instructions to the officers involved.

"Sersant."

Fortune spun on the spot to face the source of the Afrikaans address. 2nd Lieutenant Richardson stood a few yards away resting on his cane.

"Yessir."

Fortune stood to attention staring just beyond his commanding officer.

"A word if you please, with me."

Richardson walked off through the scrub, Fortune following him, the men looking on in silence.

"Platoon is ready to move sir, at your command," Fortune offered to break the silence as he caught up. Richardson was facing the village, again resting on his cane, with his back to his NCO.

"Yes, yes, I am sure they will do everything we require of them," the officer gesticulated dismissively, "But that is not the reason for which I need to speak with you Sersant."

"I see sir. How can I help sir?" enquired Fortune.

"How does one motivate the men in our charge?"

It was not clear if Richardson's pondering was rhetorical or directed at Fortune. He remained facing away, looking off towards the village. Before Fortune had thought to reply, he turned sharply, stepping closer to his subordinate.

"I need an effective unit, a strong team, a successful platoon," Richardson scrutinised Fortune for any facial clues.

"Oh, they are sir. Very good men sir. Ready to follow your orders sir," Fortune emphasised every sir in his statement.

"Well that's good to hear Sersant, but I already expect that much at very least. They are required to follow the orders of an officer. Their submission to my commands is not in question. I seek to motivate beyond the requirements of their duty. I am asking how we, you, achieve the loyalty I am informed you, deservedly, achieve within the platoon. I wish to learn from your approach, connect with the men, and inspire them beyond the implied respect assumed through our difference in status, education and rank. So, tell me, Sersant, how should I win this privilege from the men?"

Richardson stepped closer still. Fortune did not move.

"I see sir. The men are well trained sir. They trust each other and their officers. They are well disciplined, as well as civilians can be."

Fortune's mind was racing. This line of questioning was unusual. The officers of the battalion were there to be obeyed. It was more than a soldier's life was worth to consider otherwise. Their place was not to think but to follow. The training they had all been through slowly eroded any belief in self direction. The section, platoon, company and battalion had to act upon orders without thought. Respect or not, and in many cases there was not, held little relevance. Following the order of a superior was intrinsic to army doctrine.

"Allow me to elaborate," Richardson inhaled sharply with some frustration.

He backed away and turned again to face the village.

"The men might respect their NCO or officer and in return said NCO or officer would benefit from their improved loyalty, if said NCO or officer were to allow certain freedoms which would be considered," Richardson paused momentarily and waved his hand impatiently as he searched for the correct words, "Inappropriate or illegal, let us say."

Fortune immediately realised the situation he was now in. He had to get a message to Sergeant Fitch.

"I'm not sure I follow sir. Army regulations are army regulations. We uphold them to the letter. The men have free time in the town and the occasional picture show. We engage them in sporting activities with regularity, between companies and sections to keep them stimulated. All above board sir. No funny business."

Richardson slapped his cane against his thigh, clearly agitated. Turning once more to face Fortune his face featured an almost sneering smile which faded as he revolved. Raising his cane, pointing directly at Fortune with its tip, Richardson raised his voice for the first time.

"I am aware, Sersant, of methods being employed within this camp, within our company, my platoon, aimed at building the morale and camaraderie of the men through illegal activities," his voice calmed to its original tone, "Which a court martial would find of great interest."

"I see sir. This is concerning if you have evidence, we need to act upon it. I was not aware of any improper conduct," Fortune maintained his composure, his stomach in knots.

"Indeed. We should act. Should we not? Unauthorised excursions to local drinking establishments, contraband goods traded openly, women smuggled onto the camp, gambling, narcotics. Not a list worthy of the Somerset Light Infantry, I dare say?"

"No sir, not at all sir. Shameful sir if any of it were true, sir."

Richardson took out his pocket watch, glanced at the time and snapped it shut.

"Familiar with Wellesley's work, Sersant?" noticing Fortune's confused expression he continued, "The Duke of Wellington, at Waterloo. The main body of his force was hidden from view beyond the ridgeline. Napoleon's cavalry charged again and again, dashing themselves on the square formations of Wellesley's infantry. Concealing them beyond the ridge their true intention and number were masked from the enemy."

"I am not sure I follow sir," Fortune was bemused by the lecture.

Then came the sudden realisation that Richardson was referring to the platoon resting in the scrub while waiting for the order to advance. Had Richardson been watching for some time from an unseen vantage point? Fully expecting to be charged for the indiscretion Fortune was surprised when Richardson took one last look at the village and moved away, calling out behind him.

"Good work Sersant. Ready the men, we advance shortly."

Chapter 8 - Roof tiles and recollections

16th August 1915

Aldershot, Village of Cove

1800 hours

Fortune took a deep breath as he slowly moved up the grassy bank, allowing him to peer through the hedge. The lane looked deserted. Rooks were busy in the branches of the Elm tree which stood sentry on the bend in the road. Blackbirds sounded the alarm, darting from one side of the thoroughfare to the other while insects buzzed incessantly over the decaying remains of a pheasant only a few yards from where Fortune lay. Beyond the bend in the lane, a few buildings were visible. A thatched cottage and an arched entrance to a courtyard marked the boundary of the village of Cove.

"See anything?" called Private Henry Hamblin excitedly.

Fortune looked back at the men who crouched beneath the shallow bank behind him. He shook his head slowly. Henry looked disappointed, sitting back on his heels drew a cigarette from a battered tobacco tin. Henry was 18 years old. He had attested in Taunton the day the war broke out, just over a year ago, underage but mature enough in stature to pull it off. The son of a butcher in the village of Stoke Sub-Hamdon he had spent his adolescence poaching with his father on the Montacute estate. He was the best shot in Fortune's section, bringing with it impetuosity for adventure and excitement, which made him dangerous unless sternly managed. Naturally, everyone wanted their chance to kill a German or two, but Henry was determined to finish off the entire Imperial Army singlehanded. He was brash, acting on instinct with little fear for any repercussions. Fortune could use someone like that.

Fortune stared into Henry's expectant blue eyes. Was there a similarity here with a distant memory of himself? He too was eager to serve and fight and even die if that was indeed his destiny, for Queen and Country they used to say. Fortune chuckled under his breath. There were far more exciting opportunities to be explored now the country was at war.

Fortune began to pull himself through the hedge. They had cut many of the brambles with a wire cutting tool Corporal Hope always carried. His mother had sent it to him in his most recent parcel. A private purchase, mail ordered, from a penny magazine. The base of the hedge now featured a reasonable passage through which access to the lane could be gained. Part way through Fortune froze.

There was movement ahead, by the buildings beyond the bend. Two soldiers ran from out of sight, across the lane and under the archway into the courtyard beyond. Waiting some moments, Fortune continued his crawl. Once through he looked back and Henry passed him his rifle and his webbing. Fortune beckoned for the group to follow. He crouched watching the buildings, while slipping effortlessly into his equipment. Propping himself up on his Lee Enfield, he stood guard as the group passed through the opening. Once clear of the hedge each soldier was directed to a position either side of the lane, where they crouched or lay prone, rifles readied.

Corporal Daniel "Danny" Hope was the last to emerge. He had a broad smile on his face as he caught Fortune's gaze. Fortune knew little of Danny Hope. A Welshman from the mining village of Llanhilleth in Gwent, he was a short but strong man in his mid-20s. It was said he had joined the Army in 1912 to avoid trouble with the law, although this tail was never substantiated. He was a good-hearted soul who cheered the men by his presence. It mattered not what secrets his past held, he was a good soldier and could be trusted.

"Take 'em up the lane Danny," Fortune instructed.

Without a response the corporal began his work. The section split into smaller groups which worked their way slowly to the base of the elm, covering each other as they advanced. Fortune stood to his full height momentarily and looked around him. Satisfied they had not been watched he doubled up and joined the back of the section.

The street leading into the village was now visible. A cart and its horse stood patiently outside a large house. Cottages and barns lined the lane as it worked its way towards the church. Figures, far-off, could be seen standing in the street conversing. It was quiet save for the birds and a dog barking some distance away.

"What do you think Danny?" asked Fortune in a whisper.

"All good I reckon. Let's do it."

"No, I mean, we'll be for it for sure if we're caught," Fortune added.

The corporal nodded.

Fortune sent Private Edwards down the lane to calm the horse. Two more men dashed to the archway and peered hesitantly around the corner into the courtyard beyond. They soon beckoned for the others to join them and the entire section moved rapidly across the lane and through the archway. Finally, Danny waved Private Edwards to join them. The target of their steady advance was soon in sight, the Black Bull tavern, an old coaching inn, already teaming with soldiers. Piles of equipment had been unceremoniously heaped either side of its low beam entrance. Groups of men congregated, deep in conversation, beneath the old wooden sign which had hung there since the 1700s. Excited civilian soldiers shared their war stories from the exercise in Cove, with wild gesticulations they gave their expert analysis as if the day's proceedings had been a cup final football match. Fortune rubbed his hands together gleefully and stooped to gain entrance to the tap room.

A short while later Fortune raised the second tankard of pale ale to his lips, pausing in recognition of their objective secured, before gulping down the cold refreshing drink in one go. The packed, low beam tavern erupted in cheers and as many men as could reach out to him patted him soundly about the back and shoulders.

"Many happy returns of the day," one man shouted in the din.

"Happy Birthday, sergeant," came another.

"Get him another," hollered Corporal Hope.

"Thanks Danny, we did well today didn't we?" Fortune chuckled.

"It's a wonderful war," Danny expressed in his rolling welsh accent.

His broad grin disappeared behind his tankard as he gulped down the beverage, "Righto, I'll get some more."

Fortune watched as Danny shoved himself through the throng of men towards the bar, disappearing behind a wall of shoulders. Out of sight his strong voice could still be heard above the cacophony of sound in the small room. Fortune sighed. Conversations around him became muffled as he withdrew into contemplation.

His eyes scrutinised every joy filled face. Lips contorted in an upturned snarl, teeth exposed by retreating flesh, eyes wide and dilated. A man in pain, he thought, was not so dissimilar. Surrounded by happiness Fortune suddenly felt uncomfortable. The alien display of merriment was now stifling. Looking for the exit he caught the eye of Private Pocock. Pocock had a grim look upon his face amongst the revellers, he had positioned himself in a corner beneath the large wooden beam in the ceiling. Fortune sensed refuge and made his way over.

"Come on, shift," he frowned at some privates who blocked his path.

"Sergeant," Private Pocock acknowledged.

"Charlie," the two men exchanged glances which immediately confirmed they were both feeling the same way, "Come on, with me."

Pushing their way around the room, displacing soldiers as they progressed, Fortune headed for the end of the bar. A short opening in the wall to the right would offer escape here towards the rear of the building. There was a hinged section of the bar here, currently resting in its upward position as the barman had been darting back and forth to the cellar to replenish his stocks. Fortune had been eyeing the activity from a far since they had arrived. Without a word he looked at Charlie, ensured he had his attention and then moved his head slowly from left to right, eventually looking down his nose at a bottle resting at the rear of the bar, beneath a framed picture of the King. Charlie squinted momentarily to acknowledge his orders.

"We's did show 'em proper eh sergeant?" came a slurred West Country accent from behind Fortune.

Private Henry Hamblin, with one eye visibly wider than the other, had an expression akin to someone with a bowl of excrement being waved under his chin. With mouth up turned, nose recoiling from his lips and nostrils flaring at random intervals, the young lad was clearly very intoxicated indeed. He could barely stand; the withering capabilities of his mind managing a circular swaying of his knees and hips to maintain balance. Fortune smiled at him, albeit briefly, oh to be young again without a tolerance for alcohol.

"Piss off Hamblin!"

Fortune chuckled and gave the lad a gentle push into the crowd. The boy spun on an invisible and unstable axis and crashed into some men from 2 Platoon. Beer and cider gushed from jostled tankards to the great distress of those slighted by the young lad's drunkenness. Shouts and jeers erupted as the boy was shoved and cajoled between aggravated men, finally collapsing to the flagstone floor amid a deafening cheer.

Charlie Pocock made his move as soon as Fortune initiated the diversion. Nobody saw him duck down into a crouch, sidestep behind the bar and grab the bottle of scotch whiskey from its solitary sentry. Within a simple series of movements from his supple body the target had been acquired and Charlie stood hollering at the child who had caused so much disruption in the small room. He tugged discretely at Fortune's tunic from behind to indicate success. Both men slipped unseen into the rear of the building and out into a narrow yard skirted by a high wall.

Charlie kicked a ginger cat from his path with the side of his boot and pressed on towards the rear of the enclosure. Waiting for Fortune to catch up, beside a stack of empty crates, he pulled the stopper from the bottle with the few teeth he still had in the side of his mouth. He offered the bottle to Fortune as he approached, who took it without hesitation and guzzled its contents eagerly.

"How old?" asked Charlie, needing tobacco into the bowl of his pipe.

"Old enough to know when it's time to seek refuge from the crowds," replied Fortune, handing the bottle to his accomplice.

Charlie shook his head and nestled his pipe into the corner of his mouth.

"I'll take it when you're finished."

"Suit yourself."

Fortune took another large swig of the orange-brown liquid and stared transfixed by the red and yellow light pulsing in the pipe as Charlie expertly stoked the contents. A large cloud of smoke billowed from between his remaining teeth and swirled about his features, the grey blanket churning as it dissipated upwards. Further smoke then issued forth from his nose, carving the original cloud in two and expediting its movement across the yard.

"Rumour is we'll soon be sailing," Charlie probed.

Fortune handed the bottle to Charlie.

"How long has it been?" asked Fortune.

"Long enough for me to know I still don't miss it," Charlie replied bitterly.

Charlie drank the half bottle of whiskey in one action and dropped it into an empty crate beside him.

"Damn good job I took two."

Charlie smiled and pulled the second bottle from his belt behind him.

"They don't last as long as they used to," he added.

Fortune took out his pocket watch and checked the time, its casing only partly open.

"There's still time, why not!" he added.

Charlie tugged at the stopper, spitting it onto the cobbles.

"We used to scrounge what we could in Rawalpindi. The ration was fine mind you but never enough. The local brews were made from rice, sugar cane if you were lucky. You could buy it from the blacks for a few pennies but even that was a rip off. Not a substitute for good scotch by any means. Officer's mess had plenty of the nice stuff of course but not for us scrotes. Not legitimately anyways," Fortune reminisced.

"No such chance on ship. You were either G or T. Grog or Temperate. I dint know anyone on the books as a T. Some would get theirs and pass it about for favours. Not I. I were on the receiving end all the time. Looking out for the young shits, looking after stuff, putting myself between so and so and whoever. Nice little earner in rum I can tell you. Oh and the excitement when we came into port. What could we get our hands on this time? The pilfering when we were ashore, it was spectacular. Officers dint have a clue, we were all in on it below decks. If they'd seen what we'd brought on board, well, it wouldn't have been pretty," Charlie chuckled to himself as he recalled the sordid details.

"They don't really know do they Charlie? They can't have a clue how we survive can they?" Fortune asked rhetorically, receiving a nod in agreement nonetheless.

"Sergeant major knows, course he does, but he won't say ought unless he has to, makes him look bad dunnit. And he's prolly working his own schemings himself. Nothing will get in the way of him getting his meritorious service medal."

"Likely yeah, likely. There will be opportunities when we get where we are going Charlie. Thousands of men means supplies and a lot of it. And there is always a buyer to be found."

"How be on with todays?" Charlie asked quietly.

Fortune pulled out his watch once more and reaffirmed the time.

"I'll head off shortly and see it through. The waggon should be up at the drop off, just after dusk."

"Need help?" Charlie offered.

"Nah thanks, Fitch is meeting me."

"I've heard stories about that one," Charlie looked concerned.

"I'm well aware of them Charlie. He's alright, just need to manage him right."

"There are three sorts of men Fortune. There are some lead, many that follow, and then there's those that get in your way. Them's the ones to look out for," Charlie warned.

At that moment, the door to the yard swung open, crashing against the wall. Three soldiers staggered through, conjoined at the shoulder, tankards sloshing their content onto their uniforms and boots as they advanced.

"Eh!" one announced.

"Here he is!" said another.

"What be on back 'ere then?" enquired another.

Fortune turned to face the young recruits with a broad smile, his pipe finally prepared with a fresh supply of tobacco. Charlie on the other hand was not able to disguise his displeasure at their entrance. The wiry man approached them at speed before they could reach their sergeant. With his big hands splayed beside him there was no way through to their quarry, the fisherman had netted his catch.

"Come on lads, back in with ya," Charlie insisted.

"Aw come on sergeant, av a drink wiv us, it yur birfday!" pleaded one of the men.

"Ah twas near...says in...ahh," was all that another soldier could formulate before doubling over to be sick.

"You dirty shits. Sort him out or you'll be for it," Charlie demanded.

"Leave 'em be Charlie, leave 'em be. They deserve a good send off."

Charlie looked back at Fortune acknowledging the confirmation of his rumour. He sighed and relaxed his stance. After taking two long swigs of the whiskey he handed the bottle to Fortune.

"Come on, let's slip out," suggested Fortune.

Without responding, Charlie made his way back to Fortune, testing the latch on the door at the rear of the yard. With a light shove it opened and they both moved into another slightly larger yard, emerging beneath a lean-to roof which sheltered chopped wood from the elements.

"This way," said Charlie with confidence, "We'll go around to the front for our kit."

Fortune closed the door behind him and they both made their way across the yard to a more substantial iron braced door. A large iron lock mechanism bore a heavy key. No sooner had Charlie unlocked the door and passed beneath the stone archway he stopped dead in his tracks. Fortune slammed up against him, his momentum insufficient to unbalance the bare-knuckle fighter.

"What is it?" barked Fortune.

"Red Caps![15]" replied Charlie with some alarm, closing the door quietly and locking it.

"Shit, back in!"

They both sped back across the yard and through the flimsy door. Once through into the narrow yard they could hear a commotion in the bar beyond. Charlie instinctively began to climb, like a rat escaping a sinking ship. Up onto the crates the nimble man went and within moments was crouched on the tiled roof of the kitchen. With outstretched arm he assisted Fortune while looking carefully at his surroundings. Over the perimeter wall of the tavern enclosure he could make out two horse-drawn military transports. The distinctive red helmet coverings of the Military Police could be seen at the side and corner of the tavern.

"Keep low, this way," Charlie whispered as he scampered up over the ridge of the roof and down the opposite slope.

Fortune followed closely behind, dislodging tiles with his heavily placed hobnail boots as he climbed. As they crested the ridge and dropped down out of sight two Red Caps barged into the narrow yard below them. Charlie followed the ridge of the roof towards a large brick chimney, a prominent feature at the end of the building. From here they could see into the large courtyard and stables which accompanied the tavern. Here Red Caps could be seen escorting revellers out of the building towards the covered transports, prodding their captives with the tips of their bayonets.

"Fuck, our stuff's down there!" Charlie exclaimed.

---

[15] Members of the Royal Military Police, known as 'Redcaps' due to the scarlet covers on their peaked caps

"Gone now, fuck it. Back this way Private."

Fortune dispensed with informal address and assumed command of the situation. They moved back along the length of the roof towards the out-buildings at the rear. The two Red Caps had completed their search of the lean-to yard and were proceeding back towards the beer room. As soon as they had disappeared back into the stone building, Fortune made his way carefully down onto the wooden shed roof and into the yard. Charlie waited for a moment at his vantage point, registering the position of any Military Police he could see. Fortune beckoned him down, dropping effortlessly onto the cobbles.

"Time to make a run for it, across the lane and up towards the mill. We'll split up there."

"Understood," Charlie nodded.

Fortune slowly unlocked the heavy door and with an unspoken agreement between the two men the door was swung open. Charlie rushed forward and out into the lane. Fortune emerged to witness a Red Cap collapsing to the cobbles like a discarded rag doll. A single upper cut from Private Pocock had rendered him unconscious before he even knew what was happening. Two more Red Caps at the end of the lane were now alerted as Charlie sprinted off in the opposite direction. One of them blew on his whistle and the other fired his rifle into the air before pursuing the fugitives down the lane.

Charlie leapt over a short garden wall, shoulder barging the front door of a cottage. Fortune thought better of adding yet another offence to the day and continued down the lane another fifty yards. There he spotted an alley between two houses and darted into it. A dog snapped at him angrily from beneath a gate as he ran around the back of the dwellings and up over a wall, landing on the other side in a small allotment. Having jogged the length of the vegetable patch he exited the fenced garden through a wooden gate, shutting it carefully on the latch behind him. An old metalled trackway bordered the village here, running alongside a culvert, edged with stooping weeping willows. A group of moor hens ran for cover up the opposite bank as Fortune hurried along the lane. Charlie came into view up ahead, vaulting a low wall onto the track. He did not wait for Fortune to catch up, instead proceeding at speed towards the mill which lay at the bend a few hundred yards from where they were.

The mill was an ancient building straddling a weir which fed into the mill pond. Its wheel slowly tumbled beneath the leaning medieval timbers of the upper story mill room. A two-wheeled cart and its mule stood patiently at an open doorway. Ducks and a swan paddled lazily on the pond while carp occasionally surfaced to scoop insects into their gaping mouths. The rhythmic drumming of the mill's mechanics blended musically with the chirping of birds in the willows. Beyond the wheel the opposite bank was dark and steep beneath the trees. A dilapidated fence at the summit marked the boundary of the fields beyond, and safety for the fleeing soldiers.

Charlie quickly progressed to a short ladder, at the base of a low stone wall, which led up to a platform above the wheel. Fortune was now only yards behind, the short distance to their escape motivating a quicker pace from the old sergeant. Charlie edged his way across the walkway, the wheel turning on its endless journey beneath him. Fortune approached the thin and ancient board with more trepidation; he could not progress beyond the low stone wall. He was anchored to the ground where he stood, his feet denying him movement as if the earth had opened before him revealing a deep fissure. Fortune stared at the wall, the texture of the stones and the mortar which held them. He reached out slowly, confirming the wall was not a figment. Suddenly, dark crimson blood ran like oil over its surface, broiling from atop the stones and congealing in the cracks between the larger rocks below. Fortune gasped at the spectre.

Muffled and eerie voices of panicked men surrounded him, shouts for help and cries of pain, disturbing the tranquillity of the mill pond. Unseen bullets cracked into the wall, sending fragments of stone whistling into the air. Now his legs overcame their initial fear with a great surge of energy. He leapt the wall and shielded himself from the withering gunfire which had descended on the low cover. Within an instant the scene had played out in Fortune's mind and reached its terrible crescendo.

"No!" shouted Fortune at the top of his voice, sending the swan into noisy flight and the moor hens fleeing the scene with equal bravado.

"What is it?" called Charlie trying to distinguish what had mesmerised Fortune below him.

A response was not forthcoming, so Charlie hurried on. He clambered down the other side of the weir and dashed up the bank towards the avenue of trees. Throughout the escape his mind had been examining the possible outcomes of their folly, all of which ended in the same manner, being put on a charge in front of the sergeant major. Capture now was largely irrelevant, their equipment and rifles bore their regimental numbers and were now in the possession of the Military Police. At very least, avoiding arrest before returning to camp could afford enough time for someone like Fortune to come up with a well thought out excuse or alibi.

Fortune remained pressed against the wall for some time, until the apparition faded and his terror subsided. Charlie was now nowhere to be seen. Fortune found himself drenched in a cold sweat. He rubbed his eyes with one hand furiously trying to understand what was real and what was not. He felt lightheaded, physically unstable and afraid. He staggered across the platform to the other side of the weir and climbed down to the muddy bank. There he stood for a while, both arms resting on a rung of the ladder, unable to let go for fear he would fall.

"Sersant," a muffled voice recalled Fortune to reality.

"Sersant Berriman," the voice was more distinct now; recognisable.

Fortune looked up from his defeated posture to see 2nd Lieutenant Richardson glaring down at him from atop his horse, several yards up the bank and along the ridge. Two mounted military policemen accompanied him. Fortune turned and stood to attention, looking directly ahead of him towards the muddy slope. Richardson made his way carefully down to the mill leaving the mounted police behind on the ridge. Having ridden up to where Fortune was standing the officer dismounted, handing the reins to Fortune.

"Sir?"

"Walk with me Sersant, if you will."

Fortune, stunned, took care of his officer's mount.

"I can explain Sir," Fortune began.

"No Sersant, I will explain, you will hold my horse."

"Yessir."

"There has been a troubling incident today with which I would require your advice to resolve," Richardson explained as he walked slowly beside the mill pond.

"Yessir."

"I have been informed, by a credible witness, of an unauthorised requisition of military property which occurred this afternoon, while we were on manoeuvres. A waggon was intercepted, carrying milk churns, which had all been filled with army ration jam. Can you believe such a thing Sersant?"

Richardson paused and looked directly at Fortune with his piercing gaze.

"No sir. Definitely not sir."

"Initial questioning has concluded the jam was intended for a trade, with a civilian brewer. Said brewer was to supply a significant quantity of beer. It would seem some individuals had concocted the scheme and over time built a large quantity of Army rations jam for this purpose, knowing such a luxury was hard to come by outside of the fence. In time we will discover all the perpetrators, once we allow the Provost Marshall time to execute his investigation fully. All involved will be apprehended."

Richardson continued walking. Fortune followed behind.

"Yessir. Let's hope so sir."

"Let me be clear Sersant, these men will be punished and punished severely, should the Provost be notified and allowed to pursue his investigation to fruition," Richardson stopped once more to face the sergeant.

"Sorry Sir, I don't follow."

"There is still time, while the charges and details are not entirely clear for all to see, to nip this sorry affair 'in the bud' as you say here, and put it behind us…should all parties be willing to concede to my way of thinking on the matter. There would be no need to involve the authorities at all."

"I'm not sure I understand Sir," Fortune prepared himself for the lash of Richardson's whip.

"I have in my pocket here orders for the Provost,[16] detailing the crimes so he can begin with his investigation. Undelivered. Orders can be lost, my pocket can make room for another more valuable commodity. The loyalty of my men. To have a resourceful Sersant such as yourself here," Richardson patted his tunic pocket lightly, "Would ensure this distasteful episode is behind us."

Fortune did not reply. He stood anchored to the spot holding the horse as it nudged him forcibly, much to his annoyance.

"What do you have in mind, Sir?" he asked finally, his resolve broken.

---

[16] Older title for Military Police, Provost staff specialise in custody and detention.

Chapter 9 - Over a barrel, or two
16th August 1915
2 Miles west of Aldershot Military Town
2150 hours

Fortune reached over and took the reins from Private Leake, slowing the waggon to a stop. The two soldiers sat quietly surveying the dark road ahead. Looming on either side of the thoroughfare were sprawling trees of an ancient copse. The light from the lantern, mounted on the waggon, could not penetrate the vegetation; the flickering illumination casting eerie shadows. The horse whinnied and stomped the ground.

"Calm now," Fortune called in a soothing tone.

"What do we do next sergeant?" enquired the fresh faced Private Leake.

"I'll worry about that, you sit tight lad. It's all part of the exercise. Just need to work out where we are heading."

"I didn't expect war to be like this sergeant," Private Leake confessed.

"War is full of surprises lad. It's never what you expect it to be."

Private Leake seemed comforted with this and lit his pipe. Fortune looked at his pocket watch. Nearly ten o'clock. They were an hour later than planned. Fortune checked once more that his Webley service revolver was loaded. He went over Richardson's instructions one more time to himself. The contraband exchange was to go ahead as originally planned. Richardson and his aides would apprehend all involved once the transfer had occurred and if Fortune assisted in the new plan then his role in the affair would be a nameless one. Richardson wanted the black marketers banged to rights and now Fortune was his pawn in a new endeavour, any thought of profiting from the scheme was a distant memory. Dealing with Richardson's unique approach to leadership was one challenge, but the thing Fortune feared the most was how Sergeant Fitch would take the news of the botched deal.

"One problem after another."

"Sorry sergeant?"

"The war," Fortune paused, "One problem after another. That's why we train lad, so we can deal with them when they crop up."

"I see. So, what am I supposed to learn from this?"

"To keep quiet and stop asking questions," Fortune pressed for silence with an angry tone.

"I don't like this one bit," Fortune thought, but he had little choice but to press on.

The waggon proceeded into the woods slowly, its lantern revealing sinister figures and dangers to their imaginations. The roadway, more of a track now, slowly twisted and turned through the trees. After several hundred yards a light-source could be seen ahead. They continued onward. Before long, the track entered a long clearing in the wood, logs piled to the height of a man lay in large pyramid formations to either side. A ramshackle wooden hut was situated at the far end of the clearing. A lantern, hanging from a large four-wheeled waggon, driven by two shire horses, swayed in the light breeze. A lone man stood impatiently beside the waggon; a civilian, senior in age, short and wiry. Fortune could barely make out his facial features in the poor light, but he recognised him none-the-less.

"Michael," Fortune called as their waggon came to a halt.

"Young man," replied the civilian with a strong local accent, "Who is this?"

"My driver, nothing more."

"Where's Old Man Smithy?"

"Drunk. Dead drunk. A liability to have ever included him in this endeavour Michael. I shan't be again. I'm late because of his antics. We are better off without him."

Michael stood frowning, silent for a moment.

"So, you have it?" Fortune instigated.

"Do you?" came the reply.

"Of course. What do you take me for?" Fortune scorned.

"That remains to be seen young man."

"Stop pissing about, shall we get this done?" Fortune tired of the game.

He clambered down from the waggon leaving Private Leake nursing his anxieties in silence.

"Keep your wits about you lad," whispered Fortune.

Fortune walked towards Michael stopping by the large waggon. He tugged at the tarpaulin to reveal rows of barrels which had been neatly stacked and secured beneath it. Michael came to join him, supervising the inspection closely.

"Let's see it then," prompted Fortune.

Michael moved further around to the rear of the waggon uncovering a barrel, a tap already attached. Turning the tap fully, its contents began to spill upon the wood chippings beneath.

"Steady!" Fortune called as he quickly placed a cupped hand beneath the flow.

Bringing the liquid to his lips several times, a smile spread across his face.

"Perfect. Very good!"

Michael stemmed the flow of the golden merchandise.

"It's all here, you'll not find better in the whole county," he boasted with pride.

"Oh, I'm sure. There's more jam here on ours than you'll know what to do with. Decent stuff too. Do you want to see?"

"Naturally."

They both walked over to Old Man Smithy's waggon, Fortune and Michael climbing up onto the flatbed. Private Leake turned to catch a glimpse of what was happening, Fortune snapped at him in response to look out for the horse, to which Private Leake dismounted and soothed the horse with gentle petting of its nose and head. Fortune removed the cap of the nearest milk churn and plunged a hand inside, withdrawing seconds later with a large clump of red jam clinging onto his fingers.

"Oh yes!" Michael could not contain his excitement and explored the contents of the churn himself.

"So, we have an accord Michael?" Fortune pressed, licking the jam from his hand.

Before Michael could offer his hand in agreement another voice, with a strong Irish accent, joined the conversation.

"I can take it from here Mickey."

Fortune and Michael looked up to see a young clean-shaven man, dressed in a long black pea coat and cap, standing beside the beer waggon. He levelled a pistol towards them. Appearing from around the woodsman's hut another man, older and stocky with a weathered face, stood in similar dark garb. He brandished a shotgun at Private Leake. Finally, a taller man in similar vestments leaned against the woodsman's hut with a shotgun over his shoulder, smoking a cigarette.

Seeing this Private Leake instinctively turned on his heels and ran back towards the waggon, where his Lee Enfield rifle was resting on the driver's seat.

"No!" called Fortune, whipping out the Webley revolver concealed in his belt.

The young stranger took aim, bringing down Private Leake with a single round from his pistol; shot through the back between his shoulder blades. The young soldier fell face down against the front wheel of the waggon, lying there motionless. Fortune recoiled back behind the milk churns while Michael jumped down behind the waggon before Fortune could stop him. Taking a deep breath, he popped his head up to fire but was driven back down by several shots from the young man's pistol, which smashed into the wooden planking inches from his face. The stocky man moved behind the beer waggon and levelled his shotgun but did not fire; instead waiting, poised to attack. The tall stranger by the hut moved out of sight behind the building, throwing his cigarette to the floor as he hurried, while the young Irish man with the pistol moved close to the beer waggon and crouched behind it.

"Come away wid you Micky," he called.

Michael scurried away to the tree line, behind a log pile and then back towards the chaotic scene heading for the beer waggon, where he hunkered down behind its massive form. Fortune tried to catch sight of Private Leake by looking over the side, but the burly man let off a barrel of the shotgun to keep his head down. The dairy waggon horse began to panic and attempted to back up, struggling against the weight of its load, only serving to turn the waggon on its axis.

"Shit, Leake? Can you hear me Leake?" Fortune called to no avail, "Leake are you alright?"

"Terrible thing to see such a young lad cut down in the prime of his life," the young man goaded.

The movement of the waggon had given Fortune a brief advantage, he moved quickly to the right side, now exposed to the assailants. Sitting up he fired his revolver at the beer waggon then returned to the safety of his wooden fortress.

"Calm yer shooting now, throw yur weapon over. Let's not get carried away and get yous killed," shouted the young man.

"Fuck you, you paddy prick!" Fortune spat in response.

"Come now man, there's no need for any of this, we can talk this out between us."

"You fucking cunt Michael. You bastard traitor!" Fortune fumed.

"Leave me out of this Fortune, it's nothing to," Michael was cut short in his exclamation by a short jab at his forehead from the Irish youth's pistol.

"Traitor!" Fortune's shouting went unanswered.

The young man rolled his eyes at his burly companion, waving him forward with his pistol, ignoring Michael who now lay beside him clutching his head in pain. The burly man slowly made his way around the beer waggon and prepared to move between the vehicles, however, anticipating such a manoeuvre Fortune had backed himself out of the waggon's confines and lowered himself to the floor. Crouching behind the waggon's wheel he caught sight of the burly man's legs moving towards him. By the time the stranger had sprinted over to the jam waggon and around to its left flank, Fortune was ready.

The burly man was expecting to be able to finish Fortune at close range over the top of the waggon's side, his attention firmly up above where he had last seen the soldier. Fortune was down low and immediately leapt up at the man taking him off guard, grabbing him by the collar with his left hand Fortune brought the pistol grip down upon his face with his right hand, fracturing his jaw and smashing several teeth from the force. The burly man, despite his size and resolve, decayed unto the ground grasping his bloodied face in agony. Without question or remorse Fortune unloaded his remaining rounds into the man's head at close range, killing him instantly; the victim's thick brow blasted into bloody pulp, the back of his skull disintegrating entirely over the carpet of wood chippings beneath.

"Sean?!" his companion called, "Sean, wots doing?"

Fortune did not offer up a reply instead dashing to the rear of the waggon once more. Delving into his pocket he quickly accounted for several loose rounds and reloaded the Webley. His chest heaved and throat burned, the veins in his forehead felt like they would explode, his mouth was devoid of moisture, his senses were overloaded. A twisting knot gathered in his stomach. These symptoms were all too familiar to him.

"The cunt ain't no use to you no more!" Fortune finally reposted.

Several shots smashed into the waggon sending wood splinters arcing into the air. The young man was shouting, something, but to Fortune he was far away and inconsequential. An invisible bubble had descended on his senses. He sat there panting, his head resting back on the waggon wheel, eyes tightly closed. The young man had stopped shouting, the area became quiet. Fortune's breathing sounded disconnected from himself, like a hidden presence close by as he hid from a lurking menace. Swirling red shapes darted and twisted before him as he held his eyes shut; the flash from the Webley having scored a bright fissure across his eyelid kaleidoscope. This dark world he had made for himself offered comfort and respite. A lethargy had overcome his limbs and neck, his extremities weighed down with an invisible load.

"Come on, stay with me you old fool," he thought to himself wearily.

His mind began to wonder, once more he was plunged into reminiscence of a past once his. Images formed in his mind, morphing from the red light behind his eyelids. He was crouched, bent double and almost foetal, beside a low stone wall. The sounds of battle pressed at his senses, to no avail. He was encapsulated in an intangible muffling blanket. Stone chips erupted from small arms fire impacting on the masonry, forcing his tight form to become more and more constricted. Fear compressed the human ball to the point of agony as he grasped his ears tightly to block out the cacophony. He then remembered a hand, shaking him about the shoulders and a rough palm slapping him about his face. Opening his eyes, he saw the blackened face of his sergeant screaming at him above the din, while forcing his Martini Henry rifle at his chest. Fortune stared at this furious man with wonder and astonishment, watching his large moustache crumple and flex as the mouth articulated its curses. He looked down at the rifle as a baby scrutinises a toy, marvelling at its presence but without knowledge of its purpose. The bewilderment faded the memory into blackness and the red swirling lights returned.

His body jerked as if forced from an exhausted slumber. Looking about him, he quickly registered where he was, when he was, with a grunt he reaffirmed his grip on his weapon which had fallen discarded to his side. He caught sight of Private Leake, lying against the far wheel of the waggon.

"Get a grip Henry!" he blurted to himself, banging his head against the waggon wheel rhythmically to exorcise his vision.

"Give it up now, come on now, give it up," the young man's voice could be heard once more.

"Please Fortune, it's not worth it," pleaded Michael.

Fortune squinted and rubbed his eyes, shuffling on his knees to bring the blood back into his legs. The phantoms were there no more but a tall man, dressed in black, was creeping through the undergrowth in the tree line to his left flank. This threat was very real.

"Call this prick off Paddy or he'll be the next to go, cos I'm not stopping till all you bastards are done!" Fortune raged.

He urged himself to his feet. The tall man saw him standing and let off both barrels of his shotgun, the range too significant to reward him with a kill. Pellets pinged off the waggon, its wheel and the ground around Fortune. He let out a groan as his left arm began bleeding beneath his tunic, several small puncture holes having appeared in the sleeve. Fortune steadied his arm and fired at the tall man who had ducked behind a tree to reload. Two rounds struck the tree and splintered the bark.

His location was now untenable, so he heaved himself around the side of the waggon. Where was the young man in all this? Had he remained in his position or moved around? The potential for being surrounded was a very real concern now in Fortune's mind. He looked at the tree line for a route of escape but then cursed himself at the thought. The horse whinnied and pulled at the waggon, which once more shifted its position.

Fortune glanced underneath and saw Private Leake fall away from the wheel which then became trapped on his lifeless form. He could see a pair of legs, the young man or Michael he was not sure, moving around the scene in a wide and cautious path. As he peered through under the waggon another blast from a shotgun slammed into the wooden frame beside him. Instinctively he sunk into a ball clutching his head as wood splinters rained upon him. Moments later he turned to see the tall man had made a significant ingress towards him across the clearing. Before Fortune could react and level his revolver the tall man was upon him. One barrel of the shotgun was smoking from the previous shot, the other was still primed and ready to fire at point blank range. A calming relief immediately filled Fortune. His limbs relaxed and anxiety lifted. He welcomed an end to it all, urged it, demanded it. Without shame he raised his hands in submission, his Webley dropping to the earth. As the revolver clattered by his feet, a shot rang out.

The tall man lurched to one side dramatically and fell lifeless and limp; the bullet from 2nd Lieutenant Richardson's revolver punching through his heart and killing him instantly. Richardson rode into the clearing, sitting up in the saddle with his revolver poised above the horse's head. Behind him two military mounted policemen galloped into the fray, firing their carbines into the air as a warning to anyone witnessing their advance. Fortune slumped to one side and recoiled. Richardson wheeled his horse around the jam waggon and through the gap made with the beer waggon, firing his revolver once more at Michael and the young Irish assailant. Wheeling once more to the right he galloped around the woodsman's hut. The two policemen dismounted and using their horses as cover fired above the heads of the now cowering conspirators. Michael plunged to the ground covering his head with is hands in total submission whereas the young Irish man threw down his pistol and stood with palms out-facing at his sides, glaring at the policemen defiantly.

Richardson brought his steed around, triumphantly skidding to a halt in front of the young prisoner, his horse impatiently snorting and chomping for more action.

"Join us if you will Sersant," Richardson called.

Fortune got to his feet, gathered up his weapon and rushed over to Private Leake. The poor lad was clearly dead, his lifeless eyes staring blankly from his muddy face.

"Was this in your god damned plan, sir?" Fortune gnarled and grated under his breath.

"And what sorry fellows do we have here? Caught red handed pilfering from His Majesty's provisions," Richardson gloated.

The young Irish man glared into Richardson's eyes and spat upon the floor in front of him.

"Paddy bastard from Ireland sir, did all the shooting. The old man is Michael Fowler, my contact I spoke to you about," explained Fortune as he inspected the wound upon his left arm.

"Ah yes, the contraband dealer, black market entrepreneur. Stand sir, so I might look at you," Richardson commanded.

While Michael clambered to his feet the mounted policemen returned to the saddle, keeping close eye on the captives as they did so.

"Now, listen, let's be fair," stammered Michael, "I don't know what your sergeant here has been saying but my part in this was purely commercial. I have no dealings with killing I can assure you, I diddle and dabble but this chap here is…"

"Never-the-less, one of your companions or associates," Richardson finished Michael's statement.

"No, I…"

"And as such you are intrinsically linked, to the acts of violence and murder which have befallen a soldier of His Majesty's forces. By association your guilt is clear to see, for all bearing witness to your confession," Richardson's voice reached an authoritative climax.

"Now wait, let me just…"

Michael stepped forward to plead his case, but before he could say another word Richardson had shot him in the head from only several yards away.

The bullet entered its target just below the left eye, the old man's head crumpling like a piece of scrunched-up paper. Fragments of skull, brain matter and bloodied hair spattered across the young Irish man's face with unremarkable impact on the glare which was fixed upon it.

"Jesus Christ!" blurted Fortune, now anchored to his spot beside Private Leake.

His body shifted slightly now to face both the young man and Richardson squarely, both of equal threat and as unpredictable as each other. With careful and hidden movement Fortune gently pulled back the hammer of his revolver, priming it for a quick reaction.

Richardson relaxed in the saddle and crossed his arms at the wrist on the horse's neck.

"Regardless of the meticulous nature of your planning Sersant, and the dedication and fortitude of your men, there is always a scheme of greater scale and calibre than your own. A worthy lesson indeed," Richardson rejoiced.

He waved over the policemen with his revolver.

"Take both waggons to the railway siding and oversee the loading personally. You need to be there by midnight, no later, or the train will depart."

"Yessir."

"My god," exclaimed Fortune, bewildered.

"Your praise is not unfounded Sersant. You realise now, there is no insuperable task before us the likes of you or I cannot overcome. A great team you and I will form, no?"

Fortune had no response which was suitable for a commanding officer's ears, remaining silent he watched as the scene played out before him.

"Your name sir, I would have your name," enquired Richardson to the young man.

"*Téigh trasna ort féin*," the young man replied in Gaelic.

Richardson found some amusement in the unintelligible repost, his unconscious shifting of weight in the saddle giving away his frustration.

"Very well. It is of no consequence to me. Your part in this affair is played out. Now if you would Sersant, tidy this up," he gesticulated at the young man, "You'll find a shovel in the hut and a flare gun. You will have to work quickly, a patrol is due in the vicinity before two-hundred hours. Raise the alarm with a flare."

"Alarm sir? Sorry sir, what do you need me to do?"

"The deserter you apprehended," he pointed at Private Leake, "A secure plan in case of unfortunate outcomes should always be carefully considered before the off. You can thank me at a later date for considering the finer points of this operation. No witnesses to our scheme now. That would be folly indeed."

Richardson wheeled his horse and spurred it into a gallop. The policemen had secured their mounts to the waggons and they drove them out of the clearing after Richardson, leaving Fortune, his captive and four corpses alone in the wood.

D.G.Baulch

Part 2 - Exodus and Epiphany

"Nothing is more wretched than the mind of a man
conscious of guilt."

-

Plautus (c. 254 – 184 BC, Roman playwright)

Chapter 10 - Mary is coming
Sheol Care Home

The old man emerged from a room, escorted by an orderly whose name he felt he should know but did not, it was of little importance. The old man shuffled down the stark corridor, his slippers barely lifting from the white tiled floor with each step. The orderly pulled on the old man's elbow several times to indicate his impatience but to no avail, his actions merely indicting the old man's strategy had worked. Another victory he thought, another victory. The old man's temples were throbbing in pain from the treatment just received, his eyes failing to focus in front of him. He would need the orderly for now, at least in his weary state, to return to his room. He should placate the man for the time being rather than seek to annoy him, he decided, picking up the pace much to the surprise of the orderly. Besides, he thought, he could not quite remember where his room was. Sheol's layout must change on a weekly basis, he mused, in order to confuse the inmates. It was remarkable how efficient the construction workers must be to reorganise the corridors, redecorate and clean up their inevitable mess; all the while without disturbing anyone in the process. Yet without fail, the corridors and treatment rooms were not where he remembered them being on his next outing.

The old man continued his silent pondering. Sheol had not reckoned with having such a wily character in their midst, he had managed to secure help on the inside. He had befriended this orderly, his name still flitting about in the clouds of his mind, evading capture, it would come to him, soon, for now Jacob would be his name, the old man decided. Jacob was a large man and enjoyed biscuits of all varieties. Jacob's ballooning waist divulged a great passion for all sugar based oral enjoyments, a weakness the old man had prayed upon relentlessly to gain favour. Jacob would lead him back to his room, Sheol and its ever-changing corridors would not prevent him returning to safety with Jacob to show him the way.

The old man chuckled, raising a wrinkled, sunspot speckled hand to cover his mouth and prevent more glee from escaping. Jacob, continued in his unmistakable shambling movement towards a set of swinging double doors at the end of the polished corridor, the music from his Walkman[17] drowning out any sound the old man was making.

"Dad, Dad."

The old man's brow furrowed as he strained to look behind him. The rhythm of his laboured steps slowed causing Jacob to stop abruptly to avoid catapulting the old man along the corridor.

"Come on," Jacob bleated in an accent the old man was still trying to pinpoint.

"Tom?" the old man called behind him.

"Dad, wait!"

Jacob shoved at the double doors which swung open into a small room containing low tables adorned with magazines and a sectioned off desk at which a rotund middle-aged woman sat slurping coffee in an ill-fitting nurses' uniform.

"They have a bar," the old man exclaimed, "I've found the bar Tom. Two halves of mild love, I'll be over 'ere with my son."

The barmaid shook her head scornfully and addressed Jacob, her words not finding purchase in the old man's head. He was ignoring her now on account of her dreadful hospitality. It had been a close call. The barmaid had probably phoned the authorities at Sheol to raise the alarm, soon everyone would know that he was at large. Jacob's cover was no doubt blown. It was fortuitous then that they arrived at the old man's room soon after. Not a minute to spare, thought the old man as Jacob pulled the door closed and as a safety measure locked it from the outside. The old man chuckled once more.

"Always one step ahead," he scoffed.

"Dad, there you are, sit down, here let me help."

Thomas guided his father to the tall backed chair by the window then stood uneasily by the sideboard, turning his cap anxiously in his hands.

"You look smart today son, on parade again?"

"Are you alright Dad? I've not got long, I was worried, just wanted to check in on you."

"Oh, you don't need to worry about your old dad now, you have your soldiering to do. Don't you worry about us civvies when you are off over there, you've got an important job to do son. Focus on your mates, I'll be just fine here, I've got my things."

---

[17] The Sony Walkman TPS-L2 was the first commercially available personal portable cassette player, 1979

Thomas sat in the chair opposite in an attempt to stop his agitated fidgeting.

"What's the matter son? Tell your dad now, come along."

"Do you think you will leave here soon Dad? Mum and I would like you to come back to us, but if you don't accept their help here, it will take forever."

"Don't tell me they know what's good for me!" the old man snapped, his mood changing in an instant, "I'm working my own way out of here and it's no thanks to them, they poison me son, they'd poison you if they knew you were here. Or worse."

"That's not true Dad, they just want to help you piece it all together. Then you can be on your way," Thomas pleaded.

"Did they put you up to this?" the old man barked, "Did they send you to interrupt my stories? That's how I'm getting out son, I'm going to finish my story, this time I've got help."

"Help? Dad I told you, he isn't helping you, he's a nobody who walks you to your treatment and pushes trolleys around. He's been stuck here longer than you have with no means of ever leaving. He has been here so long he doesn't remember why he is here. He has no intention of helping you escape. He is Sheol."

"Who the bloody hell are you talking about?" the old man raged, "His name is Percy, you'd like him son, after a few beers certainly."

Thomas let out a sigh with which his upright posture collapsed into a slouch.

"Sit up straight man," the old-timer snapped, "What do you think this is? The Navy?"

Thomas stood and paced the small room, beating his right palm with his cap in frustration.

"They know I have been here Dad, they say it's not helping your present condition, remembering me in this way. They want me to stop coming," Thomas confessed.

The old man's rage subsided immediately, his already frail and slight body contracting on itself like a crushed tin can. He sobbed pitifully into his near skeletal hands.

"What? No, tell them no son, I - I have to see you. I won't stop remembering."

"They are going to send someone else to talk to you, someone you'll respond to more - positively."

"Mary."

"Yes Dad. Mary's coming."

"I don't have any time to lose son. So much to go through before Mary arrives."

The old man seemed startled by the news, the knuckles of his left hand playing an invisible instrument beneath his nose while his murky eyes flicked around within their deep shadowed sockets.

"I need more time son, Percy has to hear everything, I'll have to rearrange things. I won't be rushed and flustered - no," the old man blurted his displeasure.

"I'm sorry Dad, that it has to be this way, but it's for the best. You'll not see me again, until its time."

"No Son, don't say these things, I promise, I promise, I'll do what they need me to," the old man pleaded.

"Is there anything I can do before I'm gone Dad?"

"Yes, yes. That bitch, she has the lighter son. She took it from us."

"It doesn't matter Dad, its material."

"It matters to me and if Mary is coming, I'll need it back. No lighter, no Mary."

With several shallow nods and a sigh Thomas stepped forward, releasing a heavy object onto the bed.

"What's this?"

The old man wiped away his tears and stared in disbelief at the object lying next to him. With great trepidation he cupped the disk-shaped lighter into his old hands, drawing it closer. Before his eyes could gain focus, his fingers had traced the outline of the embossed emblem on its surface and confirmed its identity. The old man looked up through teary eyes at Thomas with an expression of shock and bewilderment, betraying the turmoil within.

"How did you do this son?"

"You gave it to me when I joined up, do you recall Dad? Something to remember you by, to give me hope, a connection to you when I was away. Now I'm giving it back, we're connected again, so you have the strength to do what you now need to do," Thomas explained softly.

"No son. They sent it me in a brown parcel, with your other bits and bobs. 28th July 1943. I was up in the top field when I noticed him walking up to meet me with this brown package under his arm. I knew what it was when I saw him, he would have left it at the house if it was anything less important. Yet there he is, uniform drenched in the pouring rain, clambering up to the top field, mud all up his legs. Your mother burned it all of course, save for the lighter, I'd kept it safe all these years until that demon took it from me. This one's with you son, from your time. It's part of you, see."

The old man held the lighter on his up-turned palm, its form slowly becoming insubstantial, as if out of focus on an old photograph. He soon withdrew his empty hand and sat in silence staring out of the window waiting for Thomas to comprehend what he had witnessed. The young soldier plunged his hand into his pocket and with a startled grunt retrieved the lighter once more.

"How do you know about this Dad?" Thomas enquired.

"You all think I've lost my marbles, that I don't know what this place really is. Well you are wrong. They are all wrong. I've reasoned it all out, thank you very much," the old man scoffed.

"You have?" Thomas expressed relief as well as surprise.

"Of course. I can't take something that isn't real. The lighter is out there, she has it, and I'm going to get it back son. Don't you worry, I'll..." the old man stopped, his chin sinking to his chest.

The room was empty.

As the bus lurched to a halt, avoiding a careless cyclist, the old man focused suddenly on his surroundings. His head had been resting against the condensation tainted window for some time, leaving a porthole of clear glass from which the high street traffic and raincoat clad shoppers could be viewed. He glanced around at the other travellers and recognised none of them, nor did he register when they had alighted the bus. Where were they now? He was not sure. Where was he going? A fascinating question, the answer to which was poised ready to leap from the confines of his mind but had been restrained by some intangible force. With a sigh the old man reached instinctively for the front pocket of his coat. Withdrawing a single and tightly wrapped boiled sweet he wrestled with its confinement for some time before savouring the sharp taste held within.

At the next stop he watched as an elderly couple climbed aboard, followed by a young man carrying his child. The elderly couple sought comfort at the front of the bus while the young man took his son up the stairs to the top deck. As they alighted the old man could hear their feet on the steps, long after they had disappeared from view; the metallic resonance changing, morphing to the sound of boots on wooden duck boards. The old man closed his eyes, recalling the winding trenches and damp timbers beneath his feet.

The bus jerked in a stop-start motion as it moved away, an angry motorist sounding his horn defiantly behind them. The old man, startled, returned to his world. He glanced at the houses which lined the thoroughfare, these were new he thought, had been fields before, he was sure. The steeple of a church loomed above thick branches, crows gathering on its angular roof. He scrutinised several figures, Watchers, standing in the graveyard, motionless and upright, scrutinising the bus as it approached. Their features were blurred to his sight, no, they were silhouettes without feature, a dark emptiness where people would have faces.

The bus stopped to allow more passengers aboard with an abrupt jolt, steeling his attention from the graveyard. Glancing back the shapes were gone. The old man now caught sight of a landmark he was familiar with, the covered calvary which stood over a war memorial on the opposite side of the road. Young men jostled each other outside as the bus waited, laughing and jeering they threw empty beer cans into the confines of the memorial garden's low wall. Loud voices filled the transport as three young men made their way up the aisle to their chosen seats. Their brightly coloured sportswear and alien hair styling could not help but disturb the old man as he watched them through the corner of his eye. The three men sat uncomfortably close to an elderly grey-haired lady who perched, with handbag grasped tightly on her lap, just one row of seats in front of them. One of the men, spotty faced and sporting a thin adolescent moustache sat straddling the aisle, deep in loud conversation with his companions.

The bus moved on, the passengers retreated into their own personal enclaves of safety, comforting themselves with their thoughts while the three youths cackled and croaked in their midst. Before long the bus was travelling along the sea front, the old man watched as they passed the pier, he stretched himself upward to catch a glimpse of the rocky shore beneath its numerous iron struts and legs but lacked the strength to do so.

With a squeal of the brakes the bus stopped. A middle-aged lady, laden with shopping, tried in her best British manner to pass down towards the doors without making eye contact or communicating the urgency of her motion. The youths disregarded her entirely. Circumstances came to the woman's aid as a young lady, perhaps just eighteen years of age, entered the vehicle.

As the seagulls outside swooped down upon discarded morsels on the promenade, the men, in unison, turned their attention to the newcomer. She moved awkwardly up the aisle towards a spare seat. The old man watched as Moustache moved aside to let her through. The patient old lady took her chance to hurry to the exit. One of the young men laughed as he pressed his chewing gum into the side of the old lady's handbag as she moved.

The young lady moved to one side to let her elder go by and as she did so the long heavy coat she was wearing breached along its front for a second. The old man remembered a time gone by when the shins of a young woman revealed in such a way was the height of titillation and excitement a man could expect. He studied the young lady rapidly, she wore her shoulder length brunette hair in a loose knot at the neck, her face was pretty with a prominent nose, her skin unblemished by age or worry. Beneath her coat she wore a knee length white dress and a red scarf around her shoulders. Her hand which grasped the rail, to steady herself as the bus embarked, appeared smooth and untainted by toil. Her fingernails were painted a deep red. She smiled briefly at the old lady, her inner kindness revealed to the old man who inhaled sharply at her beauty.

As she made her way up the aisle the youths also purveyed their muse, with a determined focus, devoid of even the mildest decency. Moustache sprung from his seat almost swinging on the overhead rail, like a perverse monkey enthralled at the approach of the zookeeper and the daily feed. His companions adopted a more subtle stance than he, sitting upright, tracking her progress intently. Her head bowed as she approached the men and yet onward she pressed with determination.

"Well look at this," snorted Moustache, refusing to move aside.

His friends cackled, the old man could instantly read their expressions, their support for their leader was sycophancy and they were just as uncomfortable with the situation as the other passengers.

"May I get through please?"

"She doesn't remember my name then," the scruffy youth gloated, looking to his companions for acknowledgement.

"You never did," one of the spotty men exclaimed.

"I did too," proclaimed Moustache.

"Please, I just want to sit down."

"Come, we'll talk," Moustache insisted, grabbing her arm and turning her back down the aisle, "You don't remember me from school do ya?"

"No, thank you, I prefer to sit alone," the young lady jerked at her restraint, Moustache tightening his grip, leading her to a seat away from his friends.

For a moment, the scene had played out before, a familiarity struck the old man in an instant. A brunette girl led away by a moustached officer. She looked back, searching for a set of eyes on which her gaze would fall. The old man stared as their eyes met, she smiled unexpectedly, she was relishing the moment. She winked and laughed and turned away.

"No!" the old man blurted.

"Ha! What? What's this Grampa?" Moustache snarled.

He released the girl, who was once again in distress. He moved back up the aisle towards the old man who, feeling his chest compress with anguish, looked far out of the window longing to be somewhere else.

"Leave him alone," called the young lady as she grabbed at the youth's tracksuit.

"Shut up, get awff!" Moustache squirmed free of her grip.

Turning to face the young woman he pushed her violently down into a seat. Her bags dropped into the aisle and their contents began to roll down the bus. Someone at the rear of the bus let out a cry. The two spotty companions rose on their heels, glaring at the other passengers, who remained silent. Moustache faced the old man, his hand reaching down into his jacket pocket for something unseen.

The old man had seen enough to enrage his sentiments. He too had a secret in his pocket which could now come to play. His grip tightened on the old army jackknife in his coat pocket, the metal warm and still sticky with blood. For decades it had rested peacefully before its sudden recall to duty today. Would what strength he had left serve him better elsewhere? After all, the prize was secured in his jacket, the lighter was his again, back where it belonged. Could he risk it all acting once more? Let it pass, let it go, this was not his fight. Coward. Afraid. No. Too old, too stupid, to be afraid.

Acknowledging the conclusion of his internal monologue with a deep breath and low grunt, he pushed downward on the crook of his walking stick and began to rise from his seat, gripping the knife more tightly as it rose up within the deep pocket of his coat. The rapid excursion caused a giddiness to take him, his mind becoming fogged at the strain. As he stood, his surroundings spun and morphed before him. His chest cramped once more, a pulsing head pain surging through his brain.

The grey blur of the outside world changed to rolling countryside beyond the windows. Fields and hedgerows took the place of pavement and car park. The momentum of the bus seemed to increase from its slow, traffic induced, lurching. The train he found himself within was moving steadily, white smoke billowing about the exterior of the carriage as it penetrated a tunnel. Where brightly patterned seats had once held their patient passengers the carriage now featured drop-down metal bunks, stacked three high and laden with sleeping men. A brass boiler mounted on the wall bubbled and spurted, providing heat and water for tea.

The Moustached man stood in a tattered uniform, precariously propped on his wooden crutches, staring back at the old man as he tried to clamber to his feet. Beside him two men were sat up on their lower bunks watching the developing scene intently. One was bandaged about the head with a covered eye, the other rested with his left arm in a sling, his hand heavily bandaged. The beautiful brunette nurse in her white dress and red shawl reached out towards the old man, her eyes wide with sympathetic warmth and concern.

"Bernice!" the old man gasped.

Suddenly his legs gave way, all strength draining from his body. Trying to grasp desperately for the nurse's aid the old man was stunned at the appearance of his arm; a uniformed sleeve and a blood-stained hand too youthful to be his own. This final effort was too much for his current condition and the carriage spun into murky darkness. Muffled voices far away bemused him as he descended into unconsciousness.

Chapter 11 - Gehennan glow

23rd April 1916

Grande Rue from Bertrancourt

1935 hours

69 days to Z-Day

The open rear of the Thornycroft Type-J[18] motor transport offered a blinkered view of the passing world. The motorised column of lorries trundled and spluttered its way along busy roads. All the accoutrements of warfare were parading for the roosting birds, which looked on with nonchalant fascination. Large siege guns, parked at the side of the thoroughfare, languished in the spring dusk, while Artillerymen petted and preened them like slumbering dragons; every whim of these terrifying beasts catered for by petrified yet compliant villagers. Waggons and horses in their multitude whinnied and fussed along the road in the care of their Army Corps drivers.

As the lorries lurched along the congested road, long columns of soldiers parted to let them progress. As Moses parted the Red Sea, the steel monstrosities carved their way gradually through waves of men; the muddy trackways revealed before them like a seabed laid bare. A staff car, its horn blaring with such rhythmic incessancy that the startling nature of its call had been reduced to musical annoyance, such that a sudden silence would have caused more alarm to the unfortunate audience. The elegant vehicle pushed at the tide of traffic but could not find its purchase between the slow-moving ugly snakes of war. The general would wait in line with everyone else.

---

[18] The type-J was designed in 1912 specifically for the British Government subsidy scheme. It weighed 3¼ tons, with a four-cylinder side-valve engine developing 40hp, giving the lorry a top speed of 14½ mph. More than 5000 were supplied during the Great War.

Mules, tugging violently at their restraints, groaned at the dying sun. Oxen snorted in displeasure; their herculean efforts required for one more hour of light. The light was precious; a commodity the coffers of the British Empire could not find a market for. Everyone on the road was behind schedule, after dark no movement would be possible for such a huge conglomeration of equipment, animals and men.

The lorry behind Fortune's transport switched on its headlights, illuminating the covered compartment with its dazzling beam. The men, crowded within and hunkered at rest twitched and stirred, their heads rising from reverent posture.

"Cor, Christ almighty, that's bright!" called Private Richard Connor.

He snatched up an empty bully beef can and chucked it out of the lorry. The broad radiator of the vehicle behind deflected the attack, its glaring probe into the dark confines of the interior not fading.

"Fuck sake, will they not let us sleep!" he moaned.

"Shut up!" came a murmur from deep within the lorry.

"I swear to ya, nobody has the slightest clue what they are doing with us. Moved here, moved there, marching, trains, lorries. I never did see such a thing. They don't know where to send us, that's the truth. One day here, one day there. Can they make their minds up? Can they hell. When is our next meal? Eh? Can someone tell me when we will have a hot meal again chaps? No. Cos nobody knows. I wouldn't be surprised if they had forgotten about us altogether and we'll nod off in the back of this bloody lorry and not wake again."

"Quiet!"

"Pipe down Prick," another heckled.

"Rich not Ric," the offended private sought to correct his peer.

"P-Rick," the heckler insisted.

"Alright, everyone shut it, don't wake the sergeant," another voice called out.

Richard continued regardless, albeit in a hushed tone.

"How can anyone sleep through this? Answer me that. The bearings on this rust bucket are shot, you'd have a better ride in a barrel full of nails. The poor old Hun won't get a look-in, the English are going to see me done before we even arrive."

Richard Connor was Irish by descent but had grown up in the English midlands, his family migrating before he was born. His father was a coal miner and his mother a sadistic authoritarian, 'good Catholics' by all accounts. His short life had been a hard one. While his home life had been harsh under his mother's draconian stewardship, the outside world had not treated him any better. The small Irish community were faced with distrust and prejudice. Any misdemeanour in the village was blamed on the Irish, seen as second-class citizens, despised and resented. Richard had been up before the magistrate on numerous occasions, only a fraction of the crimes presented to the court had had any involvement from himself or his younger brother Jack.

Jack Connor had been killed while fighting in Gallipoli in August 1915, Richard joining the colours the very same day the casualty list was posted. He did not have many who considered him a friend; he was loud, almost boisterous at times, childish and very talkative. His mouth ran with abandon until someone made him shut it. He was considered a fool by most, his opinions so freely pronounced they had earned him many momentary enemies. He was treated badly, with absolute disdain by those who took umbrage at his unique personality, but to everyone's amazement he would bounce back immediately, seemingly unscathed from verbal or physical assault.

For all intents and purposes The Army was a better life than any he had experienced to date. The way others treated him was not unusual to him, the casual insults and occasional beatings were commonplace at home. He moaned and winged about the quality of his existence in uniform, this was a protective facade; a mechanism through which to engage his peers in conversation. He had learnt to ignore hunger on those long days and nights locked in the coal shed for the forgotten transgressions committed when he was a young boy.

"I'll tell you what's happening, this much I know. We're on the back foot. They have us licked. We're pulling back, it's over," he explained.

"Really?" enquired a voice.

"For sure," Richard replied with absolute authority.

"How can you possibly know this?" the puzzled voice persisted.

"It's clear as day. No food left. Roads crammed. Everyone on the move. We're off. Leave the frogs to it and back to Blighty."

"It can't be. We aren't beaten yet. We'll show the Hun what's for this year, no mistake," another voice spoke sharply with clear annoyance.

"At least we are one of the lucky ones hey? Getting pulled back. Spare a thought for those poor sods holding the line while we make our escape."

"There's nothing in the papers about this, it can't be so!" called another soldier.

"Propaganda intit, they don't want German spies reading the truth. A lot of thought goes into pulling an army home. This is a big operation. As controlled as a rout can be mind you. Let's all pray this shit heap doesn't break down and we get left behind with the wounded."

"You are so full of it Prick, shut yur mouth and let us rest. If yer keep up your rantings, I'll chuck yeh off the back me'self."

"Mark my words boys, we'll be on a ship heading for Southampton by morning. We're going home!"

Richard paused while his summary of events bedded in. Nervous smiles spread over the faces of the men as they contemplated the safety of England, their families and loved ones. A new voice now joined the debate. The sergeant, who up until now had been feigning sleep to avoid interaction, raised his head and pushed back his cap high upon his forehead.

"We're moving south to prepare for the big push. The whole Division is on the move and no doubt many more with us along the way. No matter how well The Brass are planning, the French roads aren't suited," Fortune explained slowly in a deep tone.

Fortune stared out of the lorry at a column of soldiers who had moved onto the verge to allow the convoy to proceed. Smoke surged upwards from their cigarettes and pipes like the skyline of an industrialised city. The headlights of the lorries transformed the dissipating vapour into an opaque cloud, which hung motionless over the men's heads like a patient yet hungry wraith. There was silence in the transport. Fortune carefully prepared his pipe and struck a match on his boot. The soldiers looked on, mesmerised by his every move in case it revealed some hidden secret of the war. Richard Connor plucked up the courage to respond.

"How do you know Sergeant?"

The soldier beside him leaned in close, tilting his cap to allow unrestricted access to Richard's ear. The forthcoming private whispered in disjointed sentences, pausing to gauge if he had been heard by the sergeant after every breath.

"They say he was in the show up at Loos last September. Saw some dreadful fighting they say. Wiped out half the platoon for deserting he did. Right between the eyes, all of 'em. That's what I heard. The other half died holding a trench all night. Germans kept coming this way and that, but he wouldn't retreat. Nobody got out save him and his commanding officer, Richardson. Course Richardson was so badly beat up he's been out of the picture ever since. They say even when he ordered Fortune to retreat, he refused and that's why Richardson caught a bullet. I reckon Fortune gave it him himself. That's the story I heard anyways."

Richard turned to his confidante and looked him in the eyes, assessing his honesty with scrutiny. Deciding the story was probably true his gaze switched back to the weary looking sergeant opposite him.

"Can you be sure sergeant?" he pressed.

Fortune took a mouthful of smoke. He turned to address the filled transport, releasing the fragrant vapour with a sudden and sharp exhalation.

"Nearly twenty thousand men in The Division. Artillery, medical, veterinary, Service Corps transports, labour units, engineers, signals, mounted and cyclists and then you lot. Twelve battalions of scrotes like you. You think this looks bad? This is organised. This you see before you is the collective intelligence of the British Army at work. The magnitude of such a thing, moving so many on these piss poor roads. You should be impressed.

This ain't no walk in the park with your sweetheart. It's not a weekend train to the coast. Thousands and thousands of men, their equipment, ammunition, food, field hospitals, animals, their feed, the list is endless and out there you can see it all moving along going to where it needs to be. In a day's time we'll be in place. Up the line or in reserves, every battalion deposited where it's needed, everything here, supporting you. So you can do your job."

"But we're hungry sergeant, when will they..." Richard was cut short by an incensed Fortune.

"You think this is bad? Do you? It's bad when you get off the boat and march for near enough two weeks solid. You march for so long you can't take your boots off, you can't feel your toes, the skin on your feet would come away if you touched it. Sleep comes easily to you wherever you can get it. You sleep on the move, just the chap next to you stopping you from wandering into a ditch and dying from exhaustion. A tug on your shoulder when you waiver from course, you open your eyes briefly to see everyone is there, marching like the dead, miles and miles and miles. Your transport section gets held up of course, on the busy roads. The kitchen doesn't arrive until you are setting off again the next morning. So you make do with what you can scrounge. You hope an officer won't catch you grabbing a hen or nabbing from a farmhouse. Or you eat from bully cans and be thankful.

And when you think you can't march any more, when you are done in, ready to give up and trade your life for a moments rest, that's when you hear the guns. The guns get closer and still you march on. You march all damned day and as the sun is setting, they send you in. And you fight. You fight hard and you kill or be killed. And when you come out of it, if you come out of it, having fought for the whole night and the following day, then you might consider moaning. You might moan if your tea is cold or your bread stale. You might moan you need a bath or new boots, a pencil to write home or some francs for booze. You might say such things after all that's happened.

But don't let me fucking hear you moaning when those lads are lying out there with more to gripe about than you can know. You do your marching and you think, thank you. You take your cold bully beef and you think, thank you. You stand in the rain in a bloody hole and you think, thank you. Cos everything this war is going to throw at you is a blessing, remember that, if you can stay alive long enough to appreciate it. The Army is looking after you. Your mates are looking after you. I'm looking after you. It's the best it's going to get, being alive. Alternative is being dead. Which is shit. There's nothing else."

Fortune turned away. He allowed the pipe to console him with its soothing mist. The soldier's grim expressions sought reassurance from each other but there was none. For the first time in his life Richard Connor was lost for words or the motivation to expunge them.

The journey continued in silence for what seemed to the men an eternity. Alone with their thoughts and worries they stared blankly at their comrades in disbelief. The disturbing and yet refreshing wisdom from this mysterious sergeant contrasted so starkly with the unified message The Army had fed them like Dickensian workhouse boys. Nobody had ever spoken harshly of the war or its conduct. Furrowed brows told a bleak story. Many, after some consideration, dismissed the old man's ranting; their ambitions of heroic achievement overturning his message and discounting his words. As their minds processed distressing thoughts, the blame and anger grew towards Richard for stoking the fire so recklessly.

Without warning the column of lorries halted next to a shallow bank. A Service Corp sergeant, laden with paperwork, came along the line banging on the back plates of each vehicle.

"Get this open," Fortune instructed, "And wait here."

Fortune jumped down from the transport and stretched his limbs. A private handed down his rifle, which was snatched firmly by Fortune, turning away when his pack was offered. A London auto-bus,[19] painted in khaki, groaned and puffed alongside the column; its decks rammed with men who waved and jeered triumphantly with their caps in the air as the spectacle moved by.

"You drew the short straw riding with the new draft, didn't you?" called Danny Hope in his broad Welsh accent as he approached.

"Sergeant Hope. Yes, perhaps I did."

Fortune offered a wry smile to his old companion, recently promoted.

Danny put his arm around Fortune's shoulder and escorted him away from the column and up the grassy bank; illuminated in the failing light by the headlamps of the lorries.

"Not pulling the old sermons on them are you again? The Loos march? Or was it the murderers and fornicators one?" Danny chuckled.

"Aye, well they need it. Loos march of course. So, we're here?"

"Yeah, we're here."

"Where's that then?"

---

[19] About one third of the London fleet, more than 1,000 buses, were requisitioned for war service, often along with their civilian drivers and mechanics

"Buggered if anyone knows, 2nd Lieutenant McGreggor is nowhere to be found. All mixed up in the traffic with half the company and our kitchen. We've got half of C and some of B with us. But, um, look, we aren't far."

Danny turned Fortune to face eastward, pointing at the horizon. The sky was strangely illuminated with orange and yellow glows. Occasionally a brighter flash of white would pulse like a faraway storm.

"First platoon? First platoon?"

A corporal carrying a clipboard called out along the line as he navigated the column. He paused at every lorry inspecting the back plate with his torch, having referred to the documents he carried on the clipboard.

"Over here!" called Danny.

"Where's your commanding officer sergeant?" asked the middle-aged corporal.

"Your guess is as good as mine. France would be my guess judging by the smell. What do you have for us?"

The corporal fumbled with his torch, struggling to release papers from the strong bulldog clip with one hand. Both sergeants glanced at each other as they waited.

"Um, here. You will need these papers to requisition billets. There should be two farms just up a track to the north. Battalion HQ is situated just down the road here, on the right, in a farmhouse near the orchard. Company HQ will be," he paused as he shuffled papers, "Just opposite in bell tents."

"Thank you corporal," Danny smiled dismissively until the soldier hurried away to find the rest of his quarry.

"I'll take this one and the first two sections, you have these," he suggested.

"Aye," Fortune agreed.

"Try not to put the willies up them Fortune, they are good lads really."

"Ain't that the problem."

The NCOs began the task of unloading the lorries, assembling the men into their respective sections on the roadside. Many stood with heads crooked to watch in awe the pulsing skyline in the distance. The horizon twitched with colour and excitement at the prospect of fresh new lambs for the furnace.

"You'll have plenty of time to warm your hands on the fire, let's move," ordered Fortune.

The men set off into the dark to find the farmhouse which was to be their home for the night. At first the trackway failed to materialise in the gloom, scouts eventually discovering it some way off to the right. Within an hour of arriving the soldiers were marching. John Jacques Farm was situated at the top of a rise at the end of a boulevard of elms. The rough gravel track was unforgiving on the men's feet, but they trudged along in silence at the bequest of Henry Hamblin, one of Fortune's original recruits, who was now corporal for 3-Section. The farm loomed out of the darkness as they approached. The old buildings were constructed from small red bricks, featuring a tall wall around the exterior courtyard, which linked with the farmhouse and a barn via a broad archway. As the men passed beneath, they peered up at the keystone which was embossed with the date "1870".

A dog began to bark furiously as the men assembled in the courtyard. A light then moved rapidly within the dark farmhouse and within moments the main door opened violently. Stood in a long night robe was a burly whiskered man brandishing what appeared to be a flintlock shotgun.

"*Partez, vous ne pouvez pas venir ici, vous n'êtes pas les bienvenus. Vous devez partir immédiatement. Il n'y a pas de place pour vous ici!*" he shouted and spat.

Some of the men became alarmed, levelling their rifles at the farmer, thankfully Fortune and Corporal Henry Hamblin soon had them back at attention. Fortune approached the farmer without hesitation or fear, his brash action and careless attitude had disarmed the farmer before he arrived at the doorway.

"Now listen here you. I have these papers see. And they say you are putting us up for the night. You can be agreeable and show us your barn or you can get in the way, and that's when accidents can happen. Comprender? Either way, the men here are sleeping here tonight so lower your pea shooter and let us in."

"*Pourriture!*" the farmer spat with venom.

"Very good! Wise man."

Fortune patted the farmer firmly on the shoulder and barged into the farmhouse, leaving the Frenchman with crumpled papers and a wicked glare upon his face.

Chapter 12 - Virgins and vagabonds
24th April 1916

Grande Rue from Bertancourt

0610 hours

68 days to Z-Day

Fortune had made his way to Battalion HQ before first light to seek news on the whereabouts of his commanding officer, 2nd Lieutenant McGreggor. Word had arrived via a messenger that McGreggor had been involved in an accident on the road during the night and was now being treated at a dressing station some miles away. While only a minor setback it would delay his joining the company by several days. Captain Wilmslow had entrusted 1st Platoon to Fortune in the interim.

On his journey back up to the farm, the true scale of the divisional transport became apparent in the light of breaking dawn. The road was now little more than a muddy scar ripping its way through the French agricultural landscape. Motor lorries had fallen lame to either side of the track and there they slumbered waiting for rescue. Mules and horses plodded on regardless through the mire, their heads hung solemnly, their dark moods unabated by the irony of the fate of their motorised superiors. Hundreds of men marched onward, their faces dusted and dirty. White eyes amidst dark brows strained to glimpse the struggle on the horizon ahead of them. The guns had fallen silent for some time now, only a grey miasma of smoke hung over the hills to the east, yet still the soldiers sought some tantalising image of war to enrich their letters home.

Fortune made his way through the throng, carrying the mail for his men over one shoulder, his rifle over the other. Soon he traversed the busy thoroughfare and in seeking the track which led to the farm something caught his eye. A solitary wooden cross lay on its side at the grassy verge, where a pile of earth marked a new grave. Discarding his baggage, he crouched beside the cross, wiping the dust away from the inscription it bore. The name could not be deciphered, the plaque too severely damaged. A British airman lay here, brought down a few weeks previous according to the words he could make out. On more careful inspection of the surroundings he discovered a pair of flying goggles, which had once hung on one arm of the cross, now trampled into the earth beside the grave.

Fortune repositioned the cross and used his rifle to drive it back into the ground. With mud removed from the goggles, as best he could he hung them once more around the cross. There he stood for some time, smoking his pipe in silence. The great war machine marched by without fanfare or salute.

Up at the farm the men had been active for several hours. The night had passed in comparative comfort, the large barn providing dry housing for the exhausted soldiers. Sergeant Danny Hope and his corporals now had the men cleaning equipment and restoring provisions. A portable stove provided hot water for tea as well as warmth for the platoon sections. Two men worked the farm's pump providing fresh water for their canteens, while men shaved and washed under the morning sun. Several of the men kicked a heavy leather football around the courtyard while others took the time to write letters.

The farmer's daughter, a lithe brunette girl in her early twenties, brought the men sliced meats and cheese; food they could hardly spare in such times, but she had insisted her father make amends for the poor hospitality originally shown the night before. As she glided over the cobbles towards the barn, time itself seemed to stand still for everyone present. She walked with such grace amongst the uncouth British youth, she appeared almost regal in her bearing. She wore a pastel dress which gripped her gentle curves tightly, accompanied by black court shoes with a shallow heel. The air was cold with an April chill, yet she wore no coat or covering for her shoulders. She was young and surprisingly beautiful and every man in the courtyard fixated upon her majestic form whenever she appeared.

She approached a group of soldiers who were cleaning their rifles, under a tiled canopy, beside the barn. They passed each other excited glances as she grew near. One of them went red in the face.

"Hey up pretty lassy," called one of the Tommies.

The others chuckled like excited schoolboys.

"Pardon Messieurs," she paused as soon as she realised her stupidity and switched to English, "Sirs, if you please, we have a small offering of food, *pour vous*."

The three soldiers stood up politely.

"That's mighty kind miss. We are certainly in need of it. What you can spare would be greatly appreciated."

"You will have to forgive us, there may not be much more to go around," she explained softly.

"Oh, you er, you can let us share this out, just hand it here," the Tommies looked at each other knowingly and took charge of the platter.

"Merci, thank you."

She stood with hands clasped in front of her, the breeze teasing hair across her face. She smiled and watched the men as they froze in awkward politeness; all they could do was stare back. Satisfied, she stifled a smirk and turned on the spot to walk back towards the farmhouse. It felt like a hundred eyes were clamouring for a glimpse of her shins as she strode over the cobbles. She bit down on her wayward hair and covered her smirking with a cupped hand.

"Well I never," one of the Tommy's exclaimed.

"Did you ever see such a maiden?" enquired another.

"I should very much like to take her for a walk on the promenade at Weston," another stated proudly, "The lads would be green with envy if I had such a girl on my arm!"

"Oh yes!" a Tommy agreed heartily.

"She wouldn't go with you! Not the way you smell!"

The men laughed.

"Now listen here, I scrub up well in civvies," the affronted Tommy exclaimed.

"That ain't the end of it, she wouldn't look beyond your penguin feet."

The men laughed harder. Each group of soldiers was now sharing their own joke amongst themselves, usually at someone's expense. Many a soldier was overcome with admiration that morning and in the fantasies of their minds the farm girl was taken on promenades or a bicycle ride, hands being held and kisses planted on cheeks. Some imagined a trip to the cinema, without a chaperon, leading to a kiss in the darkness on the back row of seats. The men stared into space, daydreaming of their pretty farm girl. The scenes evolved in their minds; the unknown knowledge of female interaction kindling an innocent yet stimulating storyline in their imagination.

Private Charlie Pocock and Private Edward Cartwright sat away from the other groups of men. Their faces wore grim expressions, their eyes were blood shot and glazed. They saw things in a different light these days. Private Pocock handed his friend a bottle. Neither of them stole their focus away from the farm girl as the bottle passed back and forth between them.

Private Cartwright was a Gloucester man, from a long-standing family of wheelwrights. He had attested in October 1914, against the wishes of his father who had served in the Royal Artillery during the South African War, his experiences affecting him deeply; adamant that his only son would not follow in his footsteps but powerless to stop the tall fresh-faced youth from answering the call. He had slipped away from the workshop, joined friends in a local inn and after several drinks marched off arm in arm to the recruitment office.

Having grown up around horses, he was experienced in their care and handling, so intended to join a cavalry or yeomanry battalion. The cunning recruitment sergeant had promised him a life in the saddle yet signed him up for the Infantry never-the-less.

Private Cartwright had trained in Aldershot with the original members of the company, shipping out to France in September 1915. The war had changed him in a short time. His youthful appearance, gaiety and innocent demeanour had been tarnished by conflict and stress. His face was gaunt, his emotionally vacant eyes deeply set into leathery cheeks, a prominent scar arcing upward over his chin to his lower lip. At twenty years of age he was often mistaken for a man in his thirties.

"Now the damage I would do to that Charlie, it would be in the papers tomorrow," confessed Private Cartwright.

"Firing squad if I had my hands on her I dare say," chuckled Private Pocock.

"Oh no doubt. But it would be worth it," Private Cartwright smiled wickedly.

"Fair price to pay for getting into that little cow and showing her what's what."

"You can't go flaunting yourself like that. Not without repercussions," Private Cartwright shook his head.

"True enough. We don't need to see such things unless it's up for sale, obtainable somehow," Private Pocock grabbed the bottle back.

"Maybe, that's why she came out? Maybe, she wants us to?" Private Cartwright pondered.

"Yeah could be. Probably is. Or she is rubbing your bloody nose in what you can't have Ed. They do that. Yes, that's what this is. Little bitch flashing quim, getting her kicks from the attention," Private Pocock mischievously goaded his companion.

"As if we don't have enough to deal with. Whore."

"You should have a word," suggested Private Pocock with a nudge.

"Someone needs to do something, none of these saps will," Private Cartwright agreed.

He stood, steadied himself as the blood rushed to his head, then stormed towards the farm girl who was now emerging once more from the farmhouse with a fresh platter of food. Private Pocock smiled and finished off the bottle which his companion had been unknowingly coerced away from.

"Hello miss," Private Cartwright staggered beside her.

"Monsieur."

"Now I was thinking," he wrapped his arm clumsily around her waist, "You should join me and my mate for a drink, you have been on your feet all morning."

"Pardon Monsieur, but I have much to do," she pulled away from his grasp and continued on her way.

Private Cartwright caught up, once more his hands landed unwelcome on her person. She pulled away again but this time his grip was heightened. She stopped and turned towards him. He pulled her towards him. She resisted.

"Monsieur please," she protested.

"Just a quick drink, that's all I'm asking."

"There is work to do, for all of us. I am sorry but I must decline your offer."

"Now listen you can't be strutting up and down all morning and then go cold on us. You're a Clergyman's Daughter there's no mistake, I wants the razzle-dazzle you have been offering up."

The farm girl was confused by the slang. The platter spilt its contents on the cobbles as they struggled. The farm girl pushed with all her might and Private Cartwright tightened his grip.

"I don't know what those things are Monsieur, but I assure you I am just a farm girl and I do not wish to join *you* for a drink."

"Stop teasing, lass," Private Cartwright tried to direct her over to the barn entrance.

"Let go, you are hurting me. Monsieur!" she pleaded as they turned on the spot, straining against each other.

The men in the courtyard were now watching the scene unfold, not knowing how to react. Some had stood. They were weary of Private Cartwright, his reputation was well known amongst the fresh-faced lads.

"Fucking Hoyden you are!" Private Cartwright bellowed as they fought, turning and twisting this way and that as he lurched his head forward to try to kiss her.

Out of nowhere, a tightly clenched fist struck Private Cartwright squarely on the jaw sending him sprawling on the cobbles. The farm girl shrieked and stepped back in shock. Private Pocock stood. Fortune caught his glare and shook his head discretely. Private Pocock acknowledged the warning and sat back down immediately.

"Moore, Stendhurst, take Private Cartwright and tie him to the waggon wheel there," shouted Fortune.

"Yes sergeant," responded Private Moore as he rushed over to the unconscious Private Cartwright with Private Stendhurst following behind.

"Tie him up sergeant?"

"You heard me, on the wheel. Chuck water on him and get some tea down him. Sober him up. Get to it," ordered Fortune.

Fortune turned to the farm girl, flexing his fist to relieve the pain. She wiped away a single tear from her cheek and stared up at him, studying the man before her attentively. He stood perhaps six feet in height with broad shoulders atop which a thick sinuous neck held a large almost rectangular head. She had never seen such a broad chin in all her life. The man's brow was thick haired and furrowed, his intense frown framing hazel eyes which seemed to pierce her very being, searching for hidden secrets. The man's face was darkened from a life beneath the sun, his skin seemed thick like strong leather, his nose had been broken more than once. A thick nicotine stained moustache proudly adorned his upper lip, while a dark shadow of hair lingered beneath his cap. This huge man looked dangerous, a vicious personality must lurk behind an exterior such as this, she pondered. But as she stared up at him, she thought she caught a glimpse of something altogether more passionate, a warmth. He seemed to blot out the sun with his presence, he could envelop her where she stood. She would let him. His pupils widened; his lips parted slightly.

"Miss are you alright?" he enquired softly.

His sympathetic voice startled her. He spoke with a deep rumble in an accent she could not place.

"Monsieur, I…it is fine, I am fine. It was nothing. I will be fine."

Her face reddened.

"You are shaking miss, you should sit down," Fortune gesticulated to the farmhouse.

"Oh, no, my father," the farm girl looked anxious at the thought of returning to the abode.

"Here then, on the steps to the hay loft," Fortune suggested, "Let me take this tray."

"You are very kind Monsieur."

"Not at all."

She straightened her hair and brushed it over her ears, placing her hand on his arm as they walked to the steps across the courtyard. Fortune looked about and caught sight of Corporal Hamblin. He called him over as they walked.

"Corporal, find Sergeant Hope. Tell him we have our marching orders, we leave at noon. Take this mail bag and distribute to the men."

"Yes sergeant."

Fortune held the farm girl's arm as she lowered herself to the step. She sat and wept with her head in her hands. Fortune remained standing.

"Smoke?" he finally broke the awkward silence.

She looked up, her eyes reddened, tears now streaming down her face. Hair was stuck to her pale cheeks and her rosy lips were moist with her sorrow.

"I saved these for such times," he explained, removing the Capstan cigarettes from his top pocket.

He opened the packet and pushed a cigarette up from the group with his thumb.

"I have never...yes Merci," she plucked the cigarette from the packet and placed it in the corner of her mouth.

Fortune lit a match, shielding it from the breeze with his large hands, he moved it close to the girl's face. She closed her eyes as she took the first draw. Fortune made good use of this short moment of unrestricted scrutiny. She reminded him of a movie star, what was her name? It then came to him, Mary Pickford in Hearts Adrift, at The Picture House in Clevedon, in 1914. The last film he had seen before joining up. The girl surprised him, she smoked as if it were a full-time hobby. A natural he thought.

"Thank you, Monsieur," she exhaled to one side.

"I'm Sergeant Berriman miss and I am sorry for all this fuss today."

"Your kindness is appreciated Monsieur. I am Mademoiselle Jacques. But please call me Bernice. Will you not have one?"

"Oh, no, these are for emergencies. I smoke a pipe. Bernice, very well. I'm Henry."

There followed a long pause. She smoked and he watched.

"Do you have family, Monsieur?"

"No, I don't have family no more. Well, what was left was taken away."

"I am sorry, to pry."

"I don't mind miss, please, don't mind me. The only conversion I have is, well, men don't ask after families and such, put it that way."

"Do they not? Then what do men speak of?"

"Oh, I couldn't say miss."

"Bernice, please."

"As you wish, miss Bernice."

"I feel I have done some wrong today, enraging the men in some way. But I profess," she looked up with wide eyes and held his gaze, "I have little experience of men, stranded here with my father."

Fortune swallowed hard, his mouth was suddenly dry.

"No miss, you have been very welcoming. The lads are not used to women or their ways you see, they are but boys. Cartwright though, the soldier who offended you, is a drunk."

"Many men drink, Monsieur, they seem to enjoy it more than life itself."

"Aye well, he came out in fifteen you see, has seen a lot, been through a lot. With me. And a few others still left alive. It's no excuse for him I know. But there are few ways for those damaged by this war to deal with it, and drinking fulfils this purpose. He will be punished miss, I can assure you. What we have seen and done out here can't ever be an excuse for mischief or misdemeanour."

"Poor soul. I am sure, it is more a complexity than you make of it, *n'est-ce pas?* I am indebted to you. For saving me Monsieur," she brushed hair away from her face and over her ear, "I do not know how I shall ever repay you."

"Not at all miss. You and your father have been very accommodating, coming here and turning things up-side down as we did. The debt is mine."

"Better you than the Germans turning us upside and down no?"

"Well quite. I suppose. Well yes."

She stared far-off for a moment, pondering over the cigarette which hung limp from her lips.

"My father says it's a French war for French men and would have you thrown out, but he is naive of such things. He forgets easily how we faired before without help."

"I'm not sure I know of such things miss, if I am honest."

"The first war, 1870. The year this farm was completed. The Germans occupied this land you know? My grandfather fought them. We must have your help you see, everyone's help, if we are to drive them out this time. Or we are lost."

"I didn't know."

"Why would you? It was not a British war Monsieur, not that time. You are not taught of the plight of other nations. I know as much. We have been through this before and I dare say this will not be the last. But we have your help now," she paused with a brief smile, "And let us hope the Americans will see sense and cast aside this abandonment of the old world."

"I couldn't say miss, I didn't care much for schooling or current affairs or newspapers and the like. If I may ask, forgive me, how does a pretty girl as yourself come by such knowledge?" Fortune enquired.

"I read when I can, as much as I can. I have books and time, plenty of it stranded here with my father. I was schooled in Paris and London when I was younger. I was given an education at the bequest of my mother you see. When she passed away my father had me come home, and that was the end of it."

"I did wonder how such good English was possible miss, from a foreigner. It is impressive. I can swear in Urdu, the language of the blacks in India but profess little more than the rudimentals."

"I hasten a guess that your skills do not need to lie in that of communication Monsieur, but elsewhere in more...physical pursuits? Have you seen much, of the war? If I can ask?"

"I'm a career soldier miss, Bernice, unlike most of these boys. It's the only profession I have ever really had. It keeps me fed and occupies these hands. I have seen more of *this* war than I care to already mind you. It's not like all the others miss. But it seems I have more work to do in the coming months still."

"They say the big offensive is coming. Joffre is on the attack again. Let us hope there is more success this time Monsieur. I do not think the people of France can take much more."

Fortune stood there contemplating a response, stunned by the way in which this farm girl was speaking. His mind raced. There were, of course, serious threats from spies; everywhere according to the rumours. He had never held such a conversation with a woman before. How would a farm girl know so much and speak with such authority on the affairs of men?

"I don't know of these things miss. I just go where I am told and try to keep the boys alive," he confessed at last.

"Have you killed?" the farm girl shot the question across an unsuspecting bow.

Fortune frowned and sought an apt response, he had none which he was comfortable sharing.

"Forgive me and my silly questions," she relented, standing up beside him.

Bernice ground the cigarette remnants into the cobbles. She placed her hand on his upper arm and leaned in to kiss him on the cheek.

"It is a shame you have to leave today Monsieur. Oh, thank you for the cigarette."

With that she turned away and walked proudly back to the farmhouse. Fortune touched his cheek and watched her in wonder as she sailed over the cobbles with determined strides. He was disarmed. Unmanned. He joined the ranks of nameless soldiers who stood watching their muse glide away. The girl who moments ago was weeping and afraid drew the thick coat of confidence around her exposed shoulders once more and disappeared into the farmhouse. The disappointment felt in the courtyard was tangible.

Chapter 13 - Exodus

24th April 1916
John Jacques Farm
1155 hours
68 days to Z-Day

The platoon was standing ready, organised by sections in the courtyard for Fortune's inspection on the strike of midday. The men waited patiently in their lines, rifles at their side and packs on their backs. The sun gleamed off their polished buttons. The air was fresh, their bellies were full, a positive mood encapsulating the throng. Fortune was sat at a trestle table in front of the platoon, sifting through papers from a flat leather case. Private Cartwright groaned as his head rocked slowly from side-to-side, chin on chest, his face remaining unseen. He sat, legs outstretched before him, arms bound above his head on the wheel of the waggon forming the shape of a Y. Shifting eyes surveyed him. The men waited in silence.

Fortune's pocket watch sat open on the table beside him.[20] Every so often he would look up from his papers and glance at the time. Starlings danced in the gutters of the farm building, picking nature's detritus from the lead gullies, tossing down any fragments which were not suitable for their nesting. The farm dog paced up and down the ranks of soldiers wagging its tail like an excited general, riding his steed along his army before a Napoleonic battle. At midday precisely Fortune picked up the watch and closed its lid. He then neatly stacked the papers and secured them in their leather container. Finally, he stood, setting the chair tightly under the table. He scanned the platoon from left to right then beckoned to Corporal Henry Hamblin who approached immediately.

"Platoon ready for inspection sergeant."

---

[20] British military time used to coordinate operation during the war was London time rather than local time.

"Very good corporal."

Fortune approached 1-Section and eyed them closely. He passed up and down their length pausing occasionally to peer at buttons or insignia closely.

"Private Roberts isn't it?"

"Yes sergeant."

Private Richard Roberts of 1-Section stared straight ahead. Fortune took Private Roberts' Lee Enfield rifle and perused the weapon carefully. He cleared the breach and removed the magazine. He ran a finger down the ranging sight and then inspected it for dirt. Satisfied he returned the rifle to Private Roberts.

"Good. Well done Private," Fortune congratulated.

Private Richard Roberts beamed with pride, a tuft of a moustache he was attempting to grow turning upward at its ends as his huge smile developed. Richard Roberts was sixteen years of age, his limited years disguised by his enormous stature, that of a well-built, twenty-year-old man. He had been employed as a dock worker in Liverpool from the age of twelve, when his father, a long serving employee at the docks and active campaigner for worker's rights, had been killed by an industrial accident. His mother and seven siblings looked to Richard, the eldest son, to support the family and thus any dream he may have harboured of furthering his education was curtailed the day he walked through the large iron gates of the dockyard and became a man. Richard was physically large, with huge hands, taking after his father in stature and strength of character. While he was the youngest member of the company, he was arguably more mature and experienced in the ways of the world than most of the other men present.

His appearance had not always been an advantage. Out running errands for the family one evening, two girls had placed white feathers in his pocket, while riding on a tram. Mistaking him for an adult who had not yet taken up the King's uniform their insensitive actions had acted as an incendiary of shame within the youth. He attested the very next day. As the sergeant moved on down the line, Richard tightly grasped the white feathers he still carried deep within his pocket.

Fortune moved on to 2-Section where the process was repeated, then to 3-Section. Waiting patiently for praise in 3-Section was Private Richard Connor. As Fortune approached, he turned his head several times in anticipation.

"Don't worry boy, I'm getting to you in good time."

"Eyes front!" Corporal Hamblin scolded.

"P-Rick," whispered Private Pocock beside him.

Fortune stood close to Private Connor, just to his right, poised inches away from his face. Fortune's eyes darted over the private and his equipment, searching for some misdemeanour or infraction. Fortune sniffed. He sniffed again. Within moments he had located the source.

"What on earth have you done to your helmet boy?" he enquired.

A snigger was clearly audible from the ranks. Fortune ignored it and asked again.

"Everyone was dulling their helmets sergeant. They said I didn't want my new helmet to be so shiny in the trenches or I would get me 'ed blown off. They said to dull it like everyone else had," Private Connor explained.

"Good advice. And what pray tell did you use in this endeavour?" Fortune suppressed a grin.

"I used mud same as everyone else did."

Two men laughed and quickly suppressed their glee when Fortune looked around.

"That's enough," Fortune snapped, "Mud you say?"

"Yes Sergeant, they got me some mud to use, special mud, special prepared for me."

Soldiers shifted on their feet and winced to hold back their amusement.

"You have shit on your head Private Connor," Fortune turned to the rest of the section and for the first time revealed his mirth with a broad smile.

The men erupted into boisterous laughter and hooting. Fortune gave Private Pocock a strong pat on the back for executing his orders so precisely. Private Connor squirmed and raged beneath his calm exterior. The men relaxed, exchanging knowing looks and comforting grins.

Fortune walked out in front of the men once more, his momentary exposure of emotion suppressed once more.

"All men who have not been up to the front before step forward, form a line here. Quick smart!" Fortune ordered.

A shuffling in the ranks became an exodus as men stepped out of the group and formed up their new line.

"Remove your tunics, place them on the ground, in front."

The men looked at each other.

"Get to it," barked Corporal Hamblin, "You heard the sergeant!"

Many of the men fumbled with their equipment, some tried to perform the task while still holding their rifle, others with rifle on the floor or between their legs became muddled in a tangle of straps from their webbing. Fortune watched the sorry affair with a frown. Private Pocock grinned knowingly at his comrades.

"Eyes front Private Pocock," snapped Corporal Hamblin.

"Remaining sections will form column on Corporal Hamblin there," Fortune instructed.

Corporal Harry Hamblin arranged the men in single file and on Fortune's signal paraded them around the interior of the large yard, finally turning to head directly across the front of the new draft line. The young, fresh-faced soldiers were aghast as the column approached and proceeded to march over their new tunics. As each man passed by, they stomped and twisted their boots on the garments, driving them into the dust and dirt of the cobbled stone surface.

Private Connor's rage built once more, but as always he kept his emotions hidden, his jaw clamping shut in grim determination like so many times before, when bullied or cajoled into submission. Private Pocock turned to him as he went by, with a toothless snarl which turned to a grin as he met Connor's gaze. Stooping slightly Private Pocock spat down-wards onto Private Connors upturned tunic.

The column progressed, winding its way around the end of the small line. Corporal Hamblin brought them back to where their brief march had begun, reforming them into sections.

"Front line will take one pace forward onto their tunics," ordered Fortune sternly.

"Front line will march on the spot, at the double!" he continued.

The downbeat line of young men stamped and stomped until the order came to stop.

"Front line will re-attire. At the double," Fortune barked as he approached.

The inexperienced men took longer to re-equip then they had to undress. All the while Fortune paced the line, his hands tucked tightly behind his back in a solid embrace.

"Much better, yes, that's good. Take a look at your tunics lads, I want to see them in this state whenever we are down the line, understood? Repeat this task every day, a handful of earth goes a long way, do your own, check your mates. If I see a single gleaming button or a patch of new khaki without dirt on it, you will be on fatigues for a week. Do I make myself clear?"

"Yes sergeant," the men responded in unison, albeit with looks of confusion at the instruction.

"Return the men to their sections Harry please," Fortune asked quietly of Corporal Hamblin.

"Now, listen," Fortune's voice projected around the courtyard as he walked back out to his table, "Battalion is heading up the line tonight, we're straight in lads. We're going to be attached to the 70th Brigade and the York and Lancs are coming out for a rest. I'm told they keep good trench these northern lot, nice and clean and well repaired, so we'll have a breeze. Those of you with trench experience, make yourself known again, raise your helmets."

A proportion of the platoon lifted their steel helmets above their heads.

"For those of you not raising your helmets look around. These are men in your section who will guide you. Do what they do. Your corporal will give you instructions, listen to them. No smoking means put it out and keep it out. When we say quiet, shut your trap. Do what the old sweats do, watch and learn. Keep down, never, ever leave the trench unless told to do so. And keep your rifle clean. Breech covers on at all times. Corporals please."

The four section NCOs attended Fortune as he sat once more at the table. Untying the string binding of his leather case he revealed a map from within.

"We're joining the rest of the company here, on the main road, then marching here, about seven miles, we'll meet up with the rest of the battalion. At 1800 we meet our York and Lanc guides here, south west of Aveluy Wood. They will take us down to Blighty Valley. Then along Upper Norwich here. York and Lancs are coming out via Lower Norwich so we can't use that, we'll get snarled up to buggery if we do. Battalion HQ will be here at Quarry Post. C-Company is taking this stretch, Liverpool Avenue.[21]"

"Where's McGreggor in all this?" asked Corporal Harry Hamblin.

"Resting in a hospital."

Spends more time with his toes under white sheets than in his army boots, Fortune thought to himself.

"No idea when he will return, I'm afraid. We've done this before, we can do it again without him. So, as you know the relief is crucial. That's where the danger is. They catch us going in or coming out, well, that's it. Mess. So, keep 'em moving, keep 'em quiet. Let's get in there in one piece hey? Battalion order says relief will be complete by 0400 tomorrow, before it's light."

"Gets light by five or so though, doesn't give us long does it?"

"No Harry, not long but long enough if we do it right. Form column by sections on the arch and we'll get moving," Fortune instructed.

"Alright, what about Cartwright?"

"Cut him down and get him in line."

"Formal field punishment?"

"Nah. Not this time. We might need him."

The corporals went about their business organising the men. Fortune gathered his things from the table and a private brought over his kit and rifle. As the platoon was arranging itself into a column Sergeant Danny Hope entered the courtyard with three very young-looking men, their uniforms a crisper Khaki than anyone else now standing there.

"Danny, what's this?"

---

[21] Trenches were given names to aid navigation and identification on maps.

"New draft from depot just got in," he explained handing over paperwork to Fortune.

The three men stood nervously behind Sergeant Hope as Fortune scrutinised their documentation. Two of the men were quite obviously identical twins. They were both very slight and on the short side. Their complexion was pale and eyes a piercing blue. It would be many years yet before they could muster facial hair of any quality. Their uniforms and equipment seemed to hang on them like unsuitable clothing on a scarecrow. They held their arms uncomfortably, not knowing how to relax in garb which was obviously still alien to them. The third soldier was taller, with manly shoulders and a face which had developed though hard seasons toiling under the sun. His hands were large for his frame. Yet, regardless of the weathering of his body Fortune could tell he was young, nineteen or twenty years of age.

"Alright. Leonard Cooksley to 1-Section. Michael Cooksley to 4-Section. And him, he can join 3-Section with Harry."

"Very well."

Fortune watched as the NCOs came to take their fresh recruits into the ranks.

"Wait a minute," he intercepted Corporal Hamblin.

"Gentlemen, your attention please on this auspicious occasion," Fortune's voice boomed around the courtyard, "We have a very special dignitary visiting us today."

The men shared murmurs and excitement built rapidly. They eyed the recruit who stood before them all awkwardly.

"Down on your knees lads, the lot of ya. Get down. Know your place. Go on."

The men, albeit confused, obeyed their sergeant explicitly and struggled to their knees under the weight of their kit.

"We are fortunate and honoured to have joining us today a very important person, from the holy-land. Gentlemen I give you, the Virgin Mary. Private George Merry."

The platoon erupted into laughter once more at Fortune's teasing. They jeered and hooted and waved their helmets in the air. Private Merry immediately flushed red in the face and squirmed where he stood.

"I'm not a virgin," he pleaded directly to Fortune.

"Yes you are son, yes you are," Fortune chuckled to himself.

Corporal Hamblin shook his head at Fortune and lead the boy into the ranks. Soldiers patted him forcibly on the back and jostled him as he was arranged in the column.

"I'm not a virgin," he insisted to the men as he went by, this only sought to increase their glee.

Fortune walked the length of the column and carried out one final inspection. As each section was given the all clear their NCO marched them out of the farm under the old arch and down the trackway towards the road. The little farm dog ran with them yapping with excitement, its tail thundering back and forward as it went.

A cheering column of soldiers, waving their helmets at the departing company, marched up the track towards the farm and through the arch. Fortune stepped to one side to allow their noisy ingress, saluting their commanding officer as he passed by. The men were full of great spirit, rejoicing at their march coming to an end with yet more cheering. Their buttons and badges gleamed in the midday sun, the tiger and rose emblem of their cap badge denoting their military heritage. What was briefly the domain of the Somerset Light Infantry was now handed to the York and Lancaster regiment, without so much as a word. The men strode into the courtyard proudly as if parading at Windsor Castle for the King. As the head of the column started to release their burden onto the cobbles of the courtyard the rear of the line paused for a while beyond the archway.

Amongst their boisterous celebration a young soldier stared coldly at Fortune as he lingered at the rear of the column. Fortune caught his gaze and for a moment wondered what troubled the young man. All about him his comrades laughed together and smoked, full of nervous excitement. However, this young lad, pallid in comparison, stared at Fortune with a ferocious countenance better reserved for the battlefield. His curiosity was transitory, Fortune spotted Sergeant Hope counting out the men and beckoned him over.

"Keep those twins away from me Danny," he mumbled.

"All right," Sergeant Hope replied without further question, a sombre look passing between the two men as he rejoined the column.

"Henri," a female voice struck out at Fortune as he watched the men leaving.

He turned quickly to watch Bernice rush from the farmhouse, gathering her skirt at her side to allow her faster movement. Her face was blushed and eyes full of moisture.

"You left these," she said handing over a packet of Capstan cigarettes.

"Oh aye, well, you keep 'em miss," Fortune looked almost bashful.

"Please, they will come in handy no doubt, for emergencies," she smiled knowingly at him.

He smiled back, taking the packet from her, quickly placing them in his top pocket.

"Will I see you again?"

"Doubtful miss. But expect the unexpected. I just wouldn't like to say."

"Write to me?"

"These hands weren't never trained for writing, but I will send word, I promise," Fortune looked around feeling as if every eye within a mile was peering at him, urging his shame to be revealed.

"I will write," she confessed with excitement.

"Well see as you do miss," he forced her hands back as she attempted to cup his, "There's one thing this army does well and it's post letters."

"Why are you strange with me all of a sudden Henri?" she frowned.

"It's not for show Bernice," he whispered sternly.

"I would tell the world."

She almost squeaked with titillation and she had kissed him on the cheek before he knew how to rebuff her in front of the men. With that she turned, sweeping her skirt out to its full length, running headlong into the farm like a child chasing a cat.

Glancing back into the throng of the York and Lancasters, the curiously focused young soldier amongst the throng, held his gaze once more, as did many more of his kin. A stern expression in a sea of dirty smiles and knowing looks.

"Bloody hell," Fortune grumbled to himself and he marched down the track with determined strides.

By now 3-Section was already halfway down the track in front of the farm enclosure. From this vantage point they could see a long procession of transport and men marching to the east. Four huge traction engines, belching smoke above the road, pulled heavy guns. Mules and horses strained at the weight of their laden waggons and a long column of soldiers snaked across the landscape as far as the eye could see.

"Where you from then Mary?" asked Private Connor.

"Oh, Meare, it's a village in Somerset, but I live with mother in Clevedon now, on the coast," replied Private Merry.

"Oh I know it," declared Connor confidently.

"Bollocks do you," interrupted Private Pocock.

"What are you? Before all this?" Private Connor continued.

"I was to be a carpenter, my father was a carpenter in the village, my Gramf as well. But I'm apprentice now, in a small law firm, the place is up on Hill Road if you know it?"

"Sure, I've done that wood working lark, I'm good with tools," boasted Private Connor.

"Such bollocks. Only time you had your hands-on tools was nicking 'em!" exclaimed Private Pocock.

"That's Charlie Pocock, Navy before. Barks bigger than his bite but we're all mates here in 3-Section," Private Connor revealed in hushed tones.

"Don't go spreading my business Prick, you keep to your own. And I'll tell ya who's mates and who isn't, that's not for your deciding," Private Pocock snapped.

"Stick with me Mary and you'll be a fine soldier. There's no doubt. I'll show you the way. There's a knack to it see. Some has it and some don't. But I can tell, you're gunna be a good Tommy," Private Connor beamed at his companion.

"Oh right, thank you."

"But don't go moaning about all the marchin see. We march up and down and all over and when your feet come off you keep marchin some more but don't let me hear you moaning cos we're alive and that's the end of it."

Private Pocock rolled his eyes.

"I see. I think."

They shook hands.

"I'm Richard or Rich."

"Prick to most," Private Pocock interrupted once more.

"Pleased to meet you Richard. I'm George."

"Well, we're callin you Mary now on account of the sergeant's speech."

The men laughed together once more.

"You've done much fightin?" Private Merry enquired.

"Fuck all," Private Pocock interjected, "Don't know shit if it landed on his head."

The men continued their laughter all the way to the road. The platoon marched for just under an hour then broke out of formation to the sides of the busy thoroughfare to rest and allow stragglers to catch up. The men lazed on their backs smoking pipes and cigarettes as the carnival continued on the road. Private Connor explained the finer points of bayonet fighting to Private Merry; specifically the skills not imparted to raw recruits by the drill sergeants back home, much to the annoyance of Private Pocock. Fortune and Sergeant Hope checked the map and confirmed their location with a passing Service-Corps sergeant.

The men stared in wonder at an observation balloon which was being deployed in the field beside the road. The sausage-shaped balloon, under which a large basket was slung, ascended to the air on a thick cable, controlled from a winch on a lorry below. A large compliment of men busied themselves on the ground while two figures could be seen heading aloft in the basket. Two lorries with machine gunners stationed on the flatbed were parked defending the balloon from attack. A few hundred yards away another balloon was already deployed, now already several thousand feet in the air. Beyond this yet another balloon was airborne.[22]

"What a job!" exclaimed Private Pocock.

"And this isn't?" sneered Private Cartwright.

The platoon marched for another hour before resting beside a French community cemetery, north of the village of Mailly-Maillet. Behind its large iron gates, the mausoleums and elaborate grave-settings intrigued the men. The French graves seemed ostentatious and crass to the English Tommies. A few of the men went for a quick wonder, trying to read the names in their best French-mocking accents. They came upon three freshly dug graves near the rear of the cemetery containing British soldiers. This grim discovery sobered them and they rejoined the resting platoon with heavy hearts.

Further along the road they passed a Frenchman and his cart, from which he was selling bread and wine at extortionate prices. He had with him his young daughter and the way he presented her made some think his wares extended beyond the merchandise on his vehicle. Fortune wisely stood close-by, preventing the men from loitering, although he acquired a few bottles for himself and distributed them into men's packs for safe keeping.

At another stop the platoon had arrived at a busy crossroads before a village. At the fork in the road a painted crucifix loomed over the passing troops beneath a tiled roof. Several men knelt before it and collected their private thoughts. An open sided waggon, emblazoned with the emblem of the Salvation Army,[23] distributed tea and biscuits at the junction, boasting a much larger congregation than the image of Christ could muster. Refreshed, the column continued on its march.

Just before 1600 hours the platoon gathered in an orchard beside the road. The other platoons from C-Company filed into the orchard beside them. D-Company was already waiting, Fortune reporting to the commanding officer upon their arrival. The men set about brewing tea. A and B companies arrived together twenty minutes later and positioned themselves in neighbouring fields. The battalion field kitchen had arrived earlier in the day giving ample time to provide a hot meal for the men before the march resumed at 1645 hours. Having checked in with Battalion HQ and delivering a bottle of wine to the company sergeant major, Fortune rejoined the platoon.

---

[22] Hydrogen filled observation balloons gathered critical intelligence of the enemy frontline and acted as artillery spotters.

[23] Thousands of Salvationists worked in dangerous conditions on the Western Front on both sides, providing hot tea and food. One hut on the western front distributed over 2500 pieces of paper per week, so that soldiers could write home. Field kitchens were often extremely close to the front lines and often run by women.

"We're here," Fortune shared his map with Sergeant Danny Hope.

"We've done well to keep time with the road the way it was Fortune."

"Aye."

"What happened with that farm girl then?"

"What do you mean?"

"Come on, I know that look."

"Nothing, just being polite."

"Sure, that must be it," Danny smiled, "It's only natural."

"There's nothing natural about any of this," Fortune grimaced.

As the battalion edged ever closer to its destination, the signs of war gradually became even more apparent. Shell damage was evident in many of the buildings they passed now, frequent broken windows, holed roofs and smashed walls. Brickwork and tiles littered the roadways in places denoting the scene of a bombardment. Hardly any civilians were encountered; a man with a waggon loaded with furniture was verbally harassed by Private Pocock for being a thieving scoundrel. There had been such a warm welcome for the men when they disembarked at Le Harve but now they drew near to the front-line the civilians they did see showed no interest in their heroic cause. After leaving the orchards at Martinsart the battalion was heading south, with the edges of Aveluy wood, sitting atop a steep rise some distance east of the road.

White and yellow puffs of smoke danced over the tree line horizon where a bombardment was falling on the wood. The men watched as they marched, for any sign of battle, the distant bombardment the only evidence of the war they could glimpse before a ridgeline blotted Aveluy wood from their sight. In the cover of this low ridge the Battalion halted beside the road once more. An aid station was situated here, carved into the chalk in numerous small dugouts. A dump, as they were known, provided fuel for passing lorries. Army Service Corps men paused in respite from their toil, with caps high on their blackened heads and cigarettes hanging loosely from parched lips. They looked on in wonder at the fresh faces of the Somerset Light Infantry; their dust reddened eyes showing a weary pity.

A runner brought news that the guides from the York and Lancasters could not be located, the Battalion would have to wait. Fortune and the other survivors of Loos the year before, knew all too well the dangers of entering a battle-zone without a guide, praising Lieutenant Colonel Bradbury for biding his time in this sheltered spot while the guides were located.

"We'll be crossing the Ancre here chaps," Fortune explained to the other NCOs, "Word is it's a hot-spot, so we'll go a section at a time with one hundred-yard intervals. Let's hope it's not too windy and the Boshe gunners are asleep. We'll have a straggler post here at the entrance to Upper Norwich. No light-ups beyond this point, but we'll have someone on the corner making sure nobody is smoking, just to be sure. I want a rifle inspection in forty minutes so keep 'em busy with a full clean up while we wait. Understood?"

"Yes Sergeant."

While the NCOs were attending to their sections a dispatch rider on a Triumph 550cc motorcycle burbled along the road from the north, coming to a stop beside the dugouts. Fortune sensed something unsettling and strode over to the rider who was asking around for someone.

"What is it?"

"Message for C-Company SLI, 1st Platoon."

"Give it here, that's me."

Fortune unfolded the squared paper note and scanned the content. A deep frown spread across his brow.

"Any reply sergeant?" enquired the dispatch rider.

"No!" fumed Fortune and he stormed off without another word.

Fortune hurried to find Sergeant Danny Hope.

"What is it? You look like you've seen a ghost," exclaimed Sergeant Hope.

"McGreggor is out of it. Not coming back, infection. Shit."

"So, who've we got then?"

"Richardson," Fortune paced around Danny, staring at the paper.

"Thought he was out of it, he's recovered?"

"Aye, seems that way doesn't it. Richardson, of all the people. Fucking hell. What a bag o'shite."

"Never liked him, have you? He's brave, strict with the men but brave. That's what they need, to look up to. Did well at Loos, didn't he? Would you rather we had some fresh-faced child straight from their university?"

"You don't know him like I do Danny, he's dangerous. He takes risks that should be left well alone and that's not the end of it. You don't know him like I do."

Chapter 14 - Into the trenches

24th April 1916

Village of Aveluy

2130 hours

68 days to Z-Day

Darkness wrapped the landscape in a veil of mistrust. Where rolling country had once been only dark shapes and strange noises now lived. The world had collapsed to an island of earth only yards in diameter, now floating adrift in the void. Torch light danced on the trodden grass where the platoon waited. Beyond the illumination dark forces were at play in the minds of the Tommies. Demons stalked the outer perimeter of the sphere of light. The men were anxious, the mood had hardened. They drew their harnessed equipment close to their bodies, grips tightening on their rifles. Cigarettes burned fiercely as air was drawn through them with determination and impatience, their diminished embers flicked into the night, piercing the blackness for a moment.

"Alright lads, settle," Fortune paced between the sections, "Not long."

He looked at his pocket watch and let out a frustrated sigh.

"Where are they?" he asked himself.

Captain Wilmslow came along the company and met with the COs. Fortune was not invited to the conflab. He stood watching the junior officers debating over a map by torchlight. To the east the sky was occasionally pricked with white light, as flares soared into the air to begin their bright but short-lived life over the trenches. To the north, from behind Aveluy wood a searchlight thrust upwards into the clouds.

Before long Captain Wilmslow approached. Fortune brought all in the vicinity to attention. He held his salute until Captain Wilmslow returned it.

"At ease sergeant, walk with me if you will?" the captain requested in his soft lilting well-to-do accent.

"Yessir," Fortune followed.

"How are the men?" the Captain enquired.

"Fine sir. Ready for the off sir. Can't wait sir."

"Very good sergeant. Your handling of the platoon is most admirable without 2nd Lieutenant McGreggor."

"Thank you very much sir," Fortune lurched upwards briefly on his toes in exultation.

"You must be looking forward to seeing young Richardson again no doubt? You served together at the show at Loos, didn't you?"

"Yessir."

"Good, good. Fine young gentleman is Richardson, will do you well. Cigarette sergeant?"

The captain extended a packet towards Fortune, he did not recognise the brand but took one all the same. Fortune lit the captain's before his.

"Thank you sir, very kind sir."

"Not at all. Listen, there's a delicate request I would put to you sergeant. Some of the men might get the wind-up as we go in, we're not all as experienced as yourself here, are we?"

"No sir. I'll keep 'em in line."

"Yes well, one relies on the more experienced to pull the rest together."

"Yessir."

"I know I can rely on you to keep your cool and see that *everyone* is looked after, in the most discrete way possible of course."

Captain Wilmslow turned pointing his cigarette innocently at the group of junior officers still pawing over their maps.

"Oh. I understand sir."

"I remember your actions at Loos, Sergeant Berriman. Your coolness was a great boon to the battalion, the captain paused and smoked the cigarette in silence for a while, "Well, a good chat. The Army needs more like yourself sergeant. Good listeners. Carry on."

"Thank you sir, yessir. Good luck sir."

The captain rejoined his adjutant who stood patiently waiting in the gloom. Another hour passed slowly until the guides from the York and Lancaster battalion presented themselves, their uniforms dirty and faces darkened. They seemed more at home in the night, nocturnal animals shirking from any light or warmth. Before long, the battalion began its journey, over the crest of the hill and slowly through the bombed-out village of Aveluy. A makeshift sign declared the village boundary, beyond it the men found ruined buildings and barns. Every house had been knocked about in some way, some were in a sorrier state than others, but none had been left unscathed. Stray dogs ran between the rubble, their eyes reflecting what light there was like devilish spies from the pages of a penny dreadful.

The men marched in silence, peering into the broken-down houses for signs of life. They found none. The once precious belongings of the village folk were strewn in doorways and the rooms beyond. Smashed crockery and torn clothing were abundant, their owners long departed to the west. They descended through the village towards the river Ancre and the causeway which would lead them to the trenches. A wide marshy expanse glistened beside them as the quarter moon peaked from behind the clouds. The causeway was in a damaged state and had been repeatedly repaired by the Royal Engineers at night; duck boards and planks reinforcing the road and spanning breaks in the thoroughfare. Broken and smashed waggons lay on their sides at the flanks of the causeway. A dead horse, legs rigid like a discarded toy, rotted in a shallow pool. Here the battalion halted to allow each company to cross in groups.

An owl hooted from an unseen vantage point. To the east more Very lights punctuated the sky. The men took the opportunity to smoke one last cigarette and light one last pipe.

1st Platoon went across just before midnight without incident. At the other side they congregated for several minutes beneath another painted crucifix which dominated a low earth ridge at a junction in the road. An officer peered out at the men from a chalky dugout. The battalion padre was there giving his blessings to any who would take them forward on their journey.

"Where are the Germans?" whispered Private Merry.

"East, not far, can't be," surmised Private Connor.

"Which way is east?" asked Private Cartwright.

"Oh, that way," Private Connor pointed.

"And how the blazes would you know?" scowled Private Pocock.

"Where are we going?" asked Private Merry.

"Front-line trenches, by some wood so I hear Mary."

"And what do we do then?"

"Well, we hold 'em."

"And then what?"

"Then we come out."

"And then what?"

"Then we clean up and before you know it, we bloody well go back in," interrupted Private Pocock.

"We don't stay there? For the war?" Private Merry seemed surprised.

"No Mary, you wouldn't want to be in there for more than a couple days. You'd be no use to anyone for any longer. Two or three days and then we come out. We'll rotate with another battalion and head back into support trenches or even further back into reserve," Private Cartwright joined in.

"So, it's not all in the trenches then?" Private Merry almost seemed disappointed.

"Christ no, we spend most of our time digging or repairing or carrying. Every couple weeks or so we do a stint in the trenches. That's it. Nothing to it."

"When do we kill Germans?" Private Merry asked intrigued.

"You won't even see one, let alone get to kill him Mary," confessed Private Pocock, "Chance would be a fine thing."

"Before long we'll be back behind the lines Mary, they might let us out in a town to spend our hard-earned Francs. That's when the war will liven up!" Private Connor rubbed his hands together knowingly.

"Why? What will happen there?"

"We'll get shit faced drunk and molest their women. It won't just be your purse that's drained when you get home," hooted Private Pocock.

The men close by laughed and jeered, Private Merry frowning in confusion.

"Quiet the fuck down there," hissed Fortune as he paced along the platoon.

After several minutes waiting for the last section to cross the causeway, the platoon set off north following the low earthen ridge along a trackway. The track entered a sunken road, a disposition of earth either side of a thoroughfare not uncommon in the region. Within a few hundred yards the platoon came upon a heavily sandbagged construction. A trench opened from the east into the side of the bank at this point. A dugout entrance bore into the chalk ridge beside the trench mouth. Cables, tightly bound together, wound their way from the excavated room and up the side of the sandbag wall, leading away up into the trench atop iron braces which carried them above head height. A mesh of barbed wire criss-crossed the top of the trench enclosing it entirely from above; this unwelcoming maw poised to devour any who entered its confines.

A crudely painted wooden sign bore the name "Upper Norwich", its surface caked in brown splatters; a conspectus of displeasure recorded for posterity by passing Tommies. A lance corporal from A-Company lent casually against the sandbags smoking a pipe.

"Ditch your cigs, drown yur pipes," he croaked at the men.

Private Pocock cursed as he emptied his pipe onto the ground along with many of the others. He reached into his tunic pocket and brought forth chewing tobacco, sharing it with Private Cartwright. Fortune came to the front of the column and nodded at the lance corporal as he ducked under the communication wires, entering the trench without a word.

The feeling of claustrophobia was immediate upon entering the trench. The men slowly filed through the fissure, their vision restricted to the dark skies above and the shoulders of the man in front. The trench was perhaps seven feet in depth and four feet wide, its sides reinforced with sandbags or iron bars. Occasionally elephant iron as it was known, large curved sheets of corrugated iron, gave strength to the earthen excavation. The bottom of the trench was in places waterlogged, although for the most part the boards on which they were walking were merely damp. The walls of the ditch were surprisingly bright in the starlight, their chalk surface gleaming in the mysterious illumination offered to the men by the heavens.

Any progress made was slow. Every few yards the column would come to a halt, each man pressed up against the man in front and behind. Some unseen hindrance was then absolved and onward they went once more. Some men rested their heads on the packs of the man in front of them, gaining a few moments of comfort before having to shuffle on. Fortune stared up at the sky. Stars twinkled between small clouds. It was quiet, peaceful at times and quite beautiful to behold the heavens overhead.

"You think they care about our petty squabbles?"

"Sorry sergeant?" whispered a private, but he won no response.

The communication trench leisurely wound its way along the southern most ridge of Blighty Valley, not that the men would have known they were on a ridge. All visual acuity of the outside world was banished by the sandbags and mud that encapsulated them. They could have been in any field in any land at any time.

After what seemed like an endless wait in their morbid queue, the platoon came to a junction in the trench. Another trench bisected Upper Norwich Street from south to north. A signpost revealed this trench to be Coniston Street. Set into the wall of the trench was a small opening, framed in wood. Several shallow steps lead downward into a dugout. A painted sign denoted this was Coniston Post. The communication cables spun their web above the men's heads and branched out in different directions at the junction. A sturdy wooden frame crossed the intersection, firmly holding barbed wire in great prevalence. Looking north-wards along Coniston Street, which was devoid of any soldiers, Fortune could see a constant flow of men moving west; the York and Lancasters on their way out along Lower Norwich Street. He scrutinised them as they shuffled by. Each man with a hand on the leader's shoulder, they moved like a prehistoric centipede gliding through the earth. They looked tired, their shoulders sagging, their faces sullen.

"Sergeant Berriman isn't it?" enquired a voice from the dugout.

"Yeah, who's...oh sorry Sir. Yessir," Fortune straightened himself when he saw the officer.

It was 2nd Lieutenant Berner-Potts from D-Company. He stood in the entrance to Coniston Post, with a cigarette nestling dangerous close to the end of his fingers. His steel helmet was worn at a jaunty angle and he crossed his legs casually at the ankle. He had that air about him, Fortune thought, he carried himself like a Hollywood film star, he was dashing and debonair. Berner-Potts was in his early twenties, a graduate of Cambridge and son to a successful family of solicitors. He had made a name for himself at Loos the year before by rushing a machine gun post and killing its crew. The white-blue-white ribbon of the Military Cross he had received for his bravery was clear for all to see on his chest.

"Come on in man, no good waiting out there. Us old hats have got to stick together," Berner-Potts chuckled as he waved Fortune in.

"As you wish sir," Fortune moved between two men and into the dugout.

The space was cramped with barely enough height to stand crouched. A small wooden table sat awkwardly in one corner. Atop the table were several old wine bottles which had been used to hold candles. Pegs in the wall held a binocular case, a steel helmet and a Hessian sack, presumably provisions out of reach of the rats.

"What is this place sir?" asked Fortune.

"Take a look sergeant, up here," instructed Berner-Potts.

The junior officer pulled back a sack cloth curtain to reveal a wooden ladder pressed into the chalk wall. Fortune left his rifle in the dugout chamber along with his webbing and pack, moving cautiously into the muddy chimney to look up. Over his head a circular wooden doorway, probably a barrel top, with a makeshift handle, blocked the chimney. Berner-Potts drew the curtain across and held it tightly to the wall.

"Would not want any light getting in old chap."

Fortune climbed the short ladder up to the door, grasping the handle he pushed upward. The doorway moved perhaps fifteen inches and then would raise no more. A wooden block nestling in a shallow crevice provided a door stop which Fortune wedged in place. Taking a deep breath, he climbed one more rung of the ladder and passed his head beyond the lip.

"I can't see a thing."

"Wait for a Very light[24] to go up. Shouldn't be long."

Fortune waited. He could make out the top of the trench in his immediate vicinity, mud, sandbags, refuse and plenty of barbed wire. The landscape further on was hidden under the blanket of night. There was not a single light, just blackness. Then, quite suddenly, a yellow streak fizzed up on a high arc from several hundred yards to the east. Reaching the apex of its flight the Very light burst into a dazzling white flare. The topography of the ground became visible now to Fortune as he watched in awe. Along the front he could see bright stars whizzing up and gliding down on their

---

[24] A flare fired into the air from a pistol for signalling or for temporary illumination. Named after Edward Wilson Very (1847–1910), an American naval officer who developed and popularized a single-shot breech-loading snub-nosed pistol that fired flares

invisible parachutes. A splendid display any child would appreciate on a cold November evening back home.

From this vantage point he could see trenches, zig zagging white lines of chalk, making their way from left to right on the slope of a ridge. The pure light danced over everything, but at this distance and without time to process all that he had seen, he could not discern any detail. He thought he saw several lines of trenches, their unmistakable crenulations as they darted this way and that through the fields. The view was startling in its complexity, the white lines of trenches a stark contrast to the featureless gloom of no-man's-land. A negative photographic image of Man's belligerence was burned into his eyes.

"What a view this must be in the daylight hey sergeant?" Berner-Potts called up.

"Aye Sir, I can well imagine. Although if it's alright I will be coming back down now?"

"Certainly, please do, here take my hand if you need to."

Fortune carefully replaced the wedge in its home and clambered down the ladder after securing the door.

"Those trenches I saw sir,"

"British, German's know better than to dig theirs in a valley or in plain sight. Theirs are up on the opposing ridge, you won't catch them in the night I'm sure. But they are up there, watching and waiting."

"Waiting for what sir?"

"For us sergeant, when the time comes soon."

"I see sir, looked an awfully big hill sir."

"Yes," the officer's excitement dulled for a moment, "Yes it is."

Berner-Potts became quiet, wrestling with his internal monologue.

"Ever think much about the big show at Loos sergeant?" he asked finally.

"Not sure it's wise to sir, not more than it being over and done with. Behind us now."

"No, quite right I suppose, although one can't help it from time to time, can one? Us old hats. Got through it didn't we? Right as rain now."

Fortune scrutinised the young man.

"Yessir. Was a good show sir."

"Damn fine show. Finest yet. But," he paused and lowered his voice, "Can't help thinking about it you see. All the same. From time to time. Us old hats, olds sweats. Where were you at Loos Sergeant? Bois Hugo or Hill 70?"

"Hill 70 sir, same as you."

"Damn miracle you got off those slopes alive sergeant."

"Yessir, I owe that to 2nd Lieutenant Richardson."

"Do you relive it? That night. Could we have done any better?"

"No sir, no reason to live through that again. It is what it is. We did our best. You did your best. There was too few of us to take the hill sir. Nothing could be done."

"You are right. But I hear them, sometimes."

"Sorry sir?"

"The lads on the hill. Calling for help, weren't they? We left them, didn't we? That night we couldn't bring them back with us."

"We had to go sir or we'd all still be lying up there now, the lot of us. You can't beat yourself up over this sir, it's not healthy to. A man must stay alive, it's a purpose God gave us, same as any animal."

"But when your men are calling for you sergeant, when it's your choice to retire or press on, that can haunt a man."

"Why are you down here sir, if you don't mind me asking? Where's D-Company sir?" Fortune pressed.

"I just popped away for a bit, you see."

Berner-Potts rubbed the back of his head and squinted with fatigue.

"I understand sir. They will be missing you sir, the men."

Fortune opened his pack, drawing out a wine bottle. He uncorked it with his teeth and offered it to the officer.

"I find this is the best way sir."

Berner-Potts eyed the bottle, then the sergeant and took the bottle. He drank heartily then passed it back. The two men stood in silence until they had finished its contents.

"You best be off sir, I'll see you on your way now."

"Thank you, sergeant," Berner-Potts gripped Fortune's shoulder.

Berner-Potts straightened his uniform and Sam Browne belt and having addressed the jaunty angle of his helmet slipped out into the trench.

"Poor bastard," Fortune thought.

The officers were a different breed to the men, he postulated. A soldier gets the willies up him and he screams and shouts, worse case he runs off. An officer, weighed down by the responsibility of leadership, hides his true emotions, buries them away for a later date. Would Berner-Potts, hero of Loos, have returned to his company if it were not for Fortune? It did not warrant thinking about. Fortune sat for a while and recalled the events of September 1915.

He smoked a Capstan in the dugout and then stamped it out on the dirt. He eyed the half empty packet for a while. A cigarette bore the signs of lipstick upon its filter. She must have put one back in he thought. He took it out and carefully smelt its length. He could not recognise her fragrance over the stench of the dugout. For a moment he considered joining the ranks of the York and Lancasters, returning to her this very night. Who would reassure him and send him back to the platoon? Nobody answered his internal pleading.

Chapter 15 - A lesson in cowardice
No-Man's-Land

"So, when did Richardson arrive?" asked Percy wearily.

He had listened to Fortune's story for what seemed like a lifetime and while he was grateful for the veteran's detailed recount, he was struggling to concentrate in his current state of exhaustion. A stifled yawn and heavy eyes did nothing to counter Fortune's eagerness to continue.

"The day after the relief, 25th April," Fortune replied, "Stand-to was just before dawn, everyone was up on the fire step, weapons ready. The men were knackered from the night before and for many it was their first time in, they hadn't slept. The trenches were in a good condition, the northerners had left them clean but, well you know, you don't find much comfort in there. There was a mist, lingering over no-man's-land. Couldn't see anything through the perisher."

"What's that?" Percy interrupted.

"Periscope, lad, periscope. Anyways, it looked clear out there, but you know the Hun are doing just the same thing a few hundred yards away, getting ready to receive a dawn attack. But nothing was doing. We waited as normal, just in case they were coming. Another no show. Then the morning hate was ordered. The boys really got into it, blasting away into the mist. We sent some toffee apples over and a battery of 18-pounders joined in with a few lazy shots into their second line. Watching the lads unload clip after clip you would have thought we were defending against the Zulus."

"I fired in the air when I first had to do it," Percy confessed.

"Why?"

"Didn't want to hurt anyone. Few of us were doing that, I could see."

Fortune grunted in mild frustration.

"Morning hate is for your benefit not theirs. Get it out of your system. Help with the nerves and all that."

"Oh yes, it definitely helped."

"So, morning hate was done and the Germans didn't feel like responding. The rum came around soon after we stood down. Charlie, Private Pocock, was up to his usual tricks trading rum ration for his contraband he brings in with him."

"How so?"

"Well you know, things find their way into his pack on a long march, he had soup, gloves, toothpaste, couple of small pies, smokes. Had a proper enterprise running from his pack he did. Some would give up their rum on account of them not being drinkers. Tobacco or smokes were the most traded. Charlie would keep the rum in old wine bottles for when we wanted a blow-out."

"You knew this was going on?"

"Of course, I was encouraging it. When you have been doing this for as long as I have you bend the King's regulations and make your own. What's important to me is that the men keep their mind off the danger and don't get the wind-up. If that means turning a blind eye here and there, that's what I do."

"Alright, go on, so the morning was like any other, nothing special. Then what?"

"Yes, so breakfast came up the line from the field kitchen and I had the platoon working in shifts to clean their rifles, ready for inspection. One of the other platoons was sending over an officer to check up on us, can't remember who it was. Before anyone arrived, a messenger came to find me, I was to go to the HQ at Quarry Post."

"What's Quarry Post?"

"You must know it? Just down there in the valley, at the edge of the wood, there's these big hollowed out holes with dugouts in the side. Old quarry before the war. The railway runs up to it. No? Crikey keep your eyes open lad you might learn something from time to time."

"Sorry Fortune, I probably did see it, I don't know, sorry."

"No matter. Up to Quarry Post I go, no indications what for. I present myself at Battalion HQ and wait a while. The Quartermaster Sergeant is an old friend from the South African war and we had a smoke and caught up. That's when they start throwing over whiz-bangs and the big stuff all of a sudden. Most were long and went over our heads into the wood but after a few minutes they got them zeroed in and they were falling all about. The Quartermaster and me we legged it up over the side of the Quarry and down into the wood. There's a slope there you see, blind slope the shells can't get to, where the railway has a loading platform. Quite safe once you get to it. Lots were already sheltering there.

Well there we stayed until it lifted. Our batteries started responding, trying to find the enemy battery and shut them up. Did the trick after a while and the gunners were slogging it out between themselves all morning but it meant we were left alone. There was quite a bit of damage to clear up when we got back to the quarry. One of the dugouts had been caved in and a big group were trying to dig them out, poor buggers. Nobody realised part of a connecting communication trench had come in as well, but we were all too busy working on the dugout. They found two chaps at the bottom of that trench when they eventually got to it. Suffocated."

"That's how this war is fought, waste. Every day a waste of man, animal and machine. Like a rat gnawing at a corpse till there's nothing left," Percy postulated.

"If your time is up then your time is up lad. Not a damn thing any of us can do about that. You accept it after time, hope for it on certain days."

"I had a friend from home, joined up around the same time as I did."

Percy's recollection seemed to lift his mood immediately as he remembered fondly.

"We got our uniforms on the same day and went about in the high street showing off. He had been given white feathers you see, while standing in the queue at the cinema not long before. He wanted to show he was going to fight. We went through training together. Shipped out together. He proposed to his sweetheart on the same day as I did. Walter Beale, a year younger than me he was, a clerk at the bank. I'd known him since we were small, attending Sunday school at the church. Nice fellow, bit deaf in one ear. We were jumping off the bridge by the ford, one summer when we were youngsters. He banged his head and since then he couldn't hear well from one ear. Managed to get through the medical alright. We were all silly back then, no fear of such things," Percy's recollection became quiet and more introspective.

"What happened to him? Bought it today, did he?"

"No, no that's my point. He didn't have the chance to fight. Two weeks ago, we were marching, marching somewhere, one of the route marches you know. A lovely day, flowers were everywhere, cornflowers and some early poppies were starting to bloom beside the road. Bees and insects were swarming about on their daily chores. There were birds everywhere singing for us as we went. It was sunny, I remember marching with my head titled right back like this, with the sun on my face. A wonderful day of God's creation by all accounts. Walter had received a letter that morning from his sweetheart. She was, in the family way you see, he was rejoicing such a blessing but naturally was very worried about getting leave so he could return home and marry her."

"What happened?" Fortune was eager to reach the end of the tale.

"We'd just crossed over an old stone bridge, medieval, one of those with heavy stonework and narrow just enough room for a cart. Walter said he was going to gather up some flowers, to send home in his letter, there were so many on the riverbank beside the bridge. He waited for the right moment and then, as we passed by, he dashed down the bank. The corporal didn't see. He'd gotten away with it."

"That was lucky then."

"No, not at all Fortune. A stray shell, just one, miles off course, theirs or ours I don't know. But there it was. At the right time, right place, to take a life. We ran over, I can see everyone's face now peering over the side of the bridge. I ran down the bank but, there was nothing left. No sign. No sign he was ever there. Gone. Just hundreds of flowers, the poppies and cornflowers I can remember with clarity, floating away down the stream. Hundreds of them Fortune. Just, slowly floating off and then they were gone. There was nothing left to remind us he was ever there."

Fortune took his packet of Capstans and drew out a cigarette.

"Shit," he cursed as he scrunched up the empty container and tossed it into the bottom of the shell hole with what was now becoming a graveyard for cigarettes.

"You checked them for smokes, didn't you?" he asked already knowing the outcome.

He reached into his lower tunic pocket and found the crumpled packet he was keeping there. Only Bernice's cigarette remained, the lipstick faded but still present. He returned the packet to its pocket.

"So, after the bombardment the whole place was a mess. I said farewell to my Quartermaster chum and searched for Captain Wilmslow," Fortune continued.

"Did you find him? Who had sent for you?" Percy prompted.

"Erm, yes, the Captain and Richardson were in a dugout. I could tell Richardson was revelling in our reunion. That smile on his face, his superiority in knowing he controls the situation. We exchanged pleasantries if not only for the sake of the Captain."

"How long had it been?"

"Since Loos, the year before."

"What happened to him there?"

"I'm not there yet lad, give me a chance."

"Sorry. Do go on."

"He acted like nothing was any different to before. He wanted an update on the platoon, what had we been doing, how were the men holding up, how were the trenches, things like that. He said he was looking forward to having me serve him again. He offered me a cigarette. The three of us smoked. They shared a brandy."

"Why had he sent for you?"

"Well he wanted our introductions to be in front of the captain didn't he, must have been his plan. To show the old man we were right as rain. To fire a warning shot at me not to cause any trouble for him cos he had the old man on side. That would have been it. He wanted an audience. We bade farewell to the captain and Richardson had me lead him to our stretch. He had me carry his valise."

"His batman would do that! The cheek of it!" Percy exclaimed.

"That's right lad, see you do know how things work. Yes precisely, his batman would have done. But I struggled with it all the same, down to Liverpool Avenue and the COs dugout. I showed him where everything was and we did a tour of the line. He inspected rifles and we checked the men for bad feet. He ordered another rum ration to celebrate his return to the battalion. I could see this worked wonders on most of the lads but Charlie Pocock and I, we knew what Richardson was really like."

"So, who knew about what had happened in Aldershot?"

"Charlie Pocock and Fitch and now you."

"Why are you telling me all of this Fortune?"

"I figured, once you said you were a pious man and that, you would be as good as any to hear my confession."

"About the Irish man?"

"About all of it."

"What happened to him Fortune? What did you do in the woods that night? Will you tell me?"

"Aye, I'll tell you. I'll tell you everything. I want it gone, I don't want to hold onto any of it anymore."

"So, what happened?"

"I let him go. He helped me bury the others, then he went."

"Really? Is that the truth?"

"Aye, I let him go."

"I did not expect that, if I am honest."

"I can't say I blame you, neither did I. Surprised myself that night. Now stop jumping in and let me tell you."

"Sorry. Go on."

"The men were put to task, on the mundane jobs of trench life. Cleaning, repairing, pumping out any standing water. The German's were quiet all day, was like they weren't there. Richardson had me attend him in his dugout in the afternoon. He was sat reading when I arrived, small glasses perched on his nose, I hadn't realised he needed them."

"What was he reading?"

"I can't remember, is it important?"

"No, well, Father said you can tell a lot about a person's character by the books he reads."

"Christ Percy I can tell you about his character in abundance, I dunno, something about a badge. Um, a little red book, he said it was from another war. That was it, the American war, about a boy finding his courage in battle after doubting himself. He asked if I read, I told him I wasn't much for reading. He insisted I take it, said a man only has finite experiences in life and by reading about others we learn, or something."

"The Red Badge of Courage,[25]" Percy smiled.

"Yeah, that's it probably. You know it?"

"Yes. The boy joins the Yankee army and without experience of battle he naturally questions his courage. How will he perform when the time comes? As battle grows closer, he is tormented with guilt should he not prove himself."

"What happens to him?"

"He runs away."

"A coward then!"

"It's not as simple as that Fortune."

"It is in my books, damn coward."

"If I remember correctly, he comes across a General discussing the ongoing battle with his officers. The regiment the boy has fled, thinking they were about to be overrun, has won the day and has survived. The boy is now wracked with guilt once more, but this time it fuels him. He returns to his regiment and as the battle continues his bravery is revealed. He now has something to prove you see, to somehow make amends for what he has done in the past. He captures the colours of the rebel regiment opposing them and they are victorious. He has become a man, he has reconciled his cowardice."

Fortune frowned and remained contemplative. There was a reason Richardson was reading that book when he had arrived. Like everything Richardson did there was a plan behind it and Fortune had missed it entirely.

"Did you read the book?"

"Slung it over the parapet. Good riddance."

"So, what did Richardson want?"

"He had a scheme, of course. He was keen to show the captain we were competent. He was proposing a trench raid to the old man. He wanted me to help him plan it. He wanted me there."

"I never understood the point of those, too few men to win the war."

"The brass hats dreamed them up to keep us on our toes. If a man gets bored, and there's plenty of time for that around here, his mind wonders to happier times, to home, he asks himself what the point of it all is and before you know it we end up like the French and refuse to fight. So they came up with trench raids. You go over, stir it up, maybe capture a prisoner and come back. The men get their chance to bayonet a few of them and we get a German for the intelligence chaps to interrogate, to find out which regiment it is we are facing, if our shelling is having any impact,

---

[25] The Red Badge of Courage, Stephen Crane, Published 1895

stuff like that. Problem is, unless they go really well they often go badly. Unnecessary risk if you ask me, much safer staying put."

"You can see why they want to speak to prisoners though."

"So, he was planning this raid, to get some recognition for himself no doubt. But I could see through it."

"What do you mean?"

"Where better than to deal with someone than in no-man's-land in the middle of a war. I could tell he was plotting something and he wanted me right in the thick of it. So, it was a matter of time, once the old man approved the plan, I was just waiting for the inevitable. Whatever that was. So, that's why I told Charlie, Private Pocock. I told him most of it. I told him about Richardson and what I feared he would do. Charlie agreed to come on the raid, to watch my back and if we had to, we would deal with Richardson first."

"How?"

"If he was planning on doing me in out there, we would adopt the same approach. Do away with him, a stray bullet, a poorly lobbed bomb. Accidents happen."

"But you had no proof he was planning anything of the sort."

"I knew he was."

"Goodness, what happened next?"

"We were pulled out of the line the day after, it had been uneventful, had put the lad's minds at rest. Couldn't have asked for a better result. We went into brigade support for five days. We were working fatigues every night, repairing trenches, bringing up supplies, that sort of thing. It got hot a few times, caught by their artillery when out working, usual stuff, hardly any casualties. We kept the men busy and they were cheerful. Then we moved back out into brigade reserve, quite a few miles behind. New uniforms, new equipment if we needed it, there was a show put on and some sport in the day, we beat the Dorsets at footie. All this time Richardson was plotting his raid with the old man and it wouldn't be happening until the next time we were sent up the line. Every day we spent in reserve was a day closer to the raid, I didn't know when it was, but it was soon."

"Did you ever see or hear from the farm girl again?"

Stealthily Fortune's hand reached into his tunic pocket, feeling for the delicate artefacts he treasured within; eight pages of crumpled notebook paper. Fortune's silence and distant unblinking stare gave Percy enough forewarning not to push for an answer; these memories would not be shared with the boy.

Part 3 - Redemption and Revelation

"How sweet is life when fortune is not envious."

-

Menander, 4th century BC

Chapter 16 - Fortune's muse

9th May 1916
Village of Bertrancourt
1530 hours
53 days to Z-Day

Fortune had arrived in the village the night before, walking from camp to Forceville then hitching a ride with an Army Service Corp motor lorry convoy. The roads were in a bad state owing to the heavy traffic upon them, through sheer perseverance the convoy had managed to get to Bertrancourt before dusk. Thanking his Welsh driver with a bottle of cheap French wine Fortune made his way from the field hospital into the centre of the village. The military police were satisfied with his pass-out documentation and he set about finding his accommodation. The village was alive with activity. The *estaminets*[26] were heaving with British customers who descended upon them from the large camps surrounding the village. Men walked in groups, arm in arm, through the small streets, singing in merriment under the watchful eye of the Provost Marshal and his men. Every shop front and house seemed to be utilised for entertainment and trade. The Scots were everywhere in their unmistakable kilted uniforms. Their laughter and harshness of their voices carried through the village.

An old companion, of the Royal Medical Corps, had arranged for a room to be set aside above the *Estaminet de Josephine* on the *Rue du Bourg*. Before long Fortune had located the establishment and discussed arrangements with the landlord. Fortune spent the evening drinking *"vin-plonk"*, a nasty concoction of rum and red wine he had grown accustomed to in India. After smoking Woodbines with the Seaforth Highlanders, in the *estaminet* beneath his lodgings, he filled his belly with "Bombardier Fritz and *oeufs*" in the cafe. They shared stories from the front and swapped

---

[26] Small cafe selling alcoholic drinks

gossip on the big push, which was on everyone's mind. One of the Jocks had been sent the latest edition of The War Illustrated,[27] its twenty or so pages crammed with wonderfully presented photographs from the war, from all fronts, alongside beautifully executed drawings and diagrams.

The men discussed the ongoing relief effort in Mesopotamia, to break the siege at Kut and rescue Townsend's force. The Scots were fascinated by the terrain portrayed in the pictures, compared to that of the Western Front. A veteran of Gallipoli chipped in with stories of the Turks and the conditions they had had to endure. There was, naturally, no mention of the big push in France within the publication, so the men concluded they would have to wait until after it was all over before they saw pictures illustrating their own heroic deeds. The drunken party inevitably turned sour and a scuffle between two lance corporals brought Fortune's evening to a close. He made his escape into the shadows and found his way upstairs to his small but comfortable room.

The lodgings looked out over the main street and from behind a lace curtain he watched the military police dealing with the Seaforth Highlanders. Satisfied he had seen what there was to be enjoyed of the proceedings he retreated into the solitude of the room. It was well appointed for the price and the owner had very kindly provided an old tin bath which, he was promised, would be filled with steaming hot water the following morning. Fortune thanked the landlord profusely for the provision of means to wash but it wasn't until much later he learnt it was a surprise paid for by his old Medical Corps friend and not the usual hospitality enjoyed at the establishment; a repayment for a long forgotten debt from the last war.

Sluggish from the wine and weary from the long journey he decided to rest, slipping quickly into a deep slumber without removing his uniform. A bottle of wine and two glasses sat proudly on sentry duty while he slept. A packet of Capstan remained unopened beside them, with a fresh box of matches atop; artfully arranged on a lace table cover. The window was propped open, allowing a soft breeze to pluck and toss the curtain. Laughter from below soon faded and the night was quiet, only broken by the barking of a dog or the light patter of a rain shower on the roof tiles.

Fortune dreamed of his home before the war, of his marital bed and conjugal pleasures therein. He imagined climbing the stairs carefully so as not to make a sound. It was a warm summer's evening, the curtains flourished as a breeze probed the bed chamber. He discovered her sleeping still, lying peacefully on her front with one leg drawn up and close to her side. Her night gown had risen, her smooth, shapely bottom and

---

[27] A pictorial weekly magazine published in England containing all the latest war news. Regular issues continued throughout the First World War.

thighs stealing his breath in the candlelight. He looked at her like this sight was before now unseen, with the eyes of a man who could never tire of a woman's perfection, laid bare before him. He moved slowly around the bed and as he did so more of her intimate form was revealed to him. He begged for her repose to continue uninterrupted so he might study her soft warm creases.

Fortune loosened his britches and let them fall to the floor. His urging desperation was released from its confines and he shuddered with the relief it brought. He edged his way forward, kneeling onto the bed. It creaked. She did not move. He waited for a while with his hand at play. She slept on. He edged closer onto all fours, his face only inches away from her nakedness. He careful stroked her leg from the back of the knee to her buttock where he pulled her gently apart. His tongue moistened his lips and moving forward once more he reached into her, licking her slowly with great care. She stirred for a moment, he paused, her breathing deepened. But still she slept. His hand played upon himself once more, a great surge growing and demanding from within.

He moved again, up the bed, tracing the line of her extended leg with the tip of his stiffness. Her neck was now beneath him, he kissed it. He gently pushed his nose into her hair and enjoyed her fragrance. His hand could play no more and with a prolonged push from his buttocks he was deep within her, enveloped by her warmth. Fortune woke with a start and cursed into the pillow at his sudden flood of bliss, with a laboured sigh he lay face down and returned to sleep.

The sound of lorries moving through the village woke Fortune from a deep slumber just before 1000 hours in the morning. He took breakfast downstairs while the landlord and his daughter filled the bath. This was no small undertaking, the landlord cursing and grumbling in French as he stumbled up and down the narrow stairs with his buckets. Fortune sat outside for a while watching the transport columns lumbering through the village. Elements of the British 4th Division were passing through the area, providing a constant flow of vehicles and men. Motor ambulances, artillery, ammunition lorries and tenures choked the small street. A young child stood with her toy doll, dressed as a French soldier, gazing in wonder at the huge mechanical beasts which had invaded her village. Fortune smoked his pipe and drank whiskey, obtained in a game of cards the night before.

The landlord, a grumpy middle-aged man with a pronounced limp and a large moustache articulated in his broken English that the bath was prepared, prompting Fortune to retire to his room. He found the bath water lukewarm at best but the novelty of such a luxury was too great to let the temperature or colour of the water dissuade him. Having folded his uniform neatly on the bed he sank into the bath and let out a moan as the water displaced over his shoulders. Fortune closed his eyes and recalled the brief time spent at the farm in April. He relived the first meeting with Bernice, the cigarette seducing him from the corner of her mouth, the way she formed words with her soft red lips. He savoured her kiss upon his cheek and remembered her gliding over the cobbles towards the safety of the farmhouse; her hips moving from side to side and the bare calves revealed beneath her skirt as she moved.

He imagined waiting under the archway for her father to leave on his cart, watching the old man disappear down the slope towards the road and then rushing into the farmhouse. He remembered how startled she was at his entrance, her expression changing to one of warmth and joy. He could not recall what they said to each other, only that he gazed down into her eyes and was lost in them. Then he recalled walking with her, in the field behind the farm; anxiety eating at him that he might be seen by one of the men. She strode through the long grass with her hand playing over the flowers, gently stroking their petals as she passed. He remembered they spoke, for some time, their exact words were lost to him, only his growing feelings for her as they wondered remained a vivid memory. Her eyes fixated him, perfect porcelain white and ice blue, they begged him to come closer, to lose himself within. He imagined moving her stray hair back behind her ear, carefully looping it behind while delicately stroking its helix with the tip of his finger.

He cupped her head and drew her into him, nestling her head in his large chest, her arms gracefully wrapped around his waist and up his back, small elegant hands seeking to pleasure his shoulders. They stood in silence, beneath a tree, two souls, two incommensurable personalities, somehow connecting, somehow sharing a common bond. From the moment they had met an electricity, a hidden unexplainable force had linked them and drawn them both together. He recalled the feeling of being shut off from the outside world, displaced from reality to be locked within an impenetrable bubble, Fortune and Bernice, from where the world became a nonsense and the charged touch between two bodies and minds was everything, a new universe to explore. They sat beneath the tree, her hand on his, sharing cigarettes. They talked, for what seemed like a brief moment in time, in reality hours had passed. Fortune felt like he had known her forever and yet she was a mystery.

Fortune let his imagination unfold as he relaxed into a deep meditation. He thought of her curves beneath her dress, the nape of her neck, the shape of her thighs. He imagined her lips on his body. Her thin delicate fingers running through the hairs of his chest. Beneath the water his hand found a purpose. Bernice stood watching at the door. She made no sound and waited for Fortune to open his eyes, peering up at her from his watery isolation. Her hair was tied above her head, two plaits securing her long locks in place. Her cheeks were rouge and her lips red. She smiled from the corner of her mouth. Saying nothing she dragged a chair from the window and set it down beside the bath. She reclined, facing him, drawing the hem of her skirt up over her shins and between her legs. Bernice tilted her head, amused by his reaction. She sat with her feet on their toes thus exaggerating the wonderful contours of her calves. As she forced her feet upward, her knees raised and her legs slowly parted. She drew her skirt further towards her, every inch revealing more of her form. Fortune was transfixed, the water of the bath rippling with disturbance, as her inner thighs were exposed.

"I didn't think you would come!" Fortune exclaimed.

Bernice lent forward, holding a finger to her lips. She raised the brown envelope she was holding and waved it playfully before casting it down beside the bath. Her hand penetrated the water and Fortune gasped, his head slipping back on the incline of the bath, his chin submerging. With his hands gripping the sides of the tub he abandoned himself to Bernice and her touch.

Chapter 17 - Bite and be bitten
14th May 1916
City of Amiens
1030 hours
48 days to Z-Day

Fortune and Bernice strolled arm in arm along the towpath of the La Somme Canalisee, under the shade of an avenue of trees. The old buildings lining the opposite bank warmed themselves in the bright sunlight, gasping for cool air through their wide-open windows. Ducks swam on the Somme punctuating their squabbles with loud quacks. Cyclists raced by, along the path. Two lovers sat on a bench feasting from an open wicker hamper, sharing red wine and smiles as pigeons nodded in approval about their feet. The great cathedral soared into the skyline ahead of them, its towers and steeple pocked with holes, a sobering reminder of a war being fought not so far away to the east.

"Will there ever be an end of it Henri?" Bernice asked after a long yet comfortable silence.

"Oh, I shouldn't think so. Men have been fighting each other since long before the first stone of that grand old church was laid down. And they will be fighting long after nothing remains of it."

"It is sad no, that men do not attend to their women with such vigour and excitement? A far more gratifying use of your efforts and less dangerous."

"Oh, I don't know about that my dear, some of you have more gumption than the biggest of guns," Fortune smiled, "And a far worse bite."

Bernice slapped his forearm playfully.

"Oh, shush, it is cruel to joke about such things. When will you go again?"

"Soon, in the next day or so," Fortune sighed.

"Then we shall not think of it, this day will not end until I am ready and," she blushed, "I have been gifted once more."

Fortune squeezed the muscles in his groin tightly as they twitched into life, just as a young schoolboy seeks to ascertain the situation when caught distracted by their teacher.

"Shall we eat my love?" Bernice enquired.

"If you wish, I can always eat," Fortune confessed.

"Oh you will Sergeant, but we should find food before no?" she giggled.

"My dear, you speak softly with such eloquence, such an educated...politeness, but your mind, I dare say, is as dirty as an Amien Abbess," Fortune chuckled.

"Do I want to know the meaning of this?"

"No my dear, best not to ask."

"A modern girl speaks her mind, makes clear her wishes. You would prefer if I kept my desires to myself? You would have us seen and not at all heard?"

"No, not at all my dear, of course not," Fortune insisted.

"*Non*, the world is changing my sergeant, the war of men you fight will decide the outcome of the war of women."

"There's no war with women dear."

"No? A change of tactic perhaps but the struggle goes on."

Fortune stopped and turned to face Bernice with a furrowed brow.

"What are you talking about?"

"You have Mrs Pankhurst and her Women's Union in England.[28]"

"Oh, her. Well, they have stopped their trouble making, they're helping the government now my dear. It's all resolved."

"Indeed it is so Henri. Women are working where men once did. But what does this show you men? Here we work hard, as hard as men. We are the same."

"You don't have to die like we do, so careful what you wish for my dear."

"And why shouldn't we?" Bernice stomped her foot.

Fortune laughed and continued walking. Bernice did not follow. Fortune offered his arm again and nodded to her to join him. She stood defiantly. Fortune's expression changed immediately, he returned to her and took her hands in his.

"We are two very different people my dearest Bernice, from different times and a different place. I dare say you are right, you know more of such things that I ever will. Let's not fight, not today."

---

[28] The Women's Social and Political Union was a women-only political movement and leading militant organisation campaigning for women's suffrage in the United Kingdom from 1903 to 1917

"You sound like my father when you think you know best, you don't listen to me."

"I do, I do."

Fortune raised his hands in protest.

"You don't. Do you think the world would be suffering this way if we, women, had an equal say in its government?"

"Well, I don't know, I've never thought of it that way," he confessed.

"They know, the men that would make war. They know, don't they? They keep us away from these paramount decisions and they wage their wars and fill their pockets and we are subjugated and still without suffrage. Powerless to unseat them."

"You must calm yourself my dear, I'm sorry you are frustrated, but I am just a sergeant and I have no part to play in such schemes. I am what I am, I cannot articulate an argument with you. I settle mine with bullet, blade or fist, which have no place here today. That's all I am good for my dear. Forgive me."

"Nonsense Henri, I have found a perfectly good use for you beside killing," she smiled once more and took his arm.

Fortune rolled eyes in his mind but kept his physical self firmly glued to her expressions, looking for any signal that her mood was about to change. They walked a little further in silence, her hand gently resting on his. He imagined he could feel every cell which was in contact with her young body. His loins stirred once more as he engaged a new conversation to temper their excitement.

"I imagine your father has profited from our presence at the farm?" he asked clumsily.

"I do not wish to talk of such things Henri," Bernice scolded.

Another lengthy pause was instigated but without the comfort of the previous silences. Fortune's mind agonised on what to say next.

"You have experience, *non*, with women Henri?" Bernice broke the awkwardness.

"Well, yes, of course I have, why do you ask?"

Fortune sought motive in the young girl's face but would have preferred to read an enemy's expression in a bayonet fight than draw any conclusion from the woman's countenance.

"In some aspects Henri, *comment dis-tu*, er, you have knowledge of a woman, intimate knowledges a younger man would not possess but a lot to make up, does that make sense?" she enquired.

"Not really my dear, make what up?"

"To make up for Henri, a lot to make up for."

Fortune stopped, his arm returning to his side.

"What do you mean? Like what?" he frowned.

Bernice giggled.

"Your big frown Fortune, your two *chenille* on your face are back once more, how delightful," she spun quickly on the tip of her toes, clapping twice as she turned full circle.

"Now listen here, my dear, what are you barking on about now hey?" Fortune grabbed her by the forearm.

"I am sorry Henri, you must forgive me, you are so funny. Your frowning does not scare me."

"Out with it then, let's not cause a scene," Fortune pressed for a response.

"Talking with women Henri," she slapped her sides with glee, "This is not something you are used to *non?* You English men are so afraid of what you don't understand."

"Oh I see, more than happy to make use of me in any way you see fit but I'm no good for conversation, well, there's no changing me now, my love."

They both stopped in their tracks, staring intently into each other's eyes. Bernice held a hand over her mouth. Fortune showed colour in his face for the first time since they had met. He sighed and pulled a Capstan from his pocket. Finding some matches, he lit the cigarette and shook his head slowly.

"Now don't go making a big song and dance Bernice," Fortune capitulated with heavy shoulders.

"Oh my dear Henri," she exclaimed, looping her arm into his once more, gripping him tightly, "Walk with me."

Fortune obliged and watched her face as they wondered. A broad smile radiated joy from her beautiful visage. She made no eye contact, looking forward without flinching. He glanced several times at her, her composure had not diminished.

"Oh curses woman," Fortune stopped, "Can you not make a fuss about this?"

"Henri, my dearest Henri, we shall not mention this accident of the speech again," she patted his hand lightly.

The couple walked again in silence to a small arched bridge over the canal. Before crossing, Bernice reached up around his broad neck and kissed him passionately. As soon as their embrace was fulfilled, she ran up and over the bridge with a skip in her step, flashing the backs of her legs with a quick toss of her skirt.

"Bloody hell," Fortune grumbled, losing the battle of wills with his animal hunger which was now raging below.

Once he had composed himself, Bernice was found buying a bouquet from a street stall, in a small square surrounded by tall buildings and a shady cafe.

"Here Henri," she beamed, placing a single yellow flower in his lapel buttonhole.

"Bloody hell," Fortune groaned to himself once more.

"Come," she called, snatching his hand, "There is still so much more to see."

The couple took a small meal at an *estaminet* in the square beside the cathedral Notre-Dame D'Amiens. They watched the other couples, walking out in the mid-May sun. Officers strode with their sweethearts, carriages carried lovers beside the river, while the war still ground its lethal mortar and pestle without regard for the momentary respite some were enjoying. French motor ambulances trundled through the square. A plane crossed the sky, heading somewhere of importance. Two staff cars waited patiently beneath a large medieval building. Invalid soldiers walked on crutches escorting their nurses in a slow hobble. Horses carried staff officers to their briefings. French soldiers, the Poilu,[29] marched through the street in their striking blue uniforms. Bernice snatched up a flower from her bouquet on their table and ran to the column of men. She placed the flower in a soldier's lapel and kissed him on the cheek.

Having waved to each individual soldier, Bernice returned and poured them both another glass of wine.

"Tell me of your life before all of this? Before any wars I mean."

"Is there such a time my dear?" Fortune countered.

"*Naturellement* Henri, there is always peace before a war. This city was so full of joy, laughter, gaiety, before the soldiers came."

"I'd have to think of a time long since passed. For between the wars there was never gaiety to speak of," he confessed solemnly.

"How so?"

"When a soldier comes home, it's difficult my dear. Your women will discover this when those blue coats have done their job. There are many things a man should never see or do, which we must see and must do, to win a war. These things, my dear, are not the subject of casual conversation, and not something any soldier wishes to speak about with civilians. When you return, you must understand, you are not the same person as went away. You bring with you a hidden turmoil, so severe you want to rip it from deep inside you, but fear what would happen if it were released. We are, my dear, vessels which carry a shame, and some can carry it better than others. Sometimes that vessel is broken, see. And then all around you are broken through its contact."

---

[29] Poilu is an informal term for a French World War I infantryman, meaning, literally, hairy one. It is still widely used as a term of endearment for the French infantry of World War I. The word carries the sense of the infantryman's typically rustic, agricultural background. Beards and bushy moustaches were often worn.

Bernice reached over and extracted two cigarettes, lighting them both, passing one to Fortune. He smiled grimly at the gesture.

"And," Bernice paused to gather confidence in her pursuit of the questioning, "You struggled with what you have described?"

"Indeed."

"You wish you had never gone to fight?"

"Oh goodness no, not that. You might think that but no. I would long for the chance to do it again."

"But it is horrible *non?*"

"Yes, at times, that is too light a word."

"Then what is this compulsion you speak of?"

"To feel the bond again, a calling to return to others who share your experiences and pain, and to enjoy the thrill and pleasure only found by such a bond with other men. Pleasure is not the right word my dear, satisfaction? I am not one for many words."

"On the contrary Henri, you surprise me once more. I understand."

"You don't, and can't," Fortune snapped in an instant.

"*Non*, of course. You are right. But, before the wars, there was happiness? As a child?"

"My father would take his belt to me rather than say more than two words to acknowledge my existence. I took this as his way of showing his love, in the end. My mother, I don't remember well."

"You don't?"

"She passed on when I was young."

"I am sorry."

"Don't be, no need."

"Brothers, sisters?"

"Yes, we were all split up and handed around to aunts and uncles when mother passed on. Never really grew up with them, I knew them, they were in the village, but it wasn't anything close."

Bernice looked glum, defeated. She took a large gulp of the wine and finished her cigarette.

"The Army, my dear, was my family, gave me a sense of belonging I never had before that. Looked after me well, good feed each day and warm clothes. You can't argue with the simple necessities Her Majesty provided."

"Were there girls, women? A sweetheart?"

"Boys are kept at distance from the gentle sex, it's improper in England unless you are courting, even that is supervised. You have to steal yourself away, to meet up, you know? But once in the Army that all changed of course," Fortune smiled.

"I don't want to know," Bernice frowned.

"Of course not no," Fortune acknowledged the blunder and frowned in solidarity.

After dining they wondered into the cathedral and stood amazed at the tall banks of sandbags which now swamped the buttresses and columns of the huge vaulted space. Birds flew between ageing stone figures high in the damaged roof, the weather-worn chiselled faces staring with judgemental sneers down at the unorthodox couple. Bernice knelt and prayed, crossing herself before she rejoined Fortune at the entrance.

"What will you do after the war is over?" asked Bernice as they marvelled at the medieval architecture.

"There will always be a war to fight, that's the only business I am apprentice to."

"We will be left with this and you will go home, where the war has not scratched the skin with its terrible claws."

"Home, it has changed more than you know my dear. Granted we have not suffered as your homeland has but suffer we do. Every day more lads are buried on your soil and many more are sent home a shadow of their true selves."

"I know, I'm sorry, my comment was unkind."

"What will you do after all this is over?" he returned the query.

"Oh, I will be a teacher, in the city or a journalist for a newspaper," she twirled on the spot with a childish excitement at the question while grasping Fortune's arm.

"And the farm?"

"Farm be damned," she scowled, "I will meet a fine young Frenchman, returning from the war. Tall and dark and handsome but no moustache," she waved her finger.

She enjoyed Fortune's stern reaction immensely so continued gleefully.

"He will give me many children, three boys and two girls. We will live here in Amiens in a townhouse by the Somme. Pierre, for that is his name, will wait upon me, my every need fulfilled, while I write my newspaper column from the first-floor bedroom. I'll have a typewriter and a maid and a large portrait of my new family will hang over the fire. In the evening, when the children are resting, Pierre will take me up in his large arms and," she laughed, its intonation leapt up into the cathedral and startled the pigeons.

"Alright, alright, cease your tormenting girl."

Fortune dragged her from the cathedral under the scrutiny of many disgusted locals; their fingers entwined, an electricity maturing the bond of passion.

Once outside they alighted the ancient stone stairs to the square below. Before the last step had been reached, Fortune stopped abruptly, pulling

Bernice back from her continued descent. It was too late to avoid his gaze. Fortune's heart jumped.

"Sersant!" 2nd Lieutenant Richardson called out.

The mounted officer bade his companions farewell, steering his steed to the cathedral steps he waited, his horse impatient. Fortune remembered himself and saluted, Richardson returning the respectful greeting of the King's commission. Fortune frowned; his officer smiled. Both remained silent holding each other's stare for some time.

"Are we to be introduced?" asked Bernice.

"Forgive my rudeness mademoiselle, your humble servant Percival Gregoor Armstrong-Richardson, second lieutenant of His Majesty's Somerset Light Infantry. May I take know your name?" he bowed respectfully from the saddle.

"Mademoiselle Jacques sir, I am pleased to have your acquaintance."

"The pleasure is all mine mademoiselle, I assure you. I trust today finds you well and in good company?" Richardson glanced momentarily at his sergeant.

"It does sir, and yourself?" Bernice enquired politely.

"Indeed. What better source of exhilaration for a man could be gained than riding one's charger in the open field, with a fair city such as Amiens on the skyline, a sword at one's side and the scent of glory in the air."

"The exhilaration of love monsieur, the contented excitement of two people, arm in arm, sharing their life with no other."

"Forgive me but how does such a beautiful young girl come to be walking with one of my men?", Richardson sneered, "If I may be so bold?"

"I am sir, very fortunate to have been introduced to Henri this most recent month."

"Where do you come from mademoiselle? Amiens?"

"Bertrancourt sir, we are a farming family."

"Ah, it is explained. The proletariat, working folk such as yourselves, must have plenty in common Sersant I should wager?"

His patronising laughter sent shock waves through Bernice's spine.

"Not really no sir," Fortune replied awkwardly.

"Then what, it must be asked, should attract such a delightful young *meisie* to an old soldier such as this? I must know the secret so I may employ it myself mademoiselle," Richardson baited with a chuckle.

"I fear, sir, you would not match Henri if you knew of his secret."

"Damnation of course I could, with ease. There is nothing this miscreant brute of the lower ranks can provide for you which I could not supply tenfold!" Richardson jeered.

Fortune squeezed Bernice's hand tightly to warn her from her present course. She had never left an injustice unanswered before and this was certainly not going to be the first time she would retreat from such a challenge. She ignored the pain in her fingers. Like so many arguments with her father and her father's friends, her final blow, her *piece de resistance* was already planned and meticulously timed.

"With the utmost respect which is due sir, you are a slight man unlike Henri and one would assume you are quite impotent to provide for me the same *breadth* of attention a man of his vigour and strength can....cultivate."

Bernice was delighted with the choice of her final word, a supplementary victory on behalf of the farming community.

"Well I have never," Richardson's face reddened, his rage mirrored by the violent movement of his horse's head.

"In short sir, we are, I assure you, very intimate indeed."

"A word of warning mademoiselle, the other-ranks of the glorious British Army are not gentle-men, dallying with such scoundrels will only end in misery," Richardson snarled, tapping his cane on his thigh impatiently.

"I have read such things sir," Bernice tightened her grip on Fortune's hand.

"Oh, I am sure," Richardson dismissed her.

"*Some of our men enlist from having bastard children, some for minor offences, many more for drink; but you cannot conceive such a group brought together, and it really is wonderful that we should have made them the fine fellows they are,*[30]" she stumbled over some words and stopped several times to recall correctly but Bernice recounted the quote in full.

Richardson wheeled his horse and stared across at her, tightening his lips together without retort. His horse snorted and nodded its head up vigorously.

"They say in Amiens, a strong horse is as difficult to handle as a woman," she gloated, "It appears the saying is correct sir."

"A hot-headed girl such as this will not serve you well Sersant. In my country, mademoiselle, a woman takes the hand of a gentleman and speaks only of the affairs within which she is permitted to contribute. Otherwise she is expected to know her function and damn well stick to it. Fires should be extinguished before they spread Sersant! You will attend me at dawn tomorrow," Richardson turned his horse violently once more and rode away.

"You are in my country now sir," Bernice called after her vanquished opponent.

"What the devil was that about Bernice?"

---

[30] From Notes of Conversations with the Duke of Wellington (1886) by Philip Henry Stanhope

"The Duke of Wellington," she replied prosaically, "Of the English army."

"No, I mean what was he up to? Were you two?" Fortune was cut short.

"A minor scuffle in a larger engagement, *n'est-ce pas?*"

"I think you have just been drawn into it my dear, an antagonism exists between us and has done for some time. I had intended to keep you safe from it."

"Men such as he are easily handled Henri, they expect us to listen to their perfectly articulated discourse without wish or need for hearing our own. *Non?* A man of education is countered with words. Words with more virtue than his own."

"I don't know my dear, it doesn't work that way in the Army. He is my commander and virtue or not he'll make my life hell if he wishes it."

Chapter 18 - Town and out
14th May 1916
City of Amiens
2200 hours
48 days to Z-Day

Fortune panted and wheezed, his head hanging heavily onto his chest. His service cap lay top-down on the beer-soaked table in front of him, several stubbed out cigarettes nesting within it. His left hand rested atop a large ceramic cup brimming with beer, guarding its contents until Fortune was ready for more. Sergeant Danny Hope sat beside him, embroiled in a flamboyant discussion with another NCO. Danny's arm buffeted Fortune as he gesticulated, causing the weary sergeant to sway and lurch like a heavy tree branch tugged by a fast-moving river.

The large *maison tolérée*[31] was crammed with Tommies, all of them worse for wear. The long sweeping bar sporting a design which would in time become known as art-deco, with its gigantic mirror and shell-like gas lamps, was partially obscured by the density of soldiers crowding its length. A balding man with a handlebar moustache and white apron worked feverishly to fill flagons, glasses and cups for the men. Every conceivable shape and size of table was crammed into the floor space, each one desecrated with spilt beverages and upturned glasses. A flight of stairs, open sided to the huge chamber, alighted to the right and formed a mezzanine level above the bar. Men jostled on every step and peered down into the mass.

Across from where the NCOs were sat was a semi-circular raised area, lined with upward facing gas lamps, currently presenting a man on an accordion singing a raunchy cockney shanty. His song was practically drowned out by a group of Welsh tenors who erupted into verse beneath

---

[31] Licenced brothel

the stairs. Nobody seemed to mind the cacophony. Laughter and shouting and a hundred leery conversations overlapped to create an intense barrier of sound, a barrier to irrational thought and troubling anxiety.

Three French girls, perhaps only teenagers, twisted their hair through their fingers on the first three steps of the stairs. A larger woman, more senior in years and baring remarkable similarities to the younger girls, collected francs from men in a large glass bowl. The eager men were led away to hoots and whistles from their friends.

Privates Connor and Merry stumbled across the street from a smaller *estaminet* and grinned their way around the large Scottish corporal who stood guard at the entrance. He waved them in nonchalantly and continued his vigil for the Military Police. They met Private Cooksley floundering out of the establishment as they entered.

"Going for photograph," he spurted at them.

"Wa? Steady mate," Private Connor laughed.

"In the square, there's a bloke doing photographs, two francs. Group ones on a waggon or individuals like. I'll send one home to mother in the morning."

The wretch could barely speak let alone stand.

"Christ almighty Michael that ain't a good idea, not now. Look at yous. Poor woman will fret something silly if she knew you were in this much danger."

"Come on Michael, come back in with us," Private Merry begged.

"Ah bollocks to ya Mary," Private Cooksley raged.

The Scottish corporal grabbed him by his neck and flung him out into the street, sending him tumbling over himself into the gutter.

"See thes fanny haem ur he'll tak' his chances wi' th' redcaps," bellowed the Scot.

Privates Connor and Merry shrugged their shoulders and passed inside. Private Pocock, grinning his toothless smile, pressed his way through the swarm carrying large glasses of beer to the rear of the room. Making their way towards a vacated table near the bar he met Private Connor and Private Merry.

"I'm gunna get myself a lady!" Private Connor slurred at the ex-sailor.

"Good lad, what do ya look for in a gal?"

"Cheap and up for it," Private Connor replied over the din.

"Ha! Get yourself one of these dollymops boy and make sure Mary here butters the bun!"

"Will do mate," Private Connor beamed as his eyes rolled around his head.

"Don't fucking call me that you prick, you hear me! We ain't mates you hear!"

Private Pocock's face tensed with aggression and his mouth drew upwards into a snarl. Private Connor sank back but the weight of the crowd prevented any escape. Private Pocock started to laugh heartily, shaking his head as he pushed his way through and out of sight.

"What was he talking about Richard?" shouted Private Merry.

"Sloppy seconds after me, bloody nut-case that Charlie you know?"

"He does seem a little intense at times," Private Merry confessed.

"We go back a long way, have been friends for yonks you know. He can see a lot of himself in me I think, that's why he likes me."

"He hates your guts. He hates everyone, even himself."

"Nah, it's all for show, we're like that really," Private Connor crossed his fingers.

They reached a table where Privates Moore, Stendhurst and Cartwright were slumped in alcoholic ecstasy, but as Private Connor went to take a chair Private Moore kicked it away.

"No room here, fuck off Paddy," shouted Private Moore.

"Funny chaps, crack me up they do," Private Connor admitted to Private Merry.

Private Edgar James Moore was thirty-two years old, comparatively ancient when surrounded by such youthful men. His wife Sally and daughters Charlotte and Grace lived in relative luxury, for an up and coming middle class family, in the city of Bristol. Before the war Edgar had worked his way up to senior clerk at a prominent architect's firm. The family home was well furnished, Sally would frequently hold soirees for the society women of the same social standing as she belonged. Visitors would arrive throughout the day to take tea, admiring the cakes and delicacies their cook could muster. They would frequent the theatre, marvel at the local museums and Edgar would play cricket on every other weekend in the summer.

Life was harder now for the Moore family. Their maid had given notice to go and work in the munitions factory. The market for hired help had fallen through the floor once the young women of Bristol caught wind of the heightened pay being offered for war work and thus with no applicants for the vacant position Sally herself had taken up an apron to attend to matters of the house. The children's governess had left to join the Volunteer Aid Detachment. Food was scarce and the abundance of the pre-war boom was but a distant memory.

Edgar had refused a commission, owing to a fierce pride from his working-class background. Being the first Moore to have obtained a degree following grammar school he broke the traditional mould of factory worker or general labourer which was prevalent within his large family. Regardless of his success in education and employment he felt strongly that he should serve alongside his fellow countrymen, attesting on 1st January 1915, joining the *other ranks* soon after.

Edgar's elder brother Simon had been killed in Dublin only a month previous, serving with the South Staffordshire Regiment during the Easter Rising.[32] He was in no mood to entertain Private Connor's company.

Over on Fortune's table Private Pocock had reached the recess and deposited the beers.

"Fuck me you should get up there Danny, proper toffer. Unrigged before you know it, madge and all. Do what you like, if you pay for it. Roundmouth too, all of it. Cor, what a place, I'm never washing these fingers again!" Private Pocock babbled.

A sergeant from the Ulster Regiment turned from his table and scowled at Charlie for addressing NCOs in such a familiar fashion, soon returning to his own business when he saw there was no reprimand from either Danny or Fortune, only scowls at his interjection.

"Keep your voice down Charlie," Sergeant Hope warned with a hand on Private Pocock's sleeve.

"What's wiv him?" Private Pocock indicated with a tilt of his head.

Danny shook his head slightly while raising his bottom lip to a grimace.

"Been out of sorts all afternoon, leave 'im be."

Private Pocock was about to nudge his old friend when the sound of an altercation became audible over the debauched pandemonium. Private Pocock stood, enthused, as a fire returns to life from embers when fresh fuel is applied.

"Blimey, it's some of ours!" he shouted as he rushed into the horde.

"Fortune, wake up, there's trouble!" urged Sergeant Hope with a violent shake of the old timer's shoulder.

Those two words that rouse an old soldier from any state, any intoxication, any malaise, "There's trouble" exploded their vibrant and sobering chemistry in Fortune's addled mind. He lurched upward sending vessels of beer crashing to the floor. With an undignified and clumsy movement, he removed his service dress tunic and cast it down on the bench.

"Look after my stripes Danny," Fortune slurred.

---

[32] The Easter Rising also known as the Easter Rebellion, was an armed insurrection in Ireland during Easter Week, April 1916

"Wake up you sod, come on, wake up," Charlie insisted, "Wake up soldier."

Fortune opened one eye and immediately closed it.

"Where are we?" he croaked.

"Where else could we be after a night like that?"

"Christ," Fortune exclaimed.

"Don't ya worry, they don't have your stripes. Danny got them away."

Fortune let out a relieved sigh and dribbled onto the hard floor.

"What happened?" Fortune lisped as he felt his swollen lips and jaw.

"What do you remember?"

"Nothing, drinking, some fucking terrible singing."

"Jesus you were well out of it you daft bastard. We went whoring with the others and Moore stirred some Paddies with his profanities. Er, Moore, Cartwright, Stendhurst, Connor, Mary all beat up pretty bad."

"Mary?"

"Yeah, can you believe that?"

"And you?"

"Oh I'm alright, those Paddy pricks had nothing for us, straight fight, over before it started," Charlie boasted.

"And me?"

"Yeah and you, when have you turned down the chance to see the Irish off?"

"Shit. I don't remember. Red caps?"

"Yes, you were fightin like your life depended on it, f'ing and blinding and swinging and punching. Wouldn't have been up to pulling you off if I'd wanted to. Danny got the others out the back, but someone had to stay. Can't shift you these days, not with beer in you. You scared even me last night old mate, such ferocious fightin, Jesus, there weren't no jaws left without bruises. Red caps bust our heads and everyone else they found in there."

"I owe you I guess."

"Old sweats, never leave a man behind. That's what you taught me."

"Aye well, did we get them all? The Paddies?"

"Yeah, we got 'em. Where you hurting?"

"Everywhere."

Charlie rolled Fortune over onto his back. Fortune let out a groan and grabbed his side.

"Ribs then, your nose has gone again too," Charlie diagnosed, "What was up with you last night anyways?"

"Can't shake this gloom, you know, stuff catching up on me I think."

"Kin'ell. Loos again?"

"Maybe, something like that. I can't shake it this time."

"Sure it's that? What about the cunny?"

"What cunny?"

"Any cunny? You been getting any?"

"No. Well yeah but…"

"Well there it is."

"It's not that."

"Lobcock?"

"No! Fuck off Charlie."

"Hey, happens to all of us out here. Don't be ashamed."

"It's not that, alright."

"Richardson?"

"Maybe. No. Maybe."

"I've not known you spooked by no man before, not like this. He's got under your skin ain't he?"

"Yes. But we've talked about what I'm going to do," Fortune lowered his voice.

"Yer we have, so stop yur fretting," Charlie slapped Fortune's face.

Fortune pulled himself up against the wall where he sat, slumped, in a corner of the dark cell.

"What is this place?"

"Dunno, some old city prison no doubt. Stinks of the French."

"There's…" Fortune paused.

"What?" Charlie grabbed his sergeant by the shirt.

"There's this girl."

"Oh, for fucks sake, I fucking knew it," Charlie's eyes danced in his head, his gums glistening at Fortune in a broad smile.

"Shut up."

"You daft old cunt you, you've knocked someone up, haven't you? Christ don't worry about that we'll be hauling off somewhere new before you know it and she'll be nothing but a joke with the lads."

"I haven't knocked anyone up Charlie, calm down. It's the farm girl, I can't get her out of my bloody head. We have something, you know, when we are together. I've never felt like this before, not even with," Fortune was cut short.

"The young mot from that farm? Flashing it about for everyone. Oh mate, she was making eyes at everyone, you didn't think that did ya?" Charlie laughed.

"She wasn't Charlie, it wasn't like that."

"Cock-tease that's all old chap, you have to let that go. Hard times smile on enterprising girls. Half the bloody army has been up at that farm and she winks at anyone for a cigarette or a few francs," Charlie jested, "Word is she's been draining the army of its coin and cum for months."

Fortune, filled with a sudden ferocity, raged with primeval violence. He grabbed Charlie firmly by his neck and forced him sideways against the wall of the cell. Charlie, startled at first, pushed back but could not resist the strength and weight being exerted upon him. Fortune's grip tightened as he drove his head in hard on Charlie's forehead, grinding the back of the sailor's skull against the stonework. Sensing this was more than just a playful wrestle Charlie hit out, with upper cuts to Fortune's stomach and a sweeping punch to Fortune's right cheek. Fortune relaxed his grip on Charlie's throat and rolled back, winded.

Charlie was up in a single fluid motion and now stood poised over Fortune, he stabbed quickly with his left, then right fists, watched how Fortune reacted for a blink of an eye then stabbed again with his formidable and refined weapons. Fortune spat blood, sweeping Charlie's feet out from under him, then landed a ferocious kick to Charlie's face while he squirmed on the floor. The two men lay where they had fallen, their chests heaving for air, staring up at the ceiling of the cell.

"Well, old mate, you've fallen for her alright," Charlie began to laugh, spitting blood from his broken gums.

"Your insights of wisdom never cease to amaze," coughed Fortune.

"Booze, bum and baccy, we used to say when on ship," Charlie began.

"Ha! What?" Fortune tried not to laugh, grasping his chest in agony.

"Booze, bum and baccy. All a sailor needs to keep his spirits high. But, the truth is, the fellas with a sweetheart at home, a wife, whatever, waiting for them to come home, pining for them you know, worryin and wishing, them lads were always stronger in spirit than those of us without it. Knowing there's someone out there, no matter how far away, makes you stronger, makes a man whole. You've gone and found that wiv her at the farm. But there's a price."

"What's that?"

"Your life is worth savin now, it has value to someone. And you value them. You didn't care before, did you?"

Fortune turned his head and looked at Charlie.

"Well there you are," Charlie responded to the look he was given.

"How do I shake it?"

"You won't, not while she is in yur 'ed."

"And how would you," Fortune's eyes lit up, "Charlie Pocock you old dog, who is she?"

"Daisy Tremlow," Charlie answered after a pause.

"What!?" Fortune shifted uncomfortably to face Charlie.

"She would sit on the handlebars of yur bike and let you touch her ass as you rode along, all innocent like," Charlie grinned as he recalled happier times.

"Seems a bit tame for you Charlie," Fortune joked.

"I was twelve, she was fifteen," Charlie confessed.

"Blimey, I shouldn't have doubted you, Christ!" their laughter and joy spread pain with every pulse.

"We had it off whenever we could, after school, before school, whenever she wanted it. She had an itch you see, one she couldn't scratch without a boy. It would drive her crazy, take over her mind until it was seen to. Behind the church, up the lane, broke into the butchers once so she could get her meat, on the meat," Charlie laughed hard when Fortune frowned.

"I'm joking, we didn't break in. When mother was sleeping off the gin, we'd do it there, right there. She never had a clue," Charlie sighed.

"My God, you really are a piece of work. So you fell for her? What happened?"

"Of course, what twelve-year-old boy wouldn't. My root was always sore. It went on like that for the summer, an amazing summer, but what goes up must come down, she was pregnant. Her dad went crazy, came round and had it out with my dad. In the street they were, all the neighbours were out, a right hullabaloo."

"So, what did you do?"

"I ran away. Dad told me to. That's when I joined the Navy the first time. February 1903. They wouldn't take me though. I'd lied about my age. They sussed me out. I didn't go home. Found work in Portsmouth docks. Did some time on a trawler."

"What happened to Daisy?"

"Eight years went by quick, the Navy took me on when they finally thought I was eighteen. I sailed the oceans, saw the world. Life was good. I was serving as a stoker on HMS Gloucester when I got a letter, out of the blue like. We were in the Med, docked at Malta. It was Daisy. Father had passed on my details. She said she was in trouble, dying. Consumption she said. I had not thought about her until then, life had moved on. But, from the moment I read her letter that old bond was there see. I wanted to see her, to help her you know, in some way, to make things right, to be by her side. It ate me up."

"And that's why you jumped ship? The Pocock mystery is finally solved."

"If any of the lads find out it was for a lass, I will kill you."

"I know you will, I know you will. So, you went back then?"

"Yeah."

"And Daisy?"

"Daisy died the morning before I arrived. I didn't show my face at the funeral. Watched from a distance. That's when I saw William."

"William?"

"My son. She'd kept him, not given him away as many were forced to. Living with her parents he was and passed off as theirs. That told me she loved me you see, all that time."

"Charlie I dunno what to say to that. Did her parents know you had come home? Did you meet him?"

"No. I ran again. Got work on a freighter doing runs to Canada. Started fightin for wagers, using my training from the Navy. We used to box all the time, shilling a bout. I started fixing my smile," he grinned, "You see I had nothing left, nothing in here, my life's love was lost, all those years wasted when she was there waiting for me. And a boy who would never know me."

"What point are you making now Charlie?"

"Ah I dunno, I'm done making a point. I'm just makin misery now."

Chapter 19 - Interjection
No-Man's-Land

As Fortune had been talking for quite some time, Percy had for the most part remained silent, listening intently to the old soldier's story. He politely waited until a break in the tale before asking his next question.

"So how did you get out of it?"

"Richardson. He had all the papers drawn up and everything. As usual not a detail had been left unaccounted. What could the Provost do but turn us over to him," Fortune revealed.

"But, how did he know you were there?"

Fortune pondered the question.

"Good point. Well - He had dined with the captain and a few other officers from the battalion, in Amiens. Some of them had retired to a blue light, officer knocking shop, you know? In the early hours they had gone their separate ways and Richardson, riding through the now quiet streets, had come across Danny and the others making their way back to billets. They said he was with a girl, local lass. Lady's man by all accounts. Anyways, they didn't have the knack for spinning yarns as I do so, they told the truth."

"You must have been in for it?"

"Well that's just the thing. His papers were bogus, he buried the whole sorry affair. The old man never knew. Nobody was reprimanded."

"And why pray tell would he do that?"

"Nothing was going to get in the way of his raid and I needed to be there. I was no use to anyone locked up awaiting discipline."

"What did you think to all of this?"

"It just confirmed my suspicions, was obvious that his plan for dealing with me was centred on the raid and me being there, not rotting somewhere waiting my punishment by someone else's hands."

"You haven't explained why he wanted to Fortune, what had happened to steer him on this murderous course? The evidence suggests your CO was compassionate and pulled strings to have you saved from charge. This evidence does nothing to support your line of reasoning."

"I have more, I'm getting to it," Fortune snorted.

"Was it Loos? What happened there Fortune?"

"Like I said boy, I haven't got to that yet," Fortune scowled with frustration.

Chapter 20 - Into darkness

19th May 1916

Front-line trenches east of Authuille Wood

2300 hours

43 days to Z-Day

"We'll assemble in Bomberbridge Street here," 2nd Lieutenant Richardson indicated on the map, "Then proceed to the Russian sap here and await the off. At 0100 we move out into no-man's-land and make our way to the German wire here. Sixteen men in total, four bayonets, four raiders, six bombers and two with charges for the dugouts. A flare for each pair of men. Wire cutters for the riflemen. They will make a path through the wire and we enter the front-line trench at this point, where is it, here. Photographs show there is some sort of strong point, dugouts and a machine gun post perhaps. We make our way along this trench and on arrival we send a green flare up.

The forty fifth battery Royal Field Artillery and the heavy trench mortars of U8 will lay down a box barrage cutting off their lines of reinforcement here, here and here. Once we have acquired prisoners and we are ready to cross back over, a red flare will signal the battery commanders to bring their barrage down on the front-line, here and along here, thus protecting us from any fire in our rear as we make our escape. Upon reaching our wire the password Bentley will signal our approach. Sersant Hope you will have the remainder of the platoon on the fire step ready to throw back any counterattack they may muster. Any questions?"

"Just two sir," Sergeant Danny Hope requested.

"Go on Sersant."

"How many of them are you likely to find in this stretch of trench?"

"Unknown at this time. Nothing we can't handle I shouldn't wonder."

"And, what time should we expect your return sir? We've heard a number of German patrols over the last two nights and wouldn't want to mistake you for the enemy."

"I want to be clear, we should not rush to get into their lines, the period prior to entering the enemy trenches is crucial. If we make good time we could be back home for 0300 hours. But I will not pin a time upon it, it is my view that we cannot go about our business effectively with a specifically defined schedule. If the plan deviates and we have a set timing for each stage, we would surely risk failure."

"The Captain is happy with this sir?" Fortune probed.

"Naturally," Richardson frowned.

"What happens if anything goes wrong?" Fortune waited eagerly for Richardson's reaction.

"Nothing will go wrong Sersant, it has been meticulously planned as you can see," Richardson boasted with confidence.

"*A secure plan in case of unfortunate outcomes should always be carefully considered,* sir," Fortune recalled precisely.

Richardson smiled.

"Very good Sersant. Very well, should we encounter difficulties before entering the wire the red flare will indicate our position is untenable. As I have mentioned before, the gunners will bring down their barrage on the front-line here, allowing us to make our way back to safety."

"I see sir. And what if we run into trouble once we are inside? What then?"

"This is why you must select the best men for the task Sersant. There is little the artillery can do to help us if we become stuck here. If their numbers are superior, then we must make the best of it and pull out. But gentlemen, this is where the element of absolute surprise will serve us well. Once they realise what is happening, we will be passing back to our lines, with our prisoners."

The telephone rang suddenly and Richardson's batman, sitting patiently at a small table in the dugout, answered it immediately.

"It's Captain Wilmslow sir."

"Thank you Squires. Richardson speaking. Yes sir. Yes of course sir. Thank you sir. Yes, that's correct. Thank you sir, goodbye."

"Captain Wilmslow sends his best wishes for the operation. Squires, the captain will be attending once we go over, he wanted to be here upon our return. Please make sure he is comfortable. There's a claret I've been saving."

"Yes sir, of course sir."

"Gentlemen, have you selected your men?"

"Yessir, they are ready sir. Very keen sir to get at it," announced Sergeant Hope.

"Very good. Ensure you have everything you need from the Quartermaster stores and we shall reconvene here at, let's say midnight thirty."

Richardson closed his pocket watch and walked over to the cabinet. He poured himself a whiskey from a dusty bottle, sipping it casually while the sergeants waited.

"That will be all for now Sersant."

"Very good sir, thank you sir."

Sergeant Danny Hope came to attention and saluted his officer, once the salute was returned he left the dugout through the thick leather curtain.

"Sit, Sersant, please, sit," Richardson waved at a chair.

"Thank you sir, if it's all the same to you I will stand," replied Fortune.

"Sit. I insist. Squires, bring over another glass would you. Thank you. Why don't you go for a smoke?"

"Very good sir."

Richardson poured Fortune a large whiskey, handing the tumbler across the table, he sat. Fortune took the glass and drank the whiskey in one large gulp. Richardson tilted his head slightly in annoyance but continued sipping his drink.

"Have you done anything like this before Sersant?" Richardson broke the silence.

"Yessir."

"And it was a successful enterprise?"

"No sir."

"What happened?"

"They must have heard us when we were at the wire with our cutters. Before we knew it Very lights and star shells were going up, it was like daylight. They caught us point blank sir."

"Many casualties?"

"Four dead, seven wounded, three missing. One crawled back in two days later, the others we never found sir."

"I see. What do you owe to the failure of the raid?"

"They heard us at the wire sir and as we were all grouped up when the alarm was given, we didn't stand a chance."

Richardson sat back on his chair having finished his whiskey. He pondered for a while, pressing both hands together at the fingertips.

"You and I shall go forward from the group and see to the wire ourselves, with the utmost caution. Should anything go awry, the others will be safely dispersed."

"You shouldn't risk yourself in such a manner sir, let me sort the wire with someone else."

"No, that won't do Sersant. I will lead from the front, set an example of bravery to the men and should anything untoward happen to me I dare say there is a MC for my action."

"The Military Cross is no good to you dead sir."

"Quite the contrary Sersant. I don't expect you to understand."

"I can try sir."

Richardson reached back to the shelf behind him and selected a small leather-bound book. He fingered the pages for a moment and came upon a page where the corner had been turned down. He read a short passage.

"For the whole earth is the tomb of famous men; not only are they commemorated by columns and inscriptions in their own country, but in foreign lands there dwells also an unwritten memorial of them, graven not on stone but in the hearts of men. Make them your examples, and, esteeming courage to be freedom and freedom to be happiness, do not weigh too nicely the perils of war.[33]"

"What do you want of me sir?" asked Fortune, puzzled.

Richardson poured out two more glasses of whiskey.

"I want you close to me Sersant, I want to watch you, I want you to prove to me you have the fortitude for what is coming."

"Anyone would have done what I did on that hill," Fortune slammed the table with the palm of his hand.

Richardson smiled, fingering the small book once more.

"He is a man of courage who does not run away, but remains at his post and fights against the enemy.[34]"

"Stop playing these games with me sir," Fortune stood.

"Sit down!" Richardson raised his voice, carefully enunciating each syllable. Fortune recovered his chair and sat once more.

"There are no games out here Sersant," Richardson snarled, "We do not play games with the lives of our men. We have a responsibility, a great duty to perform Sersant and that is to wage this war to the best of our abilities. And yet not one, not one of these men is to be wasted for another man's folly. Do you hear me? Am I clear? My NCOs are to be the best I can foster, I will not tolerate cowardice, insubordination, torpidness, indolence of any kind. My platoon, when the big push comes, will go over knowing we have the bravest officers and NCOs in the battalion. They will trust their superiors implicitly and look to you, to us, for cool, calm, carefully considered instruction."

"They do trust me," Fortune insisted angrily.

"Oh I am sure most do, but those that remain from last year, do they know what happened?"

"They know what I told them."

---

[33] Funeral Oration of Pericles - Thucydides, History of the Peloponnesian War
[34] From a dialogue between Socrates and Laches

❖   ❖   ❖   ❖   ❖

The men walked in single file along Chorley Street, turning into Bomberbridge Street. A drizzle fell on the trenches and the boards beneath their boots were slippery. They passed a sentry post, the two Tommies they encountered there, standing with their waterproof ground sheets wrapped around their shoulders, wished the party luck. As they moved along Bomberbridge Street a Very light shot into the sky in front of them, bursting into its radiance and slowly falling to the earth, disappearing suddenly out of sight. A machine gun rattled for a moment in response. Fortune, at the head of the group, threw down a sodden cigarette with a curse. Sergeant Hope waited for them at the end of the trench where it formed a T-junction with the front-line, the platoon arrayed in several bays, presenting their arms on the fire step, waiting patiently as the rainwater ran enthusiastically from their helmets.

"Danny," Fortune greeted his friend.

"Fortune, good luck. We'll be waiting. Ready," Sergeant Hope patted Fortune on his helmet.

"See that you are, we might be in a hurry. Has the wire been moved?"

"Yes, just a few moments ago."

"Thanks. Richardson?"

"Down the sap waiting. He's keen."

"He's early. Right you lot, rifles first, raiders and bombers then you two last. Don't lose them bloody charges. Remember the password, you might need it."

Fortune counted the men through into the Russian sap, a covered trench, quite invisible from above. Private Pocock grinned his toothless smile as he passed.

"You remember the bloody password as well Danny," Fortune requested with a smile and he disappeared into the tunnel.

Fortune pushed through to the end of the sap where he found 2nd Lieutenant Richardson waiting, crouching beneath the opening.

"Sersant," Richardson called softly.

Fortune nodded. He looked back at the men crowded in line.

"Fix," he whispered, the four riflemen carefully attached their bayonets.

Richardson looked at his pocket watch and then up into the rain. A Very light pierced the night again, drifting down into their view at the head of the sap. Once it had completed its journey Richardson clambered up the short incline and was gone.

"Come on lads," Fortune beckoned, he too clambered up and out into no-man's-land.

Stakes struck into the earth around the sap entrance supported barbed wire. The exit of the sap was muddy, but after a short crawl Fortune came to the grass of the field. Richardson was crouched looking east. Seeing that the others were following he moved away slowly, walking on bent legs. Visibility was extremely poor, perhaps ten feet in every direction, the void ahead of them was absolute. Richardson led the way slowly forward, finding a gap in the wire where Sergeant Hope had said it would be. The party moved on, crawling and crouching in the darkness, stopping and starting, waiting and watching. Fortune's ears rang within his head, he could hear nothing.

The four riflemen spread themselves at the head of the party, creeping silently forward, straining their vision desperately into the night for any sign of danger. The others followed on behind, keeping their companions in sight as best they could. A man would move forward, stop, crouch, look back and ensure he was seen by those following before moving on again.

Fortune approached Richardson, who had paused in a shallow shell hole to check his compass bearing. As he slowly closed on Richardson, he calculated his deed to come. There were two other men in sight, behind. He could slip quietly into the hole and without warning cut Richardson's throat, they would not see. Too obvious he thought. Not yet. Richardson turned and caught Fortune's stare. He indicated to move onward then clambered out of the hole he was gone once more.

The party scrabbled and scraped its way slowly through the field and up a slope. All concept of time or distance escaped the men. On and on they moved with no sign, save for a few shell holes, that they were anywhere near the war. Richardson looked at his watch, 0143 hours.

"You still with me Mary?" whispered Private Connor.

"Yeah," replied Private Merry.

"Still got them charges?"

"Yeah."

Whether it was a reaction to focusing on his crucial role or sheer clumsiness Private Merry dropped the bag he was so carefully bearing. The satchel rolled once, then twice, into a shell hole. Private Merry ran in after it, falling against the opposing side, his equipment fussing and clanking together as he did. Private Shaw glanced nervously at Private Connor, both freezing where they stood in terror.

A Very light shot into the sky from a hundred feet or so to the east. It fizzed and crackled into the rain then burst into brilliance. The landscape all around them was bathed in light. The field's dimensions grew a hundred times before their eyes. Fifty feet or so ahead a belt of barbed wire, held in place by numerous iron piquets, could be seen blocking their route. Beyond the mass of industrial thorns, shapes loomed from the shadows, piles of earth, a parapet perhaps of a hidden trench. Shell holes, more concentrated here, near the enemy line, pulsed and morphed as shadows were traced across them, the dazzling light delved into their depths from above.

Fortune froze and looked back at the party, his hand outstretched, ordering them to stop. They had all been briefed before the raid began. When illuminated by a flare the instinctive reaction was to get down, to move out of sight, however, the correct response to such danger had by now been well documented and circulated. Movement of any kind draws the attention of the enemy scrutinising the landscape. To remain still, even if upright, had been seen to produce startling results. An observer sees many shapes in no-man's-land as a flare moves through the sky. If something moves it is clearly alive and warrants a bullet. The shapes that manifest and remain still could be anything, mundane detritus of war discarded in no-man's-land. It was a chance worth considering, taking every ounce of bravery from the men to avoid flinging themselves on the ground. They all held their pose and composure.

A machine gun rattled into life some distance away to the north. It continued to spit for some time, the light from its muzzle-flash clearly visible to everyone in the party. By luck or fate it was firing due west of its position, presenting no threat to the group. Several distinct flashes were observed from the British lines. Sergeant Hope's men had started to distract the Germans with rifle fire.

The flare floated down out of sight, the landscape returned to darkness and the field shrunk back to its former size. The weapons, so vocal and angry, now held their tongue. Fortune dropped prone when the light had extinguished. He breathed heavily, recovering from the surge of adrenaline. Private Pocock crawled up to where he lay, moving with his trench club before him, between both hands. The club had been fashioned from a wooden truncheon, a hollowed-out Mills bomb casing fixed to its end, it resembled a knight's mace from a long forgotten medieval war. Charlie revered the weapon, talked to it at times and had even named it, "Temperance".

Richardson indicated that it was time for the wire party to advance, making a scissor like motion with his fingers. The men passed the message to each other and lay down in the grass. Fortune glanced nervously at Private Pocock and crawled forward. The two men came together some twenty feet before the wire belt. Holding their wire cutters in front of them the pair crawled forward. They came across a body, a German, lying headfirst into a shallow hole. He had been there for some time, the rats had done their bit for the war effort, recycling the poor man's flesh. Giving the gruesome discovery a few moments of inspection, Richardson and Fortune moved on.

Fortune watched the officer with suspicion. Every move Richardson made was a potential sign he was about to enact his plan. While Fortune observed, Richardson crawled forward, oblivious to the paranoia racing through the sergeant's mind. The belt of wire was thick, a multitude of different reels interlocking, woven around thick iron posts, twisted into the earth using their distinctive corkscrew like shape.

"It's too thick here," Richardson whispered directly into Fortune's ear.

Fortune nodded. They made their way north, skirting the wire closely. Every few feet of movement was accompanied with a longer pause, to listen and watch. Foot falls on wooden boards anchored the men to the ground but were distant and soon indistinguishable. Further and further they crawled, the party behind them became a fading memory. It was so quiet and so dark their minds began to play tricks on their senses, indistinct sounds drawing their attention. They waited then moved. After some time, they reached a small depression, a series of shell holes all interlinked, which although unsuccessful at cutting a route through the obstruction, had forged a chalky gully beneath much of the wire. Richardson indicated this was the spot and both men began to delicately cut through the wire which hung over the culvert.

It was interminable work, every click of the cutters warranting a pause to listen. Before long, they had developed a system, by which one man was cutting and other listening for danger. They took turns. The evening progressed. The German's sent up numerous flares during their toil, they could only hope that the party, stuck in no-man's-land, were now safely obscured from sight.

Fortune plotted as he watched Richardson cutting more wire. He could easily dispatch the officer, quite silently and suddenly, then make his way back to the party claiming he had fallen to a German in a heroic yet futile hand to hand struggle. He imagined plunging a blade into the back of Richardson's neck, or thrusting his bayonet into his fleshy side, twisting it remorselessly as Richardson expired. That would be too noisy, a slit throat was certainly the most efficient method. Fortune's jubilation at the successful selection of method was short-lived, his mind raced faster, what if the body was discovered, by a patrol one night, or in the advance which was surely not far-off? A cut throat, could that be explained as a wound acquired in a tussle? Perhaps. Perhaps not. It was not important. Richardson had to die.

Chapter 21 - The trench raid

20th May 1916

South of the Mittenwald redoubt

0245 hours

42 days to Z-Day

Fortune slowly and discretely removed his jackknife[35] from its pouch. As Richardson continued to snip wires, Fortune carefully deployed the Marlin spike, once fully extended and locked into place, Fortune held it tightly with is thumb pressing on the base of the point.

"I'll make this swift for you," he muttered.

Richardson looked around. Fortune's heart pounded, his chest heaved. Richardson looked beyond the immediate threat, as if distracted. Fortune looked behind; Private Cartwright was crawling towards them. Fortune's eyes widened with anger as they watched Private Cartwright making his way along the depression.

"What are you doing?" whispered Fortune.

"Came to find you, we thought you had bought it," Private Cartwright confessed, "It's been forever."

Richardson was visibly annoyed. He passed the cutters to Fortune, indicating it was his stint at the wire. Fortune slipped the jackknife away.

"Get back to the others," Richardson whispered, "Bring them with you, we are nearly through."

Private Cartwright scampered away quickly, like a disturbed beetle fleeing from an upturned stone, moving on all fours rapidly until he was out of sight. Fortune squeezed up into the opening which they had carved, beneath the wire which remained taught between its fittings above. They

---

[35] The Army issue jackknife featured two blades and utility tools such as a Marlin spike, a two-inch polished metal cone tapered to a sharpened point designed for rope work. Similar to Swiss Army knife multitool.

had created a low passage under the wire, which proceeded into the dense belt for some seven feet. Fortune, encased in barbed walls of iron, began his tedious task.

By the time the party had found their way to Richardson, the tunnel through the wire was almost complete. Richardson went out to assemble the men in the order he would have them arrive in the trench. Fortune, now finished with the cutters, discarded them to one side, carefully parting the loose ends of wire to make ingress easier for the men. Privates Pocock and Cartwright were sent up into the shell hole gully, each brandishing their raiding weapon. Pocock with Temperance and Cartwright with a crudely fashioned punch dagger on his right fist, consisting of a sturdy gripped handle and a blade which projected three inches forward from the wielder's hand. Behind them two riflemen prepared to advance.

Passing up the chain of men, a message reached Fortune via a tug at his trouser leg. Private Pocock pointed forwards. Fortune began his crawl, out of the wire and onto an open space, littered with rusting cans and general refuse, his fingers sinking into damp soil as he cupped each can and moved it delicately to one side. Moving forward on his belly he could make out timber just in front of him and a sharp drop into blackness. A German trench.

Looking behind, he beckoned Private Pocock to join him. Once alongside, his eyes met Fortune's and held his stare. Fortune slowly turned his head and nodded slightly. Private Pocock followed his gaze until he saw them, two German soldiers, stood all of three feet below. The trench was deep, well made, with thick wooden supports giving strength to the boarded walkway and fire step. As they watched, a rat scurried along the bottom of the trench, pausing when it sensed the Germans in its path. One of the soldiers turned, kicking out at the animal, cursing as it moved quickly away in the other direction. Private Pocock remained still, watching.

The Germans were talking quietly together, one of them lit a pipe, the other laughed at a joke. Their rifles remained slung over their shoulders, waterproof coats of some kind protecting them from the drizzle. Private Pocock slowly turned to face Private Cartwright who was watching him intently for a signal, chewing a long blade of grass in the corner of his mouth as he waited. Private Pocock pointed along the trench to the south then held up two fingers. Private Cartwright nodded, making his way ever so slowly up onto the earthy parapet, then to the right of Fortune, stopping once he had caught sight of his prey, taking care not to disturb any of the discarded cans which littered the scene.

As the German sentries turned to walk off down the trench, Fortune signalled the attack. Privates Pocock and Cartwright leapt down into the man-made channel, either side of the Germans. Private Pocock swung

Temperance downward onto the shoulder of the first German, crushing it. Private Cartwright lunged forward with his punch dagger, catching the second German in the neck. He punched again slicing into the man's cheek. Once more, as the German was falling to his knees, Private Cartwright attacked, forcing his blade into the soldier's chest, finishing with a twist. Private Pocock beat at the first soldier's head and face, the protective barrier formed with his outstretched arms no match for the heavy weapon. Privates Pocock and Cartwright crouched over their victims, looking up and down the trench for movement, for a reaction, a response, to their murder. There was none.

Fortune dropped into the trench followed closely by the riflemen who formed sentry for the remainder of the party. The remaining men filed out of the gully and clambered down into the wooden channel. Richardson came last, helped down by Private Merry. Richardson drew his Webley service revolver, urging the men onward by waving the weapon. Private Pocock moved quickly to the traverse in the trench, without pausing he darted around and into the next bay followed closely by Private Cartwright. Privates Moore and Stendhurst, armed only with a satchel of Mills bombs followed quickly.

The party moved rapidly. The next bay contained a pair of German sentries. One was sitting on the fire step, one boot and sock removed, delving in between his toes for some unseen distraction from monotony. Private Pocock smashed his skull apart with one blow upon entering the bay. The other German readied his rifle, too late to rebuff the British, Private Cartwright was on him, punching him repeatedly in the groin and stomach with his short blade. The riflemen now poured into the confined space and on to the next traverse. The speed at which the trench fighters were moving risked stretching the party across several bays. Fortune rushed forward to stem their violent progress. The party reconvened, waited for a moment, a reaction, a sound. They heard footfalls from the next bay. Several voices. They were not the sounds of an alerted foe, however, their number was a concern.

"Do not risk anyone," Richardson whispered into Fortune's ear.

Fortune rearranged the party bringing up Privates Moore and Stendhurst with their bombs, supporting them with two other men who carried supplies of yet more Mills bombs. The men all looked at Fortune for direction, their eyes wide with fear and exhilaration. Private Cartwright chewed his length of grass feverishly. Private Pocock ground his gums together to alleviate the adrenalin surge.

"Now," ordered Fortune.

Privates Moore and Stendhurst lobbed their bombs into the following bay, not stopping for a reaction before throwing two more. Their support, standing close by, resupplied them instinctively. The bombs exploded with a sharp thud and a cloud of debris. Two riflemen charged headlong around the traverse into the next bay followed closely by Privates Pocock and Cartwright. The riflemen bayoneted everyone they discovered, living or dead.

"Send up the flare," Richardson ordered.

Private Connor raised a flare pistol into the air and fired. A green light lazed above the trenches. The men stared up at the wonderful colour, a pure and mesmerising hue in a world of bleak monochrome.

"It's on lads, let's get to it!" Fortune shouted.

The party stepped over the bodies of the unsuspecting Germans and rushed to the next traverse. From fifty yards away to the northeast, a red flare arced into the sky followed by the sound of an alarm being raised. A metal bar rattling within an old shell casing, clamoured for attention into the night, the German second line of defence was now rallying.

"What does red mean?" Private Merry shook Private Connor's arm.

"It's their alert for them further back," Private Connor replied.

"No, what does it mean in our plan?!" Private Merry screamed.

"Sergeant!" Private Connor wailed.

"Keep moving!" Richardson bellowed.

Around the traverse, the head of the party discovered a large square area into which several trenches connected. A platform, disguised with earth and wire, provided the Germans with a raised observation point. Set into the side of the timber wall was the entrance to a dugout.

"This is it," called Richardson, gesticulating his revolver he distributed the men.

Riflemen crouched at the entrances to each trench, waiting for the inevitable rush of Germans. Private Stendhurst primed a bomb, looked to Fortune for his approval and rolled it into the dugout entrance. A thud denoted its discharge of death, Private Moore instinctively sent another into the dust filled timber maw.

Shouting now erupted from all directions. Voices called out in panic from the dugout, orders could be heard to the northeast and heavy footfalls and yet more yelling from the trench leading north.

With pompous arrogance a sudden loud bang signalled the arrival of the British artillery, the sounds of the smaller ordinance shying away to the great noise of the 18-pounders. A shell burst with a violent yellow light several yards east of their position, the trench walls shielding the men from the shrapnel which dispersed downward into the soil. Another shell exploded to the north, followed by another further east still. A fourth explosion, just west of the trench, sent debris raining down upon the party. Within moments, trench mortars came into action. A large explosion of orange and red erupted just west of the trench. The men were covered in falling soil, recoiling into near foetal positions while clutching their helmets tightly to their heads.

"What's happening?!" screamed a rifleman.

"Stay at your post private, look to your trench!" Richardson shrieked.

Fortune grabbed Private Pocock and they rushed down the dugout stairs. The concrete steps were scorched from the two bombs. At the landing, Fortune peered around and downwards into the next flight. He waved for Private Moore to throw another Mills bomb. A plume of concrete dust surged upward. The group rushed downward once more, at the next landing Fortune was nearly caught by several bullets as he traversed, ducking back into safety just in time. The Germans below were shouting in panic. Private Moore once again, rolled his bombs into the dusty aperture. Fortune and Private Pocock rushed down to the end of the staircase, closely followed by Privates Connor and Merry.

They emerged into a large room, filled with dust and several bodies. At the foot of the stairs three Germans lay upon each other. To the immediate right, concealed beneath the stairs, was an open doorway leading to a tunnel. Along the right wall two cot beds were set back into bolt holes. Opposite the stairs a tired French dresser stood with some pride still left in it, while to the left was a table, covered with mundane items. Four chairs, once huddling at the table, had been scattered by the blast. Further around to the left a smaller table was set in the corner, a field telephone sitting squarely on its surface, wires and cables leading up the wall and into the ceiling. A German soldier sat in the corner here, his knees up by his face, his head covered in his dusty hands. Beside him another soldier lay groaning, a pool of blood slowly oozing onto the floor.

Fortune waved for Privates Connor and Cartwright to explore the tunnel. Private Pocock looked hopeful that Fortune would send him to deal with the Germans here, Fortune denied him this pleasure, instead sending him after the others into the tunnel. Private Merry remained, standing at the bottom of the steps, aghast at the scene of horror before him.

"Give me your rifle son," Fortune instructed.

Taking up Merry's rifle, Fortune pulled back the bolt to inspect the chamber. Confirming it was loaded he pushed the bolt back into place with a sharp movement and raised the weapon to take aim at the German soldier. The German reacted with panic, scampering with feet and hands moving himself backwards further into the corner of the dugout.

Fortune emerged from the dugout entrance and rushed to Richardson's side. The breastwork strong point was strewn with spent rifle cartridges. A rifleman lay injured at the mouth of one of the trenches, his blood-soaked trousers indicating a severe wound to his stomach. Richardson was firing his revolver at a traverse several yards away. Private Stendhurst was hurling bombs into the northern trench, his face bleeding from a wound in his forehead. Private Shaw sat foetal screaming into the night. Everyone was fighting, firing, throwing, shouting. Overhead shrapnel shells were bursting, raining their contents down over the scene, a lethal confetti at a wedding turned sour. Fortune tugged on Richardson's tunic, the cacophony of war invalidating his speech, forcing Fortune to indicate their task was complete with his hands. A trench mortar round found its mark on the north eastern trench and from out of sight two bodies twirled a macabre dance in the air.

Privates Pocock and Cartwright emerged into the din, leading with them two Germans, the cowered man from below and an officer they had overwhelmed in the adjacent chamber. Both prisoners were bruised, the officer clutching his right forearm, its sleeve shredded and damp with blood. At Richardson's order the party retired along the southern trench. Fortune looked down at the injured rifleman, but Richardson shook his head and vacated the pit. Grabbing the fallen soldier with his powerful hand, Fortune dragged him down the trench after the others.

Watching as the party departed Private Shaw's eyes widened in panic, he was quite alone now, Death was poised above him preparing his sweeping scythe. Dashing back through the nearby opening, Private Moore took hold of the weeping recruit and heaved him to his feet. With frantically blinking eyes Private Shaw regained his senses, a final chance at survival had been offered, instinct took hold. He ran. A sudden, powerful, explosion rocked the earth as the charges set within the bunker detonated. Dust surged from the mouth of the dugout and the entrance collapsed.

The men rushed south, the gunners had done splendid work on the front-line here, leaving several wounded Germans in their grizzly wake of brass, iron and lead. The party passed them by, leaving them to claw at the bright lights above like primitive trees. A shell burst close by, opening the shoulder blades of Private Moore, but he struggled on, assisted by Private Merry, having thrown off the helping hand offered by Private Connor. Private Shaw pushed passed them all on his dash to safety.

Within moments they arrived at the bay into which they had dropped only fifteen minutes before. The weary men helped each other scale the trench and onto the parapet. Their prisoners, stunned and afraid, did as they their captors instructed, dragging with them the injured riflemen who Fortune had saved. A Very light shone its starlight over the area, allowing several Germans in the second line trench opportunity to open fire on the party, as it heaved itself over the parapet and into the wire gulch. Fortune looked back, catching sight of a row of helmets some way off, the flashes from their rifles briefly revealing faces to the night. Private Merry caught a bullet in the bottom of his boot as he crawled away, rolling over within the wire, yelping in pain, now protected in the confines of the depression.

Fortune counted the men out until only he was left with Richardson. He mounted the fire step and had no trouble making the climb to the parapet, heaving his huge body over and around to face down into the trench. A bullet impacted on the timber beside him, he jerked to one side as another struck the plank just beneath his chin. Glancing down at Richardson who offered up his hand for assistance, Fortune slid himself backwards and into the gully.

He discovered Private Merry rolling about, in the first shell hole, with his leg pulled up to his chest, his boot shredded at the heel, a moistness revealing a wound lay beneath.

"Come on, it's not so bad, I've seen worse, let's get you out of here Mary," Fortune grabbed the lad by his shoulders and started to pull him.

At that moment an enraged Richardson appeared over the parapet, his face contorted with the venom of his cursing. His eyes revealed his intent, a purity of rage. Richardson now released his vengeance. A Mills bomb rolled forward and into the first shell hole of the depression. Instinctively Fortune pushed with both legs, moving his torso rapidly backwards, clearing the lip of the first crater and rolling down into the next shell hole. The Mills bomb thundered, shaking the wire above. As the dust settled from the sudden explosion, Fortune raised his head and peered into the adjacent hole. Private Merry lay dead.

Chapter 22 - Muddled memories
Sheol Care Home

"What happened in that dugout old friend? You seem overly preoccupied with it," came a voice suddenly.

The old man looked up from his contemplative posture, lowered his hand from his eyes and stared at the soldier who stood over him in a tattered and dirty uniform, his head slightly cocked to one side, a wry smile upon his muddied face. The bright tube lighting of the care home canteen forced a painful squint.

Private Merry stood patiently holding a plastic tray before him.

"Is this seat taken?"

"You again," the old man sighed and bashed his forehead with a clenched fist.

The old man looked around the canteen, quickly ascertaining that the other diners were paying no attention to the scene unfolding before him. Venerable inmates sat quietly; some staring off into space in a pharmaceutical haze while others prodded the dull food with plastic cutlery, mumbling curses beneath dry wrinkled lips.

Private Merry placed his tray carefully on the table, sitting in the chair opposite. The old man slid his seat back suddenly as Private Merry began to bleed over the table's surface, his dark crimson essence streaming from his mutilated left hand and from within the sleeve of his tattered tunic.

"I was told you were coming. What do you want Mary?" the old man asked in a whisper.

Blood continued to pool on the table, reaching the old man's tray and congealing about its edges. The old man moved backwards instinctively with a screech of his chair.

"Do you wonder, old man, as to why your story is meandering, so far at times from the truth?"

"What do you mean?"

The old man sounded exasperated at his haunting spectre, a steady flow of bloody drips now splattering on the tile floor between his feet.

"Percy and Fortune fight in the dugout. A charged discourse over the life of a wretched German. The same scene unfolds on Richardson's trench raid. I'll wager we'll be back there again before this has played out."

"What of it?"

"You are misleading the facts old man, points in time that you should not avoid so deviously. You negotiate the truth skilfully, but you will not evade me."

"It's not complete in here," the old man snorted, tapping his forehead with a gaunt finger, "I remember the dugout clear as day mind you."

The old man probed his food with his fork, pushing it around the plate. He was not hungry. He cursed himself for not being able to remember the details. The pieces of his story were there, he could sense their presence, but an absence of linking memories made them float without anchor, like icebergs adrift until some other recollection pulled them into place and secured them.

"You have a memory of it, that much is clear. Is it accurate and in the right place? Well, I could call into question most of your story with the same line of interrogation. The important facts, old man, are of grave interest to me. The mundane details which you sculpt to delay and deceive, are not. If you need more time, there is plenty of that here."

"Damn you! I'm doing what I can," the old man barked, slamming his fist on the blood drenched table.

For the first time his raised voice provoked a reaction from someone else in the room. An orderly, standing by the wire-mesh windowed door, looked on with furrowed brow, his hands tightly clasped behind his back. After prolonged scrutiny he lost interest as no further outburst was forthcoming.

"Let us return to beneath the wire once more," Private Merry demanded.

"Go away," the old man pleaded with his eyes tightly closed.

"Your twists and turns only delay the inevitable. Focus. I want my story old man, my patience is wearing thin this time. We'll return to the raid, before you move on. For completeness you understand, humour me."

"Why should I do anything for you? Leave me in peace," the old man pleaded.

"Peace? What do you know of peace? Look around you, nobody is at peace here. You've been here so long you've forgotten what this place is. You flaunt the rules, you twist everything to suit your desire to remain here, your stubborn crusade to delay the inevitable. Goodness knows I have better things to do, better people."

"I'm not stopping you, go on, shuffle off. I can take care of myself," the old man snorted.

"Is that so old man? The mess with Nancy, caused me considerable issue. You were lucky to stay here after that furore. Don't you understand? I am here to help, not hinder."

"Who's Nancy?"

"The cleaner."

"Ah. Worth it. Deserved it."

Private Merry paused for a while, tracing shapes with a mutilated finger in the blood-soaked tabletop. Occasionally the old man would look up from his plate to confirm the apparition was still there, choosing to maintain an awkward silence.

"Listen, old friend. We're linked by your actions. I must stay, until we are concluded. Delay and avoidance simply prolongs your suffering here. Can we not agree a path of minimal resistance?"

"Suffering? Is that your intention?" the old man scoffed, "After all the things I've seen and done, nothing here can be described in that way. The shock therapy, the pills, the ice baths and the isolation, none of this is real. My stories, what's left of them up here, old memories and distant friends, they are real. They are alive as long as I recount them. And as long as I retreat in here," the old man tapped his temple, "I stay alive and so do the others. If I lose them, I'll have nothing, I'll be nothing."

"And what of us?" enquired Private Merry, tapping a blood-soaked sleeve on his chest asserting the reality of his physical form.

"You?"

"Yes."

"An unfortunate memory I can't misplace."

"Charming."

"You know Mary didn't talk like this, like you are, don't you? Nothing like it. You aren't him, you aren't real," the old man sent an accusatory glance at his companion.

"What is real when memories are so old, the only point of reference you possess?"

The old man sighed deeply through his nose.

"It's all I have and have come to cherish, I'll not banish you with the pills. To send you into the haze also condemns the others to dreamlike oblivion. I'll not do it."

"Tom?"

"Yes. A father and his lost son, spending time, remembering. How is that suffering? It's heaven for the brief moments I am allowed. I'll not risk another parting. Real or not, I don't care anymore. For all the times I've been through it, repeating the tales and finding new details, again and again you torment me with this, but I don't care. Let me see him and the rest of the shit in this shell-hole is inconsequential."

"In Sheol," Private Merry corrected.

"Same thing!" the old man scathed.

"Hmm," Private Merry nodded slowly in acceptance, "Then the path ahead is a difficult one old man."

"I have a proposal," the old man relented at last, "But not here. Meet me in the gardens."

"As you wish, friend."

The old man hurried as best he could to the small enclosed cloister they referred to as the garden. Private Merry was waiting for him, standing over the small rectangular pond marvelling at the fish which swarmed and darted around each droplet of blood he allowed to fall into the water.

"Stop that, please," the old man requested,

"Very well. We shall hear your request," Private Merry gesticulated with his mangled hand.

"I want to be with Tom and his mother when this is concluded. Can this be done? If you agree I'll do what you ask."

"Your request betrays you. You fear that this journey, the truth, will not end well, in your favour. That you will be denied the same, liberties shall we say."

"Perhaps."

"And therefore, your stories have, until now, taken a meandering twist on the facts. Inconclusive and evasive, only to your detriment I may add."

"Perhaps."

"How long have you been here old man, reliving your torment?"

"I don't know. My incarceration seems eternal."

Private Merry smiled grimly.

They walked for a while in contemplation, around and around the pond, the old man with his hands clasped behind his back and Private Merry cradling his injured arm with his good hand, his gaze fixated on the troubled face of his venerable companion.

The old man broke the silence causing Private Merry to stop abruptly.

"You sent Percy to the hole, didn't you?"

"Why would you think that?"

"Forget I said it."

The old man resumed his amble, but Private Merry remained where he was, waiting, sensing this was not the end of the old man's questioning. The old man's chin dropped, his arms falling weakly by his sides as he turned to face the apparition.

"I had thought, for a moment, I knew him, or of him, Percy I mean. A memory, lost, driven from the light, yet resurfacing. The face familiar yet not, more like remembering a smell or a sound than something I have seen. Does that make sense?"

"Go on, please."

"There was a pastor, in South Africa. With the regiment. I can't recall his face, or a name. But as soon as Percy spoke about his father, I knew it was him. But for why, I could not say."

"Then you need to go deeper into your story and Percy will help you remember."

"So, you did send him?"

"Perhaps," Private Merry chuckled, "Or maybe you have brought him into the light, for your finale, knowing him to be of great importance."

"Hmph," the old man scoffed stoically, "Will my request be honoured or not? You'll hear it all, but I'll see them again, be with them, once this is done."

"Very well. We are in agreement. Now, are you ready to continue? The truth is imperative, the details old man, are vital," Private Merry instructed sternly.

"What is it you want, exactly?"

"There are details you often avoid old friend, which this time need to be corrected, if you are to leave this place and move on, to gain your prize. We'd want everything in order would we not?"

The shattered soldier continued to pace slowly around the edges of the pond.

"I want the truth, for clearly your most recent recount - was not," Private Merry expressed his frustration with a change in tone.

"I told you, I struggle to remember some details."

"I am sympathetic, although also easily enraged as you know old friend. I am here to help you remember, rather than seek to punish. I urge you to try again."

As the light faded, the old man grunted in acknowledgement.

"Let's bring this merry dance to a fitting end," he scoffed at the darkness.

Fortune reached down and grabbed Richardson's forearm. He heaved and strained, pulling his officer out of the trench in two movements. Both men retreated from the rifle fire which continued to smash into the trench and crack through the barbed wire overhead. Richardson escaped into the depression, pausing beside Private Merry, he offered some words of sympathy.

"Get him out of here Sersant!" Richardson shouted before clambering on.

Fortune filled with rage, internal cursing contorting his face with hatred. He could not let Richardson escape to the rest of the party, who no doubt waited on the other side. The time had come, there would be no more chances to take. He scurried down beside Private Merry, franticly reaching to grab Richardson's ankle, arriving too late to make contact. Richardson, oblivious to the move, crawled deeper into the wire tunnel. Lying beside the wounded Mary, a Mills bomb had fallen from one of the escaping men. Fortune snatched it up with his spade like hand and with his other he wrestled with the pin, trying at the same time to crouch up on his heels with his back against the wire above.

Sensing the ferocious demeanour of his sergeant, Private Merry lashed out, catching Fortune under the chin with a hobnail boot. His windpipe compressed, the sergeant released the Mills bomb too soon, lobbing the lethal device pathetically with a weak jerk of his restricted arm. It fell, rolling back into the depression where he crouched. Fortune reacted instinctively, pulling Private Merry with all his might, placing him directly over the device, then, pushing with both his legs he managed to clear the lip of the first crater, slumping down behind the earthen berm. Just as he reached protection the bomb exploded, Private Merry absorbing the blast.

As the dust settled, Fortune's face appeared at the edge of the hole. The battle seemed to retire from his senses, all becoming quiet around him. He watched for a moment. Private Merry did not move. Richardson shouted back enquiring what had happened, his voice distant and distorted as if under water. Fortune simply shook his head at the officer who disappeared out of view further down the wire tunnel. After a short pause to regain his senses, Fortune crawled in beside the mangled youth.

"Mary?" he exclaimed in grief.

Blood gurgled from Private Merry's mouth in thick gouts of dark crimson. He coughed and spluttered and moaned. His left hand was almost gone, a deep wound flowing beneath his sleeve which bled profusely onto the earth, forming a viscous puddle. The mutilated boy moved his right hand, slowly, then in forced spasms over to his left pocket. Fortune aided, rummaging in the pocket. A letter, a single page of notepaper.

"Alright, alright," Fortune confirmed he understood.

Tragically his voice was unheard. Private Merry was dead. Fortune continued his search recovering some cigarettes and coins and finally, there in the depths of the right tunic pocket he discovered a lighter. A brass disk embossed with the regimental badge; a photographic image of a woman inserted on the inside of the hinged, keep-sake lid. A family heirloom or good luck charm, ether way it was no good to the lad now. Fortune stashed the letter and the lighter and scurried into the next hole. Soon he was through the gully and out into no-man's-land, the landscape around him filled with a deep and sorrowful groan as artillery shells began falling disparately into the field of death, expressing their relief from restraint in bright fury.

Part 4 - Tribulations and Wrath

"The hour of departure has arrived and we go our ways; I to
die, and you to live. Which is better? Only God knows."

-

Socrates (BC 469-BC 399) Greek philosopher of Athens

D.G.Baulch

Chapter 23 - Sirens

20th June 1916

The road to Bertrancourt

2355 hours

11 days to Z-Day

The night was still. The moon was in its third quarter, but unable to spread its silver illumination due to the clouds which hung at low-level. A creature of the gloom shrieked from a field to the right of the road. Fortune crouched beside the trackway which led up to John Jacques Farm. He had hoped to pay his respects once more at the lone airman's grave, however, no evidence of it could be found in the nocturnal abyss. He made his way slowly and cautiously up the trackway, beneath the trees which lined the avenue, methodically approaching the farm as a cat burglar stalks his bounty. The farm showed no signs of life, the lights were extinguished, all that should be hidden from the night was secure.

Fortune waited for some time just beyond the great archway. He took care to note any smells upon the breeze or detect any sounds which would divulge any intelligence on the farm and its occupants.

"Where's that damn dog?" he muttered.

The dog was sleeping soundly up in the hay loft, but the mere threat it posed, unknowingly in its slumber, incurred a prolonged delay on Fortune's advance. He crouched for a while aside from the track, squatting in the darkness slowly confirming to himself it was safe to proceed. Just as he was about to move closer there was a noise, a door creaking. A light shone momentarily into the courtyard beyond the arch, followed by an exchange of muffled voices. Before long the door was heard closing, returning the yard to darkness.

"Shit!"

Fortune cursed under his breath as he made his way hurriedly towards the high wall to the right of the arch. If someone were coming out, he would need to be concealed by the wall, in total darkness, as they passed by. Sure enough there was a figure emerging from the beneath the arch, a soldier, in British uniform, racing off down the track on a bicycle. Fortune had not been spotted.

Once satisfied that the unknown cyclist had cleared the scene, he approached the archway. Rather than enter the courtyard directly, he skirted the exterior of the farm to the opposite wall, away from the track and any roadside scrutiny, where he knew a smaller entrance existed which would lead to the kitchen and scullery.

Upon reaching the old iron-braced wooden door he paused once more, listening intently to the ringing in his ears. With no other sound to stimulate his sense the ringing intensified. His imagination fought with the high-pitched hum to produce spectres of acoustics never issued from a natural source. The more he waited the more flamboyant the paracusia[36] became. He could, in his state of frustration, not recall a time where his hearing was devoid of ringing of some kind. Naturally, his exposure to loud noises in the firing line had taken their toll, however, the problem was deeper rooted than any medical officer would care to investigate.

He suddenly remembered concealing himself in a game of hide and seek, his friends trying to locate him in an old barn they used to frequent after Sunday school. All around him the darkness was impenetrable, only one's hearing could offer any signal as to the approach of the others. Yet, his sense could not provide the forewarning he required and his short tenure as "the one that did the hidin" was soon curtailed. Fortune cursed his disability and forced the door open, jamming the thick marlin spike of his jackknife between the frame and wooden portal.

Moving silently within the dimly lit corridor, Fortune pulled the door securely behind him, ensuring no sound would reveal his penetration. Once more he waited for signs of danger. A light flickered near the end of the passage which was adorned with a large, age-speckled mirror and a coat stand. He stood, slowly, to his full extension. With careful paces he moved deeper, along the narrow lobby towards the light and the kitchen beyond. At the corner he peered around into the large chamber. A candle sat beside the window, dancing joyfully at his approach. A cup, its contents still steaming, sullied the glass windowpane with condensation. The kitchen was otherwise devoid of interest to the soldier.

Taking a deep breath through his nose, Fortune crossed the kitchen and entered the formal hallway of the farmhouse, with its large ascending staircase and stone tiled floor. Another light beckoned in the chamber across the hall, highlighting his next target of exploration. At the base of

---

[36] An auditory hallucination, or paracusia, is a form of hallucination that involves perceiving sounds without auditory stimulus.

the grand staircase Fortune paused and looked up, portraits lined the walls, a chandelier hanging miserably between the balustrades of the staircase's confines. Judging the path was clear he pressed onward, his hand outstretched before him to contact the door which was left ajar. Within, through the gap in the entrance, he could see a carpet, threadbare but refined, a mantelpiece and its cold fire, a circular table sporting a vase of flowers and a short bookshelf.

He pushed the door, lightly at first, it would not surrender to his strength. Another force and the door moved slightly, revealing more of the room. Sitting by the window, overlooking the courtyard, a slight brunette woman, dressed only in her nightgown, began to sing softly to herself while pulling a stocking over her foot, unravelling its folds up her slender leg. With careful, deliberate and silent movement, Fortune moved toward the unsuspecting woman. When within reach of his victim the time for subtlety had vanished and his actions became rapid. With a hand rushed in front of her face and firmly over her mouth, his free arm grappled with her waist and spun her to confront him. A stifled shriek alerted none but his large palm of her peril.

"It's me," Fortune announced himself with a large smile and excited whisper.

Bernice beat her fists upon his chest as he released his grip upon her mouth.

"Henri!" she squealed, a frown descending upon her candle lit features, "Why are you here? How did you..."

Fortune pressed his body onto hers, kissing her passionately to prevent further discourse. Her arms ceased their attack and wrapped themselves around his bulk. She returned his passion with vigour. Fortune lifted her from the floor, supporting her thighs with his large hands and sturdy wrists. He pushed forward once more placing her onto a table beside the window, its contents scattering to the floor. Bernice suppressed a giggle and held a finger to her mouth in a brief attempt to stem the disturbance. Fortune pushed forward again, the young woman's legs wrapping themselves around his lower back.

The couple struggled in an amorous panic to relieve the girl of her night garments, Fortune pausing to pull her gown over her head while she feverishly pulled at his trouser buttons. The tall soldier cupped the back of her neck with his powerful grip and pushed forward once more, filling her with his expectant lust. The light of her candle played mischievously over her naked form as Fortune's power came to bare on her petite body. Bernice lay back upon the table, her back arched upwards towards her accomplice, while his hands explored her breasts and the curvature of her waist. Bernice gasped and ran her gentle fingers up the middle of her stomach and around her bosom. Leaning forward Fortune placed his hand over her mouth once more without objection. His pace now quickened, the savagery of his strokes displacing the table which ground against the wall as his young mistress groaned in ecstasy.

"Bernice!" a call came from a distant location.

The entwined lovers froze and listened. Bernice's eyes widened, not in fear but exhilaration. Fortune slowly pushed forward to reach his full potential and Bernice yelped into his hand.

"Bernice! *Où es-tu?*" came the voice again.

Her response surprised Fortune utterly, removing all focus on the jeopardy which lurked in the hallway. She moved her hand beneath her thigh and clutched him firmly, pulling at him rhythmically while staring intently into his large blue eyes. Fortune convulsed, the enforced silence manifesting itself physically in uncontrollable spasms of his entire body. She held him tightly with all aspects of being.

"*Va te coucher papa, je vais apporter ton café,*" she bellowed.

Fortune staggered backwards, clumsily attending to his britches while staring at her in disbelief.

"Go!" she whispered, "I will join you in the hay loft, be quick my love!"

Without a word Fortune scurried to the doorway but dared not proceed. He glanced back at Bernice who, with her back to him, was donning her gown once more. The cotton vestment flowed effortlessly over her figure, gathering around her shapely bottom. Fortune groaned.

"Go!" she waved him away dismissively.

Fortune sat within the entrance to the hayloft, the small farm dog resting contentedly on his lap. The large door was open enough for him to scrutinise the farmhouse from his hidden location. The candle in the kitchen had moved and the drawing room was now devoid of illumination. He kneaded the tobacco into his pipe with his thumb and withdrawing the circular brass lighter from his pocket brought fire to his creation. The hound looked up momentarily from its slumber and with a bewildered expression gazed into the smoke cloud which issued from the soldier's mouth.

"Henri?" Bernice whispered loudly at the entrance to the hay loft, "Henri?"

Her intrusion startled the little dog, which leaping up from Fortune's lap began to bark. Bernice, rushing into the interior, grappled the small pup and soothed it from its panic with loving caresses.

"Bloody hell," Fortune snapped.

Bernice dropped the puppy onto a bail of straw and leapt upon her desire. Sweeping her thick coat aside she revealed herself to him, drawing her night gown up her thighs as she attempted to straddle his form and envelop the broad man in her arms.

"Hang on now, woman, who was that Tommie leaving just now?" Fortune pushed her away.

"Henri, what is this? Him, I don't know, someone who came to see father about expenses," she scorned.

"Oh, alright then. Just, please, will you sit a moment my dear," Fortune pleaded.

The young beauty drew her coat angrily around her and sat down with the frustration of a child denied its favourite toy.

"You don't trust me, *n'est pas?*", she thumped his thigh with her response.

"No, I mean of course I do. Stop this. Look, can we talk? For a while, I need to talk," he grasped her cold hands in one of his.

"My father is at rest and the night is drawing out before us and Sergeant Berriman wants to talk," she scoffed.

Judging the look upon the soldier's face her petulant repose shifted to one of guilt. She sighed and accepted his request with silence.

"It won't be long now my dear, we'll be off soon and there's no accounting for who will return."

"Oh nonsense my love, you mustn't talk this way."

"Let me finish, I shouldn't say but, it's happening soon, we're going over, a bigger thing than any of us have ever been part of before. They say it will be a piece of cake but us hold hats, we've heard that all before. Men will die, many men will die, and when you have dodged the reapers scythe for as many years as I, you know when your time is up. I had to come and see you, one last visit, before it's done."

"The big push, yes Henri, everyone is speaking of it, it is no secret. The British have been arriving for weeks. It will be a success, *non?* You will save us, you will be heroes!" Bernice shook his grip.

"Heroes are for books my dear, there are no heroes out there, only fools. And many a dead fool before this is over."

"You must believe Henri, you must survive for me."

"Your life is still ahead of you, you must live it and you'll see that what we had is soon not worth remembering. As if it never happened. You must move on Bernice, your life can be so much more than mine is capable of. What we have, what we had, is just a blink of an eye and then it's gone."

"Henri, I have had little cause for you to anger me until now, but I cannot make use of you in such a *malaise*," she attempted a smile but could see Fortune would not react as intended to her playful remarks.

Her shoulders dropped and her chest lurched with a heavy sigh.

"I want you to have something, here take this," Fortune revealed his gift from within a deep pocket.

Bernice handled the disk-shaped lighter with admiration, tracing the outline of its embossed markings with her delicate fingertips. Opening the case, she gasped with momentary joy at the crudely cut sepia photo of Fortune which had been inserted within the hinged lid, the shoulders of other soldiers still visible beside his uniformed torso.

"Oh and these, for emergencies," he smiled sombrely as he handed over an unopened packed of Capstans.

"You say I have my life to live and yet you wish a cough upon me, like my father's," she half smiled, "Share one with me Henri?"

The pair lay in silence upon the straw and smoked a single cigarette, its embers tracing time as they chased the tobacco to ash, a fleeting moment shared by two souls, in a world forged in fire.

Fortune woke with a start, alone save for the small dog who tugged frantically at his tunic sleeve with a heroic little growl. In contrast the world outside the barn was alive with noise. Horses whinnied under torchlight beyond the open door, while men were shouting from different vantage points, English voices, brash and authoritative.

"Shit!" Fortune exclaimed as he leapt from the straw, his small companion staring expectantly upward at the towering soldier.

"You're on your own little man. Make your own fortune, you don't need mine."

In crouched yet rapid movements Fortune hurried to the doorway, seeking shelter from the torchlight behind the old wooden frame. Several military police, weapons in hand, could be seen holding their horses in the courtyard in front of the main house. Lights flickered in the windows on both floors while the voices issued their orders from within. Having ascertained there was no obvious exit other than the main barn door, which would surely lead to detection and arrest, Fortune shot back the way he had come to the rear of the building, the little hound matching his pace at his ankles.

"Not now little man," Fortune hissed at the unshaken pup.

Napoleon, a good name for the brave little mutt Fortune had decided, snarled in frustration and then bounded up onto the hay as high as his short yet powerful legs would propel him. From there he disappeared.

"I asked for that I spose," Fortune fumed under his breath, "Good luck to you. Traitor!"

Within a moment the dog reappeared, higher now on a thin horizontal ladder near the roof, which had been strung between beams, yet unseen by Fortune's scrutiny. Without pausing for further debate, Fortune clambered up the hay, scurried over its elevated plateau and lifted himself upward to the beams of the barn, where Napoleon waited triumphantly.

"Now what?"

Napoleon bounded over to a secluded space on an old wooden mezzanine far above the hay; flopping down on some old rags which formed a perfect hollow for his little body. He sat wide eyed and tongue proud, congratulating himself at the revelation of his little hiding place.

"Perfect!" Fortune scorned.

His course frown lifted as quickly as it had swept across his face. From his new vantage point Fortune could see where a patch of the roof had been hastily repaired, with little expertise or thought for durability. Lying on his back, balancing across the old ladder, he thrust his boots upward, through the tiled roof and into the night's sky. As Fortune hauled himself out of the barn, Napoleon yapped a midnight serenade to mark his departure, joined by the horses who accompanied the men raising their own shouts of alarm into the night. By the time the police had mustered, Fortune had slipped away into the darkness of the fields and was away, leaving little Napoleon, Bernice and the unknown commotion behind him.

Chapter 24 - Forced marches and foul play
22nd June 1916
Forceville, 6 miles from the front-line
1335 hours
9 days to Z-Day

Fortune stepped out of the column and clambered up a steep grassy bank which massaged the road as it wound its way across the farmland. Taking out his pocket watch he frowned at its dusty face. 2nd Lieutenant Richardson pulled his horse alongside, the exhausted men of the Somerset Light Infantry swerving their march and tightening the column in order to pass by without slackening their pace.

"Well Sersant?" enquired the officer, his steed shaking its head in knowing disappointment.

"Too slow again sir," Fortune sighed, closing his watch case angrily.

"Then we shall do it again," announced Richardson sharply.

"With all due respect sir," Fortune was cut short by his CO before he could finish.

"You have an hour to prepare, no more," warned Richardson as he swung his horse about and galloped off along the road and into the village of Forceville.

Fortune ordered the men to wheel off the thoroughfare before entering the village proper and just south of a small copse of trees they rested in the long grass, out of sight from the earth-enclosed roadway. The soldiers lay smoking their pipes, their packs and equipment piled between them. Fortune stood on the high bank watching the congregation for a while, with their tunics unbuttoned and sleeves rolled up anyone could have mistaken them for farm labourers taking a short break from their toil. He marvelled at how they teased and joked with each other, even after such a hard day of forced route marches and training exercises. Was there nothing these young lads could not do with a smile still blazoned on their faces?

"We shall see soon enough," he said out loud to himself.

"What's that?" asked Sergeant Hope, approaching with his cigarette case open, craving attention.

"Bloody well make yourselves busy you idle chumps!" Fortune bellowed, "There's a damn war on although you wouldn't think it looking at you bunch of toss bags! Get those bloody buttons done up, what is this? The French Army!?"

"Fortune, please."

Danny gave Fortune one of his stern looks, deployed when Fortune's temper had got the better of him.

"Yes, go on then."

Fortune grasped one of the slender white sticks and nestled it between his dry lips.

"We're going again, he wants us faster."

"They can barely stand as it is," Danny exclaimed.

"They will bloody well have to Danny, no excuses," Fortune raged, catching the attention of some of the platoon.

Fortune pondered for a while before responding further, allowing the refreshing vapours of the Lucky Strike to stir his cognitive powers and calm his sudden ferocity. His pulse was surging within his forehead and he could feel a great pressure in his hands and thumbs. His temper had suddenly awoken and was clouding his mind as an old two stroke motorbike strains at full throttle, filling the air with smoke and unburnt oil. This heightened state, in combat, brought about quick reactions and sound judgement, but here now, his faculties were impeded, all he felt was rage and the need to lash out at someone, anyone, whom he could pass his painful pressure onto.

His outbursts were commonplace, renowned within the platoon and indeed expected from any sergeant with a backbone. Even he could accept, in calmer moments, that they were becoming more and more irrational. Staring off at the horizon he muttered to himself angrily, talking himself down from his red tower, then in time he turned to Sergeant Hope.

"We've tried three times to get anywhere near the time he set for us. Do you think it's achievable Danny?"

"No, not a chance, not with the men so tired," admitted Sergeant Hope.

"What's he up to then? Hey?" Fortune's frown intensified.

"We're dead beat, on an officer's folly Fortune, whole day of training tomorrow to boot."

"Aye," Fortune turned again to his far away spot where he could think coherently.

Fortune's mind was racing. Since the incident during the trench raid nothing had been said directly, to implicate him or suggest Richardson's motives. Perhaps this was the beginning of a new plan the South African had hatched? Did Richardson see anything that night and if so why hadn't he acted upon it? He would enjoy an elaborate chase Fortune surmised. Defeat the men and their moral and you defeat their sergeant? Yes, perhaps that was it. Whatever the details, it was clear in his mind that something was afoot, he just needed time to figure out what. Above all the pressure being applied to the men, his worries fixated on the night at the farm, the military police and the unknown commotion. What were they looking for? Why had Bernice left him there? He did not have the answers. In the meantime, he was not going to allow Richardson any more victories.

"So, what's to be done?"

Sergeant Hope tried to catch glimpse of Fortune's muse but found nothing but fields and birds roosting over the crops.

"Get 'em ready, we'll be faster this time or we'll be at it all night. Empty their packs."

A puzzled Sergeant Hope paced around the side of Fortune to face him squarely.

"Come again?"

"Empty their packs, stuff them with grass. Leave everything we can ditch here, hidden by the copse. We'll collect it later. Lighten their load Danny, anything we can leave we leave. But we have to look fully burdened."

Fortune pulled out his watch once more and scrutinised it.

"And we don't have long."

The message soon spread across the resting platoon and groups of men were given tasks to see Fortune's orders were enacted. Privates Pocock and Cartwright prepared a suitable hiding place within the boundaries of the copse, while Privates Connor and the Cooksley twins ferried equipment back and forth. Some men were busily emptying packs and pouches while others harvested enough grass to safely complete the ruse. A circle of men sat upon the ground, stuffing grass into bags and satchels with the expertise of the finest French mattress makers. Fortune paced through the men barking his unique encouragement at the tired soldiers.

"He's raging again," Private Cartwright vented at Private Pocock.

"Aye, proper rattled he's been these last few days, keep yur head down and crack on mate, don't get caught in the crossfire, that's me advice," warned Private Pocock.

"What's doing?" asked Private Connor, approaching the small group with arms full of equipment.

"Fuck off," Private Pocock snapped.

"This won't win any war, what's his game?" Private Connor persisted unabated.

"Pricks don't ask questions, Pricks get stuck in where their masters tell them to," Private Pocock hissed.

"Richardson is trying to break us boy, sergeant is just trying to lighten the load, or we'll be marchin all damn day and night cos of you slow slackers," Private Cartwright joined the fray, his eyes betraying his true lack of venom on the matter.

"March faster than you old farts, any day," Private Connor boasted with a smile, "You wanna leave the heavy stuff to us young'uns, stick to potato peeling and washin, we'll show ya how it's done!"

"I'll fooking skull ya, dirty Irish Prick," the old sailor growled, standing to his feet.

"Ah'rite Charlie, come on, leave Prick alone, he proved himself out there with us, leave im be."

Private Cartwright grabbed Private Pocock by his trousers and pulled him back down, glancing up at Private Connor he gave him a knowing look.

"Go on, piss off Prick," he added to placate his friend.

Private Connor left his offering at the feet of the two old timers and rushed back to where the Cooksley twins were working. He stood marvelling at their astonishing similarities with his hands in his pockets, swaying in an amused fashion at some internal jape he was crafting in his mind.

"What in God's name do you think you are doing Private Connor!" bellowed Fortune, "Get away from them freaks and get on with it, or I'll have you lashed to a wheel before sundown!"

"I have to ask," Percy interjected, "Why did you have issue with the twins?"

"I thought you would never ask," Fortune sighed, sinking further down into the shell hole.

"What had they done to stir your ire in such a way?"

"Don't like twins, give me the creeps," Fortune snorted, "Why should I hey?"

"*Two are better than one, because they have a good return for their labour. If either of them falls down, one can help the other up. But pity anyone who falls and has no one to help them up.*[37] Ecclesiastes. Twins are a blessing from our creator Fortune, a multiplication of the love enjoyed through parenthood. You can

---

[37] Ecclesiastes, Chapter 4, Verses 9-10, (NIV)

see by the way twins interact, they have a special bond. This bond is God's bond between all men, twins show us how He wishes us to live, in harmony."

"Bollocks, ain't no harmony out here is there? No place for twins then is it. *So Thomas, called the Twin, said to his fellow disciples, 'Let's us also go, that we may die with him.*[38]*'* John, chapter eleven, verse…sixteen," Fortune retorted triumphantly.

"Well," Percy thought for a while, "Scriptures aside Fortune, you must have reason for your distrust for reciprocal siblings?"

"Alright, there was these two twins," Fortune began.

"Naturally," Percy scoffed.

"Borkham brothers, just twenty years of age, nice enough fellows, always went everywhere together. Joined up together, trained together, betrothed to sisters they were. Identical to boot. Went out to France, in my section they were, at Loos."

"Finally, Loos," Percy exclaimed.

"Not quite, anyways, we were right in the thick of it, Loos was burning to the right of us, whole sky was a brilliant orange like nothing we'd ever seen. Terrible in its beauty, you know? An awful scrap was going on in there, the London Scottish was it? But anyways, we had our own problems to worry about. Once over the ridge we were in plain sight, sure the evening was dark but the fire was so fierce the whole countryside was lit up, on top of that the Boshe were sending up their flares. They brought down hell on the Somersets as we moved into the valley."

"Richardson was commanding?" Percy enquired.

"I'm on the twins right now, alright? So, the Borkham brothers, there they are, rest of us in open artillery formation, shells dropping all about but we're making good headway. The twins though, sticking to each other like glue. Side by side. Almost arm in arm. I shouted for 'em to break up but you can't hear shit when all that's coming down on you. There was a German machine gun playing on the formation from a wood up to the left, the other side of the valley. You could see the flashes in the trees, you knew they were on you. You can't hear it rattling or the bullets snapping, in all that noise, but you can see them hitting the ground around you, raining it was, like raindrops hitting puddles in a shower."

"I remember that yes, funny sight, the earth jumping up around you in little spouts. Like the ground is boiling."

"Funny, yeah, real amusing like."

"What happened Fortune?"

---

[38] John, Chapter 11, Verse 16, (ESV)

"I'm sure it was a single bullet or shell fragment, passing through them both. They dropped together, both the same way. Just as everything else they ever did, they went down together."

"Killed?"

"We never found 'em after it was all done, so must have been, aye. Still out there by all accounts. It didn't need to be that way Percy, this damn bond you speak of got them both killed, and with an elder brother having bought it up in Ypres that spring."

"So, you were trying to protect the Cooksley brothers? By separating them."

"I was trying to keep them away from me, bad luck they are after Loos."

"Superstitious nonsense Fortune, you were protecting them, it's admirable," smiled Percy.

"Well, anyways shut up and let me get back to it," Fortune snorted.

The platoon assembled to the north east of Forceville where 2nd Lieutenant Richardson inspected the dishevelled men. Satisfied that his force was ready for their march the column set off, skirting around the new bell tent community of the 108th Field Ambulance, who were rapidly expanding their facility in the village. The Army Service Corps men were panting in the sun as they unloaded their waggons, while an ageing Scottish officer bellowed at them from beneath his Glengarry cap.

"Don't know they're born, this lot," Private Connor cursed, "Only danger they'd face when we're up the line, going over, is a splinter in their finger!"

"You'll be pleased enough to see 'em when they're running to you with a stretcher," Private Pocock snapped.

Richardson rode his horse alongside his column, his upright countenance signifying his authority over these men. He gazed off at the horizon as if its hidden secrets were the holy chalice, yet to be discovered, promising eternal glory for the man who plucked the great artefact from its perpetual hiding. Fortune marched alongside in silence.

Having circumnavigated the village, the men came to the main road leading east, where waggons were congregated in a great line. Royal Engineers scurried between them ensuring the guide ropes and bindings were secured. Each waggon boasted what appeared to be two wooden boats, flat topped and flimsy; de-constructed in some way to allow their travel.

"Here yar Charlie, you'll see the sea again after all, we're goin sailin," hooted a soldier to the amusement of those in ear shot.

"A pontoon bridge Sersant," Richardson called down to his sergeant.

"Very good sir," Fortune replied nonchalantly.

"They intend to cross the Ancre on it, is there nothing our great engineers cannot overcome?" Richardson beamed proudly.

"No sir, of course not sir," Fortune replied, adding under his breath, "A way through the barbed wire would help for starters."

The platoon made good time once it had cleared the congestion around Forceville, marching into the open country along a dilapidated dirt lane. The men smiled to each other knowingly at the ease at which they carried their packs, a good stride being maintained until their first rest stop within an hour of setting off.

"Ten minutes here, rest up," called Fortune.

The men dissolved into the long grass and lay beneath young saplings at the edge of the road smoking their pipes.

"They have a spring in their step to be sure Sersant, how have you engineered this revolution in attitude?" enquired Richardson from his mount.

"They only wish to please you sir, no doing of mine," Fortune concocted.

The march continued with the same successes and vigour of the original hour only pausing for the regulation rest every sixty minutes, save for a brief distraction as they watched a British Sopwith Triplane battling with a German Albatross overhead, twisting and turning beneath the heavy clouds which dulled the day. Having mourned the loss of the British airman, the troop continued on their way in silence, their deflated mood due to the aerial defeat stifling any desire to sing in merriment.

"Taking a different route this time sir?" Fortune enquired of his master.

"No Sersant, our destination will shortly be in sight, for we are expected at the practice trenches once more," Richardson beamed.

"And so there it was," Fortune sighed, "Richardson's great scheme to unhinge me, or lack of."

"I don't follow, what do you mean?" Percy quizzed his shell hole companion.

"To all accounts Richardson was a good commander, he wanted the best from his men, his plan all along had been to knacker everyone out then return to the practice trenches for one more attempt. My suspicions had consumed me and now we were heading for a live fire exercise without any of our equipment."

Percy drew a hand over his dirty face in tired frustration.

"I'm sorry Fortune, you have totally lost me."

"Come on boy, he made us route march to sap our strength, there was never any intention of meeting his target time for such a distance. He wanted us to practice the assault in a state of exhaustion. Look, how did you feel this morning before the off? Well rested?"

"Well, no. We'd been on fatigues for three nights in a row, carrying during the day, then the march into the line was maybe six or seven miles. With the bombardment going on nobody could sleep, even if we'd had any room to lie down. We were dead on our feet Fortune," Percy looked up at Fortune, a thought materialising in his mind which brightened his blood shot eyes.

"Exactly, how best to train your men for such an endeavour, to prepare them for how they will feel when expected to act? If we could muster and practice the attack in our current state, we'd be well-placed for when it was time to go over proper."

"There was nothing malicious about Richardson's intentions at all?"

"None."

Fortune turned suddenly to his left as if something had caught the attention of his well-tuned senses. He frowned and muttered to himself inaudibly.

"Fortune?"

The veteran soldier's gaze returned to Percy.

"What happened?"

"Charlie saved us, again. D-Company with Berner-Potts was there waiting, we were to practice alongside them. Naturally, Charlie had retained his contraband on his person, he never would have left it back at the copse. Cost us a bottle of scotch and most of his tobacco, but he managed to exchange for enough ammo and equipment to distribute to the platoon, not fully equipped by any means but did the job and no dubiety was aroused."

"So, everything was alright?"

"No, quite the opposite. This is what I'm leading to lad. If you'll let me get there."

"Sorry, do go on," Percy gesticulated politely.

Percy shifted his weight, reclining onto the muddy chalk bank awaiting the full disclosure.

"2nd Lieutenant Berner-Potts came over, wanted a word with me. Over friendly, you know, since that time I caught him in the dugout with the wind-up. Said he was looking out for me and I needed to know something. He was desperate to keep me on side, can't fault him for it, not that I would ever have done anything with what I knew. But at least this way he was of use to me."

Percy was about to jump in excitedly, Fortune's frown intercepting his desperation to speak.

"There was a big deal, a big fuss at headquarters. Berner-Potts was stumbling over his words, a man of such education failing on his words is never a good sign for the message about to come lad. And so, it just came out and he walked away."

Fortune was visibly shaken, his hands interlocked, straining at each other to cause a physical tension to externalise the turmoil he felt inside. His lip curled into a snarl and Percy noticed his Adam's apple rise ever so slightly before the old soldier coughed and spat. There then came a sudden change in the man. He took a great breath through his flaring nostrils and sat up, perching his arms on his knees, his legs firmly rooted on the earth supporting his torso as he leaned forward. His piercing eyes were burning with a rage so pure Percy expected the tall grass behind him to burst into flames. With the growl of brimstone grating in his throat Fortune revealed the news.

"A local lass had been murdered by a Brit. The French were blowing their top. The old man had to contain it and show we meant business, happened on our patch, see. Richardson was investigating."

Percy sat up, leaning forward enticing Fortune's every word.

"She was dead lad, killed. Murdered. She was gone. My Bernice, the one vibrant poppy in this field full of death, had been snapped at the stem," Fortune confessed gloomily, "And all the while Richardson conducted himself with the countenance of a saint, staring at me with a knowing smirk as we trampled across the practice no-man's land to the rattle of the roosting crows."

Chapter 25 - Gunner's wet dream

24th June 1916
Map Reference 57D W9D
2000 yards East of Bouzincourt
0600 hours (U Day)
7 days to Z-Day

Fortune woke from a disturbed slumber into a throng of movement and excitement. Rubbing his eyes and massaging his face with grubby hands he immediately sought counsel with a Capstan cigarette. The darkness of the dugout had been disturbed by men passing out of the canvass screen which had been draped over the entrance. His ears, ringing at first, slowly became accustomed to the sounds of chatter and footfalls on the timber floor, a deep rumbling from far-off shaking the dust from the dugout beams.

"Cut that bloody light," he grimaced, shielding himself from its glare with his forearm.

"Fortune, Fortune, come on, it's started!" called Sergeant Hope from beyond the dugout entrance.

The dugout was now empty in stark contrast from when he had sat down an hour earlier, having returned from carrying party duties up the line. What once cradled fifteen exhausted men, twitching and shaking in their exhausted ecstasy, was now merely a squalid empty box, in which the smell of unwashed bodies and tobacco smoke hung like poison gas, purveying every crevasse and crack in the crudely fashioned chamber. Rainwater from the evening's thunderstorm had partially flooded the small space, but the men had made best of a roof over their head all the same.

Fortune hoped Danny would leave him alone, allowing him solitude in this dank refuge. It was not to be. Sergeant Hope descended the short flight of chalk steps into the dugout and shook Fortune's shoulder.

"You must see this, come on," he grinned.

"I've been here long enough Danny for my enthusiasm for the French thunderstorms to have worn as thin as my tunic," Fortune moaned.

"It's not thunder, not of God's creation at any length."

Danny moved from the dark hole and passed into the light and was gone. Fortune looked at the steps of the dugout, the bright light beyond hiding shapes which moved and mingled amorphously. Rising slowly, he paused in the darkness mustering the strength to climb towards the pure brightness.

Fortune emerged, born into the light of what was a dull, drizzling morning. The men were standing up on the bank into which the dugouts had been driven, staring into the sky above them. Fortune stretched, contorting his arms and twisting his shoulders while extending his neck to both sides with a pronounced click of his joints, for a moment adopting the final pose of the Son of David; his prophetic disposition unobserved by the mortal men who stood gazing into heaven.

"There's one!" yelped Private Cartwright, pointing aloft.

"Can't see it, oh yes, bloody hell," replied Private Connor.

"Another!" called a Tommy.

"Three there," hooted Private Pocock.

The deep rumbling thunder which had been misconstrued by Fortune upon his waking was now evidently the source of the delight enjoyed by the soldiers upon the bank. Staring into the cloudy sky above, Fortune began to pick out objects speeding across the sky. A photographic negative of shooting stars, black objects tracing across a grey-white paper, unfolded above. The heavy guns of the Royal Garrison Artillery had started the bombardment, their huge ordinance travelling in elevated arcs over their heads on a journey towards the German strong points, fuel dumps and wire defences, so large and cumbersome in their new domain they could be seen with a careful eye.

Sharper, more concentrated blasts began behind them, intensifying in regularity and certainly much closer. The noise built gradually until at the point of crescendo a deafening explosion rocked the sunken lane and shook the men to their knees. A cloud of smoke billowed over the depression in which the dugouts were situated.

"Bloody hell," screamed Fortune into the din.

Racing across the road and up the taller bank of earth which encased the west of the camp, Fortune scrambled into a field. No sooner had he crested the escarpment than another roar erupted at close quarters. Dropping to the grass with hands about his head, Fortune shouted into the earth as an 18-pounder field gun spat its venom into the air only twenty yards away. White smoke poured from the muzzle as the gun team scrambled to reload the weapon. Glancing up from his position he could see several more guns, arranged in a V shape in the field. The guns had been dug into depressions, surrounded in sandbags and covered in crude camouflage applied to the defences using branches and canvass. Through the smoke and further back, horses stood with the ammunition trailers. Fortune marvelled at their cool demeanour as the shots rang out. Now fully appreciating the landscape before him he could see guns firing atop the ridge further west, great puffs of smoke marking the position of another two gun batteries.

Scurrying backwards on all fours, Fortune dropped into the sunken road. Sergeant Hope rushed over to take him by the arms and pull him to his feet. Fortune's head lopped to one side momentarily and his eyes bulged in his muddy face. Shouting at the top of his voice yet hearing nothing, Fortune recounted the peril he had witnessed up above.

"Yes, they set up twenty minutes ago, arrived late but must only be a few minutes delayed getting into action."

Fortune could only hear muffled sounds, managing to decipher much of what was said by observing Sergeant Hope's lips. He sat upon the ground and lay back groaning on the earth. Staring into the sky he watched as shells tore through the clouds, silently arcing towards oblivion. The Welshman shook him, clearly his words could rouse little attention. Private Pocock stood over him looking down, his head cocked to one side, his dark face sporting a macabre toothless grin. The two men discussed something above him and then together heaved Fortune to his feet. Confused and lacking all motivation to resist, Fortune allowed Private Pocock to escort him off down the sunken road.

The companions travelled north to the outskirts of Martinsart where they found an aid station manned by the Royal Army Medical Corp. Fortune sat outside a tent smoking his pipe while a medical officer examined him. Private Pocock used the time wisely and acquired some morphine vials from a store. Returning to the tent Private Pocock found Fortune resting beneath a pear tree, his head bandaged beneath his helmet.

"Ah rite then?"

"Eh? Yeah, better. He says it will wear off, nothing serious. Ringing like mad though, more than usual," Fortune bellowed.

"You can hear then? That's good."

"Aye. Just about."

"We'll be gettin back then?"

"You go Charlie, I have something I need to do. Tell 'em they are keeping me up here for a while."

"What are you up to?"

"I need to get to Berner-Potts. I've got to find out about Richardson and this investigation. He owes me a favour."

"You'll do no good stirring up trouble. A damn shame your lass is dead but what are you going to be able to do? Prolly caught by some drunken Tommy on his way home from drinking."

"Shut up Charlie, it's more than that, I know it is."

"You know as well as I, the damage we do to the civvies when we are about, it's the natural way of things, these things are never brought out in the open, they cover 'em up. Bad press. But we all know it happens. The boys have cravins and an anger no civvie could understand."

"Ain't no damn excuse Charlie, we aren't docked in some far-off port nobody cares about. These are real people here. This is important, she meant something you know?" Fortune raged.

"I spose. Sure, you want revenge, you want to catch this bastard and sort him, I'll help ya, you know I will. But this ain't the time to be running off on an errand. Let them find him and sort it and let's get back to the lads."

"No, I'm going to headquarters, I'll speak to Berner-Potts. If we find who did this, there is still time to do something, it'll be too late soon enough, this is my chance. I'm taking it. I'll find the bastard and end it," Fortune spat.

Private Pocock looked down at his sergeant with his hands on his hips. He could see there was no convincing the man against his course of action so picked up his kit and his rifle and walked away without another word.

Chapter 26 - Queens and pawns
No-Man's-Land

"You deserted then?" Percy interrupted.

"Not deserting no, I just took longer to get back than was hoped."

"That's deserting your duty Fortune," Percy scathed.

"I had a bloody duty to the girl alright!" Fortune snapped, "And I know that look, don't quote scripture at me again, I'm done with that."

"I wasn't going..."

"You bloody were."

"Well perhaps," Percy conceded.

"I'll jump the gun," Fortune pondered, "*It is mine to avenge, I will repay*, their foot will slip, their disaster is near, something like that."

"*In due time their foot will slip; their day of disaster is near and their doom rushes upon them.*[39] Deuteronomy. Where did you gain your knowledge of the holy text? I must say, it is far greater than any lay person I have encountered, in the Army at very least," the young lad enquired.

"There was this padre, in India. He gave me a bible, taught me reading."

"What denomination?"

"Methodist."

Percy laughed at the irony but stemmed his gaiety at the ferocity of Fortune's frown.

"Since you opened the gates with your carefully recalled quote I will counter with Peter, chapter 3 verse 9. *Do not repay evil with evil or insult with insult,*[40]" Percy rejoiced.

"He weren't a soldier though was he. What else are we here for than to repay the heathen for their crimes in Belgium? It's revenge Percy, exacted with a greater might than the world has ever witnessed."

---

[39] Deuteronomy, Chapter 32, Verse 35, (NIV)
[40] Peter, Chapter 3, Verse 9, (NIV)

"Let's not descend into our previous disagreement once more Fortune, please continue. Did you find 2nd Lieutenant Berner-Potts?"

"Aye, I did. Released by the MO I took a transport into Bouzincourt village, hopped off by the casualty clearing station up top of the ridge, around the cemetery there and into the back streets. D-Company battalion HQ was in a cellar of this big old house, iron railings, fancy tiles. All bombed out but the cellar was big, many rooms, you know?"

"How did you get through? You can't just wonder into places Fortune, this is all rather farfetched if you ask me."

Fortune smiled.

"Which is why I'm telling you the details lad, pay attention. The truth is imperative, the details boy, are vital"

Reaching into his top tunic pocket Fortune brought forth a tattered arm band sporting a red cross.

"An orderlies arm band?" Percy exclaimed.

"We all carry 'em, well, those that know. There are two people who can get through the lines without much scrutiny from the red caps, messengers and stretcher bearers. You don't want to be mistaken for a messenger or some brass hat will send you off running with a note and you'll end up shot. But who is going to stop an orderly or a stretcher bearer lad? And if the Boshe take you prisoner they won't shoot a medic, they need 'em as badly as us. I wore it today when we got into it. You also need these."

Fortune presented a cloth bag from another pocket, carefully he untied the fastening and spread the container out flat on the palm of his hand. Percy couldn't focus on the items within from where he sat so he straddled the crater and moved to sit beside Fortune, who raised his hand so Percy could inspect his treasures.

"Regimental badges, shoulder titles."

"What for?"

"If you get spotted doing something you shouldn't, in a place you should never have been, what's going down in a report? Regiment, name and number. Charlie requisitioned these when we first arrived in France. Have helped him out of a tight spot a few times. We were training in the Bull-Ring at Le Harve, after Christmas it was. A general was having a well to do soiree for his top brass chums. Well Charlie and I went out, with Army Service Corps titles and badges on. We'd had fake papers drawn up, Simmons from A-Company used to work in a bank and a was a dab hand at making papers look official, all we had to get him was a blank pad of chits from one of the regimental clerks - and enough whiskey to sink the Lusitania.

We walked right in there, showed our papers giving us charge of the waggon and off we went. Sherry, whiskey, wine, you name it. Good stuff too, not the watered-down crap they give us. Company was drunk for a month. And all they had to go on was a pair of Army Service Corps chumps had taken a waggon which wasn't theirs. In the clear lad. Always one step ahead."

Percy returned to his original perch opposite Fortune with a look on his face which told Fortune his clever story had not impressed the young soldier.

"You don't approve son, that's alright. I don't expect you to. When the judgement comes, there are bigger blemishes to concern myself with than nicked booze."

The young lad urged Fortune to return to his story, avoiding further argument.

"Berner-Potts wasn't there. I waited. I picked a derelict ruin in sight of the grand building and settled down in the rafters. Just me and my pipe. I thought of Bernice, our last meeting, the time we just sat in the barn and enjoyed each other's company, you know? There I was telling her I wouldn't return, yet it was her whose life was snuffed out prematurely."

"It is terrible Fortune, such a terrible thing to befall what sounds like a wonderful companion, snuffed out in such a terrible way at what should have been the start of her life."

Percy tried to console his colleague, his tone reminding Fortune of a priest who remains distant, rising above the troubles of his flock. The letters which had congregated in the shell hole began to stir once more, a photograph flipped over to reveal its sepia image. A swirl of air gripped the memory and jostled it into the claw like grip of one of the contorted hands which the corpses offered up, to unseen servants, begging for aid.

"I won't lie to you lad, I shed a tear for the girl. I know I shouldn't but there it is."

"Nonsense, emotions touch men as well as women. You should not be ashamed."

"By the by, my mind turned to revenge once more, and how I would enact it once my quarry was discovered."

"Can we not dwell on that?"

"Very well. That can wait. Berner-Potts arrived some hours later, I leapt up from my vantage point and raced over. He recognised my voice at once and drew me quickly into a chamber, dismissing his bat-man, leaving the two of us alone. He was a shadow of the man I knew of at Loos the year before, you could see it in his eyes, the worry had overtaken him. He tried desperately to keep his tremoring hands from my view, but I saw. Without questioning my appearance at headquarters, he started to tell me about his visit to an uncle, top brass in the Division. He'd told him much of the plan for the assault, you could see the impression it had left, far from positive."

"The plan? The attack was not planned well Fortune?"

"Oh no, the plan was detailed, in every way. Not a stone unturned, every timing and distribution carefully considered. Such detail goes into these things, he told me, however, one thing is missing, what happens if something goes wrong? Berner-Potts was afraid you see, his nerve was gone, no amount of planning could alleviate his fear of what he had to do, going over the top again, into that hell. He was broken.

If you or I get the wind up the CO sends us off to the MO, they know how battle affects us, they are clued up lad now. But the officers, their sense of duty and what they call honour, it tempers them, holds them back from causing a scene. Stood there, a recipient of the Military Cross none the less, from a respected family too and this man is a ruin of his own making to some degree. Not willing to throw in the towel, he wasn't fit to go on, but on he went. Behind closed doors he fell apart, but to his men he was a tower of strength."

"You admire that?"

"I used to. Yes, I do. The likes of you and I are too preoccupied with saving our own skin, but they have to put others first. They're the ones out in front, when we go over, and you saw what happened to 'em didn't you?"

"Yes."

"Well the opportunity was mine to use him as I saw fit. Naturally, I boosted his resolve with talk of our heroics at Loos and a bottle of plonk I had, found, lying about."

"So, did you get the answers you were looking for?"

"He told me all the details I was dreading. Bernice had been strangled, in the farmhouse. The night I was there. While I was there. Interfered with as well."

"Goodness Fortune, poor girl, that's dreadful. I am sorry."

"No matter. Grief was set aside for the task at hand - finding who did this. He said they suspected it was Somersets involved or perhaps one of the other battalions we're rotating with. Richardson had been insistent that he was involved in any investigation, he was going to work alongside one of the COs from the York and Lancs. There had been several telephone calls and wires to people he knew, red caps, some general somewhere, family members. He was desperate to have control over it all and pulled out all the stops by all accounts."

"Why would he do that? Why not let the authorities deal with it? The Military Police."

"Quite. Berner-Potts said he'd been exasperated at the whole affair. Richardson had taken it personally, a slur on the good name of the battalion was not acceptable."

"Clearly an officer with admirable intent. What was the evidence he had?"

"Berner-Potts wasn't sure, but there was talk of a ledger, a list of," Fortune paused briefly to catch his breath, "A list of visitors at the farm. Appointments she was keeping."

"Visitors?" Percy looked momentarily perplexed.

"Don't scoff lad, it was obvious I know, to everyone but me."

"Oh. Oh, I see. Private Pocock was correct about her, entrepreneurialism."

"Big word for whore, go ahead, I'm to-terms with it."

"Fortune I mean no disrespect."

"Don't you? Are you sure? What does your good book say of such women? You'd burn before you found compassion for such creatures I'd wager. I have no ill feelings for the lass, a product of war just as I am. Making what she could from this shite, it's all we can do. She was just another sacrificed pawn in his damned game."

"His game?"

"Richardson. He was coming for me."

"What? Why would you say that? Richardson had not acted as yet, nothing had been said or done directly."

"No, he hadn't. But I knew Richardson. He would be scheming. Elaborate and ruthless."

Fortune turned his head away from Percy and frowned aggressively into the bleak hole for a moment. Percy thought he could hear the man grumbling to himself.

"Fortune?"

"I told Berner-Potts he owed me on accounts of the indiscretion in the dugout, when we went up the line. He reluctantly agreed to find out what he could. If there was any suspect or news, he would get it to me. The names from her ledger for that day for starters. Until then what more could I do? I couldn't confront Richardson, not if he had it in for me. I had to be patient and my thoughts returned to what I could do to such a man who took her from me."

"Did you suspect anyone?"

"Aye, it's plain to see isn't it?"

"No, I wouldn't say it was," Percy shook his head vehemently.

"Christ. After that day in Amiens when he met her, on the steps of that great church. I saw it in his eyes then, his disdain for me and how he could hurt me through her."

"You can't be suggesting it was somehow Richardson who perpetrated this violence?"

"Damn right lad. Of course it was! There weren't any evidence, only what he would construct to see me accused. Take her away from me and have me shot for it in the bargain. Put my name on that ledger list, easy enough to do. The lads all saw me with her when we passed through."

"Fortune, I have to disagree, profoundly. Your paranoia has navigated this path before, the route march which was not just innocent in its design but quite brilliant of the officer."

Fortune brushed the comment away by scrutinising his pocket watch closely while ignoring his companion's retort.

"Huh! Look at that. She's twitching lad, we're making progress. We can start moving on shortly."

"We haven't finished Fortune," Percy protested.

"Oh alright, alright. Where shall we go next? I know. What happened to your lot, in the run up to it?"

Fortune posed the question to the young Yorkshireman to allow himself a break from his story. While he listened, he took time to prepare his pipe, the supplies of cigarettes having already reached its most dangerous level of exhaustion.

"Well, V day was brighter wasn't it, after the thunderstorms of the previous day. Warmer, I think, yes it was much warmer and brighter. But the next few days were bad again, rain and heavy mist. We were in a place called Millencourt," Percy suddenly smiled as he recollected, "We all had a bath that day, we scrubbed up well Fortune, in our new uniforms. The battalion had been up the line on working parties of an evening, preparing the trenches and digging gun pits. We'd taken the gas cannisters in a few days before, back breaking it was. Millencourt was a nice rest, of sorts. I had time to sit and read, write some letters home. For a moment, clean shaven and in our new tunics, it felt like we were back in training, you know? Like when we first joined up."

"When did you go into the line?"

"On the 28th, Y day, the day before the attack was supposed to happen. The Sherwood Foresters moved onto their assembly trenches and we took up their place in Authuille Wood. There were times when the bombardment intensified, everything was going over, and the noise was terrific. You could feel the displacement of the air, you know?"

"Yeah, they did that off and on. So as the Boshe would think we were coming over soon, that's when the smoke goes over and the gas, to make 'em think an attack is about to start, but then it doesn't come. Gets their wind up see. Well, it was supposed to."

"They replied to our noise that day, a heavy affair it was, on Chorley Street and Bamberbridge, we had quite a few casualties that day. A nice chap from my parish was killed, I never asked his name. But everyone was in good spirits, it was hard not to be confident with the show the gunners were putting on for us. Through the periscope you could see huge black mushrooms rising on their lines, blowing them to pieces, all day long. We were ready to go Fortune, we'd practised several times, everyone knew what they had to do, their little piece of the larger plan. I was detailed to help some signallers lay telephone cable across no-man's-land, they had this huge reel on a wooden spindle.

There were some nerves as the day approached, it's only natural to be anxious, but most of us just wanted to get on with it, this is what I signed up for Fortune, to do what had to be done, to throw the heathen back from whence they came. I remembered Isaiah, chapter 35 verse 4, *Say to those with fearful hearts, Be strong, do not fear; your God will come, he will come with vengeance; with divine retribution he will come to save you.*[41]"

"Vengeance hey?" Fortune laughed, "You've walked yourself into that one lad."

Percy accepted defeat with a wry smile.

"And then they pulled the plug," Fortune spared the lad any more shame.

"Yes, it was cancelled. On Y day, at the very last minute it seemed. We moved back out from the line that night and into Long Valley. It was the rain wasn't it?"

"Maybe, or did they know the wire wasn't yet cut out here?"

"Oh, we knew that, there was a raid the night of the relief, inconclusive the rumours said, some gaps but they were tight."

"Aye, same on our frontage. Enough to get through though. Down near the Ovillers end it was almost clear, further up near the Nab, it was still heavy. They had been out repairing it as fast as we were bashing it up. Anyways, carry on," Fortune steadied himself and allowed the young lad to continue.

"The two extra days we had distressed a few of us, I have to say. When you prepare yourself mentally for a great undertaking such as this and it's postponed at the last minute you cannot help but become somewhat despondent. We were not glum due to our task that lay ahead, oh no, we were disappointed that we hadn't been given the chance to go."

"I agree lad, we were relieved as well on that night, having been down there waiting for the off, marched all the way back up to Forceville and Richardson had us go through one more practise. The lads were shattered."

"Where are we going with this Fortune?"

"You said we hadn't finished."

"We still haven't. The skies darken as if to announce the finite nature of our amity and yet I feel there is still more to learn."

"Aye, the clocks ticking quickly now, you don't have long left lad," Fortune grinned.

---

[41] Isaiah, Chapter 35, Verse 4, (NIV)

Chapter 27 - Loos at last
No-Man's-Land

"On the Sunday, the 25th, we had Sunday parade and the lads went off to hear the padre. Me and Charlie didn't have to attend so we busied ourselves organising a treat for the boys."

"How did you abscond from the service?" Percy frowned.

"Oh, an old Army trick. You have the clerk change your religion on your papers, to a denomination which isn't represented by your battalion clergy. Naturally, we opted for Methodist," Fortune smiled, "So they don't force you to go along."

Percy knew by now any protest would be unsuccessful, allowing Fortune his victory over authority by remaining silent.

"We slipped off and got to work. Charlie found a waggon of petrol cans the Army Service Corps had left unattended and we made our way west, in our Service Corps badges, to where they were storing the SRD jars and rum rations. What a sight the roads were Percy, you won't have seen them being down the line. I thought the traffic on the way down here was rough but my God, it was horrendous. Ammunition waggons as far as you could see, trucks and trucks full of stretchers. Men, thousands of men, on the move. The dust and mud and smoke was awful.

This chap was filming everything with this camera, on a tripod, cranking it around and around and shouting for the lads to 'act normal' as they went by. Naturally, everyone was hooting and hollering at their loved ones back home, waving their helmets about and making a big fuss. Nothing was concealed Percy, gun crews setting up in the fields, columns of transports, for anyone to see if they had been looking, and you can be sure they were.

Anyhow, we decanted as much rum as we could into the petrol cans and the whole waggon was packed and ready by mid-afternoon. The journey back was grim, it took much longer than expected to move through the traffic. We were redirected by police, adding a few miles to the trip, but they didn't have a clue what we were up to, just another waggon in a train of hundreds."

"What about Bernice?"

"I'm getting to my point son. Patience is a virtue you certainly don't possess," Fortune grumbled.

"Sorry."

"We're heading up this lane, all congested with gunners and their horses. There's a commotion up ahead, some shells were landing all around and the column up further on was scattering. Not wanting to lose any of our precious cargo we pulled under some trees on the edge of an orchard, to wait it out. It wasn't falling anywhere close, we'd just wait for the Boshe to build up a sweat, call it off and go for Schnapps. We stood there, smoking, shouting encouragement to the chaps as they pressed on, you know?"

"Bernice?"

"Right, well down the road, towards us, comes this officer on his charger. Running him at break-neck speed. As he was passing the column ahead, the Tommies are standing up on the carriages and waving their helmets about, in a greater hullabaloo than the shell fire was causing. As he approached, we could see why. The wretched horse was trailing its guts along the road behind it but still on it ran. He's caught one passing through the bombardment you see and the officer he doesn't have a clue, he thinks the men are cheering him. Poor beast. Well Charlie, he's not one for much compassion, as you probably understand by now, but when it comes to animals, well that's different. Weird fellow, bash a man's skull in and he won't flinch, harm one of God's creatures and he'll tear your bloody arms off."

"We're all God's creatures Fortune," Percy added, without an acknowledgement.

"Charlie, he steps up all brazen, in the path of that officer and holds out his hands. Damn foolish thing to do, but there he is, blocking the path. The officer panics and pulls his horse up, right in front of Charlie. That's when I saw it was 2nd Lieutenant Berner-Potts."

"Crikey!"

"Indeed. I rushed over and took the reins while Charlie got Berner-Potts down. He was ranting and raving, waving his arms about at us, I don't think he knew at first who we were. His eyes, they gave him away, this man was running from something. I grabbed him and showed him his horse, it just stood there, steady on its feet, its entrails all muddied and drawn out around it. Berner-Potts broke down, he was blubbering, face covered in snot, it was practically billowing from his mouth. I went to take him away, put him by a tree, by our waggon and that's when Charlie acted."

"How?"

"He snatched at Berner Potts' holster, his fingers were so nimble Percy, he could have a catch or fastener undone in the blink of an eye, and he drew the Webley from within it."

"He shot Berner Potts? For doing this to the horse?"

"No, he shot the horse. Calm as anything just placed it on its forehead and bang, down it went. Then he calmly offered the pistol back to Berner-Potts, who just stared at him, he couldn't process what he was seeing. I took the Webley, tucked it away. Then we laid Berner-Potts out."

"What had happened? What was he doing?"

"Well it took a hell of a lot of our rum to get any sense out of him. Richardson and his aides had been collating evidence received from the Provost Marshal and the French. They had witnesses, some said Bernice had been seen with an officer in Amiens, some said she had been seen with many a fella, regular visitors to the farm as well and frequenting beer halls. Didn't paint a good picture of her lad, that's for sure. But what had spooked Berner-Potts was the account of her walking out with an officer, of our Battalion, in Amiens. A trusted source he said."

"Well that's not true, surely it can't be true?"

"Of course not, not by her own election but what if she had been seen with him, with Richardson, what if he had approached her."

"For what purpose?"

"To finish what was started that day on the steps of the church. I've told you what she was like, full of fire and with the intelligence to use it. What if they had argued, his rage overwhelmed him, going up to the farm that night to finish her."

"Is that what Berner-Potts said?"

"Well no, not in so many words. He said Richardson was discounting the claims about the officer, he had overheard him say to his aid. That this evidence was not relevant. It was suppressed see. Instead he was looking for a suspect from the other ranks, the likes of you or I. One of the lads on her list of appointments."

"And he had evidence, conclusive, to press the case before a court?"

"No, that's just it. He didn't have a name, well he has too many, the ledger was crammed with them, but no witnesses came forward with anything concrete to pin it on any of them. He'd done this, thing, and was covering it up. I had plenty of leverage on Berner-Potts, so I pressed the point. As soon as any name came up, he had to get it to me, especially if it was mine."

"You said Richardson wanted to implicate you, how could he achieve this?"

"Well, even if he planted my name in her list, he'd still have nothing which he could make stick to me, so I realised he would take matters into his own hands, when we went over. He'd settle for the girl's death as a fair exchange for the way she spoke to him that day in Amiens. My rage and sorrow was a bonus to him."

"You were wrong the last time you assumed such treachery from him Fortune, the trench raid, nothing came of it."

"Well, I was premature then, but the premise was the same."

"Yet again Fortune, I'm not sure I draw the same conclusions as you have, if I am honest. You asked me for my counsel on this tale of yours, I find your reasoning to be misguided." Percy declared.

"And why is that?"

"You have as much proof as you say Richardson had, it's here-say and conjecture. It's farfetched that an officer would attempt such a long-winded approach to see your demise. Besides, the motive for the hatred you describe, from what seems to be an accomplished young officer, has yet to be explained. Again, I must press the question, was it Loos?"

"Christ lad, how many times, I've told you what he was like, his scheming, how he conducted himself with my black-market endeavour. The conclusion of that was far from pleasant was it not? You've been told what he is capable of. His calm collected exterior harboured a deep-rooted desire to up-end me, he had seen my weakness, Bernice, and snuffed it out."

"All well and good Fortune, if you see it this way, but I will not arrive at the same outcome as you. Not without evidence. The poor girl was dead and that is all you have told me of any relevance. She chose a dangerous career, one frequently ending in murder, if you believe the stories which circulate. And, I must point out, you haven't explained why Berner-Potts was galloping down that road, all I can see is a suspect coincidence that you crossed paths."

Fortune sighed and drew a long and healthy draw on the over-sized Prussian pipe.

"Alright, alright. I give up. We were crouched in a shallow trench, couldn't have been more than three feet deep, at the foot of Hill 70. The battalions were all mixed up by now and anyone who had made it through the village was there."

"Is this Loos?"

"Yes lad, we're at Loos. 1915, the September following our gay summer in Aldershot. There were still pockets of Germans in the village, up the twin-towers of the great mine shaft they had there. London Bridge we called it. Their marksmen were up there taking shots at us from behind. The hill was pouring fire down on us too, from in front of us. It was dark but, like I said, the village was ablaze, the lighting was good enough for a machine gunner. Richardson and a few of us had made it through the shelling, lost the rest of the battalion a way back, turns out they had moved on to some wood further north with the 1st/8th Somersets. I can't remember what time it was, it's not important, it was late. The order came along the line, they were going to try to get up that hill and take the trenches. Richardson grouped us together, went up and down calling for Somersets, found some, even some of the 1st/8th were there. Sergeant Fitch had some men, as did I. Danny was there, Charlie, Cartwright, Arthur Leyland, Private Breslin, oh, and Henry Hamblin, was a Private back then of course before he got his stripes."

"You've not mentioned Fitch since Aldershot," Percy realised.

"Hold your horses. Very lights were whizzing up all about, shells were crashing over our heads and those machine gunners were tracing the trench line picking us off with lucky shots. You couldn't keep yourself hidden see, the trench was so badly bashed about. Richardson sent word that we would go over with everyone else and so we did. Clambered up and dashed up that damned slope."

Fortune paused to take more vapour from the pipe while Percy shifted impatiently on his backside.

"Private Breslin went down immediately, caught one in the neck I think, but the rest of us made good progress. Was nothing could be done for the lad, you don't stop, can't stop for these things, you know?" Fortune explained with a pragmatic shrug.

"You've not really mentioned him before, what do you know of him?" Percy halted the recollection, eager for more detail.

"Lad, in this business it pays not to get close to anyone. What use is it?"

"If it's just a name then why even trouble yourself to remember he was there?"

"Aye well, fair point. Young he was when we went over in 1915. I guess we were all younger, wiser, back then."

"You don't know anything about him do you Fortune?"

"No. He was just a name and number to me lad, I won't dress it up any more than it is. Good soldier, otherwise didn't make time to know him."

"Then how will he be remembered? For the part he played."

Percy seemed agitated as the reality of the mass-slaughter's legacy took hold. Fortune knew the question was far closer to home than Percy would reveal so decided to move on.

"Anyhow, the wire back then, wasn't like this, sure there were nasty spots, but not as dense you know, staked out, about knee height it was, all tossed about by our artillery, it would lie in patches where our shells had dumped it. To the left you could see some lads all caught up in it, trying to find a way around. The Germans had an easy job with them. We were lucky, there was a way through. Richardson was out in front, a good runner mind you, nimble. Waving us on with his revolver. Fitch was on my right, with his lot, thumping along on those short legs of his. Cartwright got it in the arm and shoulder going up there, but the stubborn bugger kept going all the same. We'd stop, lie down, then dash again, like we were trained back home, you remember? Move then fire, move then fire. The proper way.

Well we got to the top lad, the fire was murderous, guns flashing away in front of us, shells bursting all around, nothing like today I'll give you, but when it's flying like that you don't stop to count bullets or shells to draw comparisons later on. It was a miracle we reached the crest. The Boshe had defences on the top, but their main line was on the other side, hidden from view, on the far side of the hill so our artillery couldn't reach them. We'd thought we had sent 'em packing when we got over that hill, great lines of us rushing over, shouting and hollering, in a battle madness we were.

A few Germans were in a cutting with a big gun, Fitch dropped down in and bashed 'em in with his rifle butt. Charlie skewered a couple who threw their hands up as we arrived. I could see the others trying to catch glimpse of something to shoot at, but when you are in that fog, you can't comprehend what's happening all around, not unless it presents itself.

No sooner had we cleared up the resistance on the top than the real German line opened on us. That was when it all came apart. Field guns were firing at point blank range, machine guns, rifles, all cracking away and we were exposed. The line withered away, men were falling everywhere. Cartwright got another in the thigh and Charlie made him stay where he was. Danny took a fragment in his cheek and hand. Arthur Leyland just vanished, shell got him I think. Harry got pretty messed up too, one in the knee, two in the thigh and something lodged in his back.

Just Charlie, Richardson and me left standing and whatever remained of Fitch's section. Richardson wanted to go on, I tried shouting, protesting, but nobody could hear a thing up there. We'd got down into a hollow beside the gun Fitch put out of action. Cartwright and the other wounded were crawling back over the crest, they got away without further injury, goodness knows how. Luck is all that can save you in that situation. You could see, if you stuck your head up for a moment, other groups of our lot, crouching, in the old German forward trenches. One minute a few men would be in a hole and the next a shell came over and they were gone. And so, our numbers dwindled, just dust left, rising into the orange night."

"*They will throw them into the blazing furnace, where there will be weeping and gnashing of teeth,*[42]" Percy recounted solemnly.

"Indeed lad."

"You said Berner-Potts was at Loos, was he with you?"

---

[42] Matthew, Chapter 13, Verse 42, (NIV)

"Further along, it turns out. Had a hell of a time, lost many getting through the wire, but then he rushed a machine gun and put it out of action. That's what they gave him the MC for. He had to fall back, we all did, he left many men on that hill, injured, maimed, that's what haunted him see, tore him up inside. They called out for help through the night but couldn't be saved."

"What happened to you? Where does Richardson come into this? How did he behave?"

"He wanted us to push forward again, we could hear a field gun, close by, it was firing over open sights at anything that moved, it couldn't have been more than twenty or thirty yards away. He wanted to take it, he told me and Fitch that's what we were doing."

"A just cause, to put such a machine of death out of action, to save the lives of all those men you describe, stuck on the hill," Percy concluded.

Fortune did not respond. His eyes were fixed on his grubby boots as a severe frown cascaded over his face. He toyed with his hands, rubbing at dirt which had congealed about his nails. Looking up at Percy, the young man could, for the first time, appreciate a more fragile side to this larger than life soldier. The old man's face revealed a sorrow, a shame, which had burrowed deep into this man to find its lair.

"What is it? What happened?"

"Everyone went over," Fortune began in a quiet tone, "Fitch and Richardson tearing down the slope towards the firing gun, the rest followed, a screaming band of madness, playing its discordant mayhem, headlong into the German emplacement."

"Everyone?"

"Bar one."

Fortune recoiled into his mind once more, forced to relive the crossing of the Tugela river, north of Colenso. A scenario which had played in his mind and plagued his dreams for over a decade. Having crossed the hastily constructed pontoon bridge, the company had come under increasing fire from the Boers. Long range artillery was shelling their position and rifle bullets were falling all around in a murderous storm. His sergeant had put them behind a low stone wall from where they returned fire into the hill.

In all his self-analysis, when his morale was ebbing and his consciousness allowed such folly, he would return to this action. The unbearable heat, the incessant gun fire, the stone wall, its dusty surface still real to him even now, the texture of the masonry as he ran his bloodied hand over its features, the sergeant bellowing at him, cursing him for his inactivity. His friend to the left falling back as a bullet passed through his face. This was the moment his resolve was broken, the moment the fear enveloped him and paralysed his soldiering spirit for the first time.

"Fortune, Fortune?" Percy snatched him from his distressing memory.

"I froze lad, I let them run on. They didn't look back, for if they had, they would have seen me, watching them glide over the hill towards damnation. I dropped it all, my things, I left them there. I ran. By good fortune I caught a shell shard on the way down to our lines, right through here," he gesticulated at his lower arm, "It was enough for me to concoct a story, I'd taken the injury as we rose up to attack the gun. I limped about gathering up stragglers and isolated men. Led them back down the hill to safety."

"What happened to them?" Percy enquired, a grim expression of disappointment crashing upon his face like a dark wave pounding a resolute rock.

"Fitch was killed, three of his men with him. Richardson succeeded, they put the gun out of action. Everyone who made it home had injuries, Richardson was badly hurt, Charlie brought him back in, with Danny's help."

"Did they realise your cowardice?"

"Not the boys, but Richardson, I knew he knew."

"The Red Badge of Courage, the book he was reading in the dugout," Percy exclaimed.

"There you are, you've presented your own evidence, which I could not have provided lad. Are you satisfied? Good, then I will move to conclude."

Chapter 28 - A first for death
1st July 1916
Thorsby Street Trench
1000 yards south west of The Nab
0655 hours
Z-day - 35 minutes to Zero Hour.

Soil and debris thrown up by a bursting shell pattered and danced over Fortune's helmet like gravel scattered to the side of the road by a fast-moving cart. Yellow smoke from the discharging shell drifted over the trench as another exploded a few yards beyond the narrow aperture to the outside world. The trench was crammed with soldiers, queueing patiently for the big show while the German artillery played its violent music along its length. All the occupants could do was shield themselves from its loud destructive notes in their deep claustrophobic gully.

"Set your chin forward lad," Fortune coaxed with a relaxed grin, "There's a good chap."

Fortune had barely enough room to edge by each man on his final walk along the platoon, but he made steady progress, stopping at one man to address a tin triangle which hung loosely over his back.

"Get this tightened, won't do our observers any good with this lying in the grass now will it?" he beamed at the embarrassed boy while everyone else about him ducked from another explosion close by.

As he continued, he took time to speak to each man, albeit in veiled instructions or pseudo-criticism, the men knew full well today his venom would be spared for the Germans alone, this was his way of wishing them luck.

Private Pocock followed behind, distributing the rum he and Fortune had so expertly acquired. With the help of two others he swapped the water bottles with any man who would take his replacements, his macabre toothless grin dispersing any smile that Fortune had provoked in the men as they went.

"Hullo Danny"

Fortune stopped at the young Welshman and shook his shoulder in warm greeting, "Not long I shouldn't wonder?"

"No not long, all taken care of?" Sergeant Hope enquired.

"Aye, personal effects on their way back. Don't worry we've separated all the smutty pictures out."

"Good luck," Sergeant Hope nodded at his friend.

"Aye well, see you on the other side Danny, see you on the other side."

The assembly trench had seen better days, its sand bagged defences had been knocked about throughout the evening when the Germans had replied to the trench mortars they had sent over. Soil covered everything, the bags themselves only partially visible beneath a great blanket of disturbed earth.

"Private Connor, what pray tell do you have to say about all this I wonder?" Fortune goaded in jest, Private's Cartwright and Stendhurst sneering with enjoyment beside him.

"Ain't got no negatives to say about it sergeant, only hurry the hell up I'm busting for a piss, I hear they have better latrines than us, I intend to find out before long!"

Those that could hear erupted in laughter, even Private Pocock saw the humour at this present moment.

"Good lad," Fortune congratulated the boy, but behind the glazed expressions of the men he sensed their fear and anxiety.

"Corporal Hamblin," Fortune greeted his NCO with a handshake.

Fortune exchanged pleasantries but did not pay much notice to what was said. He was pausing within himself to look at the man who stood before him. Once a fresh-faced boy hungry for adventure Henry was now a quiet individual who would rather sit alone and read his bible than kick a ball around with the other lads. Loos the year before had changed them all, Fortune pondered, in more ways than one. Some sought solace at the bottom of a bottle, others such as Henry strived for a spiritual answer to the horrors they had witnessed. From the expression on the corporal's face his avenue of enlightenment had proved just as successful as Fortune's.

Next in line was Private Shaw. Fortune tightened the boy's webbing and moved his helmet strap from around his neck to his chin. He stared intently into the boy's eyes for a moment remembering the trench raid and his inability to keep calm.

"Alright?" Fortune asked with a tilt of his head.

"Yes Sergeant!" Private Shaw puffed out his chest.

"Here," Fortune retrieved a Capstan cigarette and placed it into the boy's mouth, "Take one of Pocock's bottles, it'll help."

Towering above the five-foot-five Shaw was Private Richard Roberts, his huge leathery hand grasping his rifle tightly to his chest in apprehension.

"Look after him," Fortune leaned in and shouted into Private Roberts' ear.

Today was Richard's seventeenth birthday, the parcels from home awaited him behind the line. He had planned a secretive ceremony upon his return to safety, avoiding any undue scrutiny of his age which would lead to his immediate repatriation. He clutched the white feathers in his tunic pocket ceremoniously, while smiling at his sergeant.

Fortune then passed the Cooksley twins and offered them only his smile, but stopped at Private Moore who seemed distressed, twisting and shaking off the hands of those beside him who tried to console him. His face was displaying an agonised frustration from within, his eyes betrayed a man with inner demons. Fortune had expected a manifestation of fear in some of the men, those that had lost the struggle with their emotions and would now present a credible risk to the cohesion of the unit if left unchecked.

"What's this?" Fortune searched the faces of those in the line.

"Edward's got a letter, her at home is in the family way see," bellowed a Tommy over the din.

"Are you sure it's yours?" joked their sergeant.

"That's just it," bleated Private Moore, "It's not mine, she's wrote to tell me."

"Then that's the best result you could have hoped for lad, one all draw on accounts of that lass you knocked up in Le Harve!" Fortune bellowed.

"Thirty minutes!" came a shout from up ahead.

The men laughed, raising their pipes and cigarettes to their sergeant. The shoulders of the young man dropped as his comrades mocked his ill fortune, but with this group consciousness came relief for the soldier, he smiled, albeit reluctantly and Fortune knew some control had been leveraged over a delicate situation. His friends jostled him playfully and patted at his grubby face, their childish support easing Private Moore's mood. Their mirth was short-lived.

A terrible roar, a guttural moan, filled the air and silenced all who heard it. The hurricane bombardment had begun. Every gun was firing, every artillery piece great or small, was emptying their terrible maws onto the German defences. The thunder-like rumbles preceding this furious venting had been distinct, a drum beat to the ears. Now the artillery was acting with such alacrity that the noise was a constant cacophony, a never reducing crash the likes of which had never been heard. The artillery gunners were reaching their final crescendo, marking the imminent handover of responsibility to the infantry who waited before them. Hell itself was emptying, its legions ripped through the sky on their way to Armageddon.

Fortune ended his journey at the side of 2nd Lieutenant Richardson, who stood patiently at the head of the line, scrutinising his watch. Richardson's batman, Squires, was nervously fumbling with a cigarette for his master. Fortune grabbed his shaking hand, giving him a stern look, lighting the cigarette himself and passing it to the officer. Fortune nodded to which Richardson frowned and forced the sergeant to remember his salute once more.

Fortune thanked the gunners silently as verbal communication with his superior was now quite impossible. He watched as Richardson used a periscope to look forward, up the trench, towards the front-line which bisected their communications trench at right angles. His defeated expression denoted his failure to see anything of importance. Further on, the defensive ditch contained one of the leading waves of the battalion; all Fortune and the others could see of what was unfolding ahead was the backs and packs of their comrades from B-Company as they waited to shuffle into the forward line, once the initial attackers had gone up and over.

This scene was repeated along the entire battle front, fourteen miles of trenches crammed with men and equipment waiting for the signal to rise up and launch the assault. The network of trenches behind them were equally utilised by those who would follow up in the subsequent waves following the initial dash. While they waited, compressed and helpless in their chalky crevasses, the German shells fell all about them unchecked, their temper growing as the expected attack edged closer to zero hour.

Richardson leaned towards his sergeant to position himself to convey some instruction which was never delivered. Without warning the trench further back heaved and burst into the air, a sudden explosion threw earth and men upwards as a howitzer shell impacted a few yards from those cowering within. Everyone witnessing the carnage instinctively flinched, drawing their hands over their eyes, crouching where possible to avoid another terrible detonation. Screams and moans, desperate shouting and cries for assistance rippled down the column of men, while the might of industrialised warfare screamed overhead, a natural wail seemed to pierce the impenetrable discord.

Fortune glanced at Richardson who released him with a nod, eager to start his fight back down the line, with Private Pocock following closely behind. Upon arriving at the scene nothing could be done for those beneath the freshly churned earth. The trench had collapsed, its reinforced sides smashed down onto part of the platoon, burying men beneath tonnes of soil and chalk. Splintered wood and twisted iron protruded from the earth pile like the arms of drowning sailors clawing at a rescuing ship. Those that could stand attempted to dig away at the mound with rifles and shovels, but there was no sign of the men who moments before had huddled here.

Some soldiers lay crumpled in the bottom of the trench, grasping their heads and moaning in pain while those who had maintained their demeanour sought to treat their inflictions any way they could. Another Tommy, his eyes bulging as his protracted tongue flashed between his snarling teeth, was being restrained by two of his colleagues, his desperate madness urging the poor man with every ounce of strength he possessed to leave this mortuary and run for safety. Fortune delivered a swift punch to the bewitched soldier's jaw, his thrashing ceasing with the same abrupt shock of the initial explosion.

Fortune quickly ascertained that Private Moore and the Cooksley twins were gone, along with several other men who had been standing nearby. Over the mound of earth Private Stendhurst appeared, waving his arm at his fellows in the forward portion of the trench, signalling that the rear of the column had survived, the shell having hit the ground away from the trench, the only damage incurred was the collapse it had orchestrated. The terrible force of the British high explosive had not ravaged the trench line itself, the inaccuracy of its blunder saving many more from being maimed.

Fortune held the palm of his hand out before him, urging Private Stendhurst to move back, there was no room for him or the rest of the men, they would have to wait for their opportunity to pass over the obstruction. Deciding he could do no more to assist those present in digging out their fallen comrades, he pushed his way back up the line. Shells continued to land and explode indiscriminately all around, failing to find their thin snake like target again. The chalk and earth they tossed into the air like a defiant child only served to keep the men firmly rooted to their crouched stance.

"They're falling short!" Fortune shouted into Private Pocock's ear, but the old sailor could not distinguish his words.

Having returned to the front of the line, Fortune discovered Richardson had gone. The rear of B-Company had moved forward up the trench and could be seen progressing slowly along its winding trail. A private handed him a note, scratched onto a small piece of squared paper in pencil. 2nd Lieutenant Berner-Potts had got the "wind up" and had to be relieved of duty, Richardson was heading forward to take his place leading one of the D-Company platoons in the first wave. The sergeant-major had caught a shell in the assembly trench and once again Fortune was placed in command of 1 Platoon. To the left the York and Lancasters had been mauled in their trenches and were low on NCOs and men. Fortune would take his charge up the line to assist.

"Bloody hell!" Fortune raged, handing the note to Private Pocock who was none the wiser for the muted outburst.

Fortune pieced together the instructions conveyed in the short briefing of the previous night. He found it hard to concentrate, his thoughts disturbed by bursting shells and the yells of his men. With Richardson gone, his quarry for the day had escaped him and regardless of orders, his actions now would need to be carefully considered. No outcome would be worse, he decided, than allowing Richardson to fall to a German bullet before he could reach him and enact the vengeance his Bernice so rightly deserved. He turned to the platoon and urged them to follow. By now the first wave would be out into the field, lying in the grass in front of the German line, while the last few minutes of the barrage shattered the wire which lay in front of them.

The second wave had occupied the space provided by the first wave's exodus and were preparing to rise out of the front-line trench and over the top into no-man's land, when zero hour arrived. Richardson would, by Fortune's reckoning, already be several hundred yards ahead of him. What is more the orders would take him further north babysitting the York and Lancasters, away from Richardson. With grim determination Fortune led the platoon forward down the trench. He looked down once more at the pencil scratched orders. Heading north now would take him too far from his goal. He scrunched the page into a ball and dropped it under his boot.

At the junction with the front-line trench Fortune stopped, men from the proceeding company were already up on the fire step looking at their commanders and sergeants for the sign to go. Wooden ladders had been brought up and were now resting against the steep sides of the trench, corporals and sergeants poised on the first few steps with whistles in their mouths. Fortune glanced back at Private Pocock who had remained at his side throughout the morning, his trusted aid fought to continue his reassuring toothless grin, even this hardened veteran could not help but disclose his inner turmoil. Fortune scrabbled for a cigarette; his comrade applied flame from a match. An officer, his wide eyes fixating on his wristwatch became the focus for all the men at the T-junction.

Fortune passed his rifle to Private Pocock and set to work redressing his webbing. Removing the entrenching tool head from where it hung over his posterior, he reattached the bag at his front, between his water bottle and helve, covering his crotch. Having completed this action, he took both rifles and helped Private Pocock complete the same exercise. The soldiers who caught sight of this watched bemused until a sudden realisation of its purpose spread down the line, instigating a frantic urgency to protect their most treasured extremity.

Fortune inspected his rifle, ensuring two full clips of ammunition were nestled firmly in the magazine, following which he placed a single round directly in the breach and slammed the bolt shut.

A movement above caught many a glance, three Morane Parasol biplanes raced overhead in staggered formation, sunlight reflecting from their polished engines as they flew southward along the front. Then the earth shook. The intense noise of the hurricane bombardment faded as a new more terrifying sound bore into the soldier's bones. The iron braces of the trench rattled furiously as displaced soil ran down the walls like water from a bursting pipe. The ear-splitting roar developed rapidly into a wall of absolute sound and from within their earthen cage all could see a huge muddy mushroom rise high into the heavens to their right flank. Like the head of some ancient monster rising from the womb of its gargantuan mother, thousands of tonnes of earth surged four thousand feet into the sky. As the scattering debris mountain reached its final height, another eruption spouted forth beside it, shaking God's creation with all of Man's ferocity and malice. The double mines at La Boisselle rang in the soldier's ears long after the millions of fragments of rock, soil and chalk had fallen on the landscape around their gaping white craters.

There followed a surreal moment of calm. The guns fell quiet, their seven days of impertinence silenced by the victor of a calamitous competition of destructive power. Fortune took a deep breath and looked back along his column of men; their eyes widened in awe.

"Get ready!" shouted the officer on his ladder.

"Fix - bayonets!" Fortune called back at his men, lifting the shining blade from its sheath and slotting it into place at the muzzle of his rifle.

Private Pocock caught Fortune's intense glare and indicated upwards with his eyes. Fortune peered into the miasma of tobacco and shell smoke which hung above the trench. Ripples disturbed the floating cloud as an unseen force pierced its confines, sending small puffs of vapour dancing in the white veil. Fortune smiled grimly at his companion in recognition of the phenomena, bullets were already passing overhead. Fortune held out his hand and Private Pocock shook it.

"May not win the war today, but I'll leave a bloody great scar!" Private Pocock grumbled.

There was a sudden commotion further down the trench, which broke the relative calm, some men were struggling. Shouting. Fortune's height gave him some advantage in discerning the source. Writhing like an eel on a fishing line, 2nd Lieutenant Berner-Potts was being man-handled by a sergeant major and a corporal. His face was red, his eyes fierce, the helmet on his head knocked off to reveal matted blond locks. Like a cornered dog he thrashed against his captors all the while maintaining his desperate gaze on Fortune.

"Silence that man, called an officer or I'll shoot him myself."

Fortune's senses crackled with adrenalin. He tried to push through, but no egress could be obtained against the wall of men and equipment which blocked his path. The men with Berner-Potts were dragging him back out of sight, back into the dugout he had emerged from only moments before, while young men around him stared in disbelief, their faces stricken with fear. He shouted incoherently, repeating the same words, a name?

Then the whistles blew, C-Company clambered up, and were gone into the maelstrom. The whole line erupted into bestial shouts and curses as they climbed into oblivion; the fear-soaked fuel that leads to murderous abandon. The noise was intense, the atmosphere charged. Berner-Potts raised his last shout, all but drowned by the pandemonium around him. Fortune glanced back at his fearful men, waiting for his order to proceed. Yet amongst the din the old soldier could only focus on the wretched officer trying to deliver his message.

"Son, something - son," Fortune mouthed the syllable he could ascertain.

A powder keg ignited in his mind and he launched himself up the ladder in two great strides, hanging from the top rung he looked back upon his men with a ferocious stare that could mean only one thing. There would be death at the hands of this man today, a great festival of death. Richard-*son* was top of the bill.

Chapter 29 - Follow, stay, damned either way
No-Man's-Land

"I watched as he opened the sixth seal. There was a great earthquake. The sun turned black like sackcloth made of goat hair, the whole moon turned blood red,[43]*"* Percy interjected solemnly.

Fortune gave no response to his shell hole companion, knowing the verse from Revelation all too well. He chose to light his pipe again rather than dwindle yet further his supply of cigarettes. Without looking at the boy for any acknowledgement, the old veteran let his head rest back on the earthen slope, blowing smoke into the night above him. Percy shifted his weight once more, then clasping his hands together in front of his face he murmured a prayer.

"The first waves made good progress, they only had a couple hundred yards to dash from where they lay in the grass you see. Made their way through the gaps in the wire easy enough and were on the Boshe before they knew what was happening. For us though, we had much further to go and by the time we had clambered out after C-Company, all hell had broken lose," Fortune explained.

"It was coming from the left Fortune, the left had a hard time," Percy recounted.

"Aye, from up at Thiepval, right wasn't much better mind you, from Ovillers and that," Fortune added, "We'd made a gap up front though, at least that was a success, we got through and they'd just kept going, marvellous it was at first."

"What did you see?" Percy asked.

"What do you mean?"

"What do you remember? What did you feel going over there? I felt, nothing, I surprised myself, I thought I would be scared Fortune, or

---

[43] Revelation, Chapter 6, Verse 12, (NIV)

unable to go through with it, but when we went over, that fear had gone, for a reason I can't explain," Percy confided.

"Oh aye, the fear is in the waiting and when the waiting is done it lifts, you see it for what it really is. Did you feel like you were experiencing it, you know, second hand like?"

"As if witnessing the event rather than taking part?"

"Aye that's it, distanced from it, like someone else is in control and you are but an onlooker."

"Yes, yes that's right. It was somehow calm in all that horror. We just walked, we tried to dash but all that stuff we had to carry, we couldn't move fast."

"Ah, we ditched all ours as soon as we were out, gave us a chance you know, to move quickly, we caught up with the other wave and moved through them in places. What did you see lad?"

"I could see the bombardment falling further back, on the rear lines, little white mushrooms popping up on the horizon, I could see the grass swaying as the bullets brushed them this way and that. I saw a man go rigid then fall down on his face, like a tree going over, just beside me. You felt like you couldn't look around, to the sides, but had to fix on a spot ahead and just march there, so I just did that and tried to resist looking for the others.

There was shouting, our sergeant, lovely man, had been in the South African war like yourself, he'd lied about his age to get back into the Army when all this started, he kept us in a line for a bit, until he went down. I did see him go, stumbled first, got hit in the thighs. One of the lads dashed to his side as he knelt there, I kept looking back to catch a glimpse of his fate."

"Receiving his final communion," Fortune added.

"He caught one in the neck and that was it, they both went down, I didn't see anything after that, I wasn't looking anymore after that," Percy lowered his head.

"It's a funny place, no-man's land in an attack," Fortune took up the reminiscence, "For all those hours before, you're with your mates, with your men, a great crowd of smelly scrotes, that you've lived with for months, been with every hour of every day. But when you go over, you are on your own, basking in the warm summer sun, wondering in the field, with just your breathing and your thoughts. You can see it all falling around you, the mud flying about, shells cracking over your head, you know that all around you the bullets are cutting the air, but for the first time in such a long time, there is a kind of solitude and your simple task of walking over that field will either end in success or failure. But either way lad, there's nothing you can do to change the course of fate, so you just walk."

"You make it sound easy," Percy protested.

"Not my intention lad, didn't say it was easy, I said it was simple. Live or die, walk or fall."

"What did you think about as you went across?"

"Bernice, Richardson, who knows, I don't recall, it all happened so quickly. There was smoke, whether it was ours or just the shelling, but when we went, I couldn't see much of what was ahead like you did. It was misty wasn't it? Yeah, there was a mist, I'm sure."

"I don't think so," Percy frowned.

"With the first waves fighting in the German lines already, the Boshe sent their bombardment onto no-man's-land. Carnage it was. I saw this young chap, coming towards me, stumbling through the smoke, carrying something. I would have shot him, but for what he was doing. He had several arms, bundled up in his, like firewood. Strangest thing you ever did see. He called out to me, I asked him what he was doing with those, terrible shame to just throw them away he said, someone might want them he said, a terrible waste he said, then he was gone, wondering back from where I had come from. He was in a world of his own, not afraid, just trying to help somehow. Making things right."

"That's awful."

"Awful? Can you assign such a word to a single event in a morning such as that? I found it amusing, all things considered."

"You led your platoon across then? You made it over?"

"I did no such thing, I made it over, that was my intention, Richardson was somewhere up there in all that. The others, no, I didn't lead them, you give any instruction out there and a sniper has a bullet for you. That's what they do lad, take the leadership first. No, I went over there for my own reasons, the war ground on in any way it pleased, but that dash was mine alone, to get to Richardson. I'd have gone over even if the whistles had fallen silent. The boys looked after themselves, they were with me, or they found me on the other side."

"You didn't care about the men in your charge?" Percy seemed aggravated.

"Care isn't the right word for it. Get yourself killed trying to keep everyone safe and what do you get for it? They just end up going west in the next show, or they survive the day and are maimed a few months later. I've seen them on the streets at home lad, begging for change in their tattered clothes, their limbs torn away reducing them to nothing but a macabre reminder for the civvies, that they're having a better time of it than us," Fortune drew on his pipe frantically.

"What happened on the other side?"

"I found myself at the head of a sap, bodies were everywhere, hanging from the wire, lying in big heaps where a machine gun had caught 'em.

Richardson's batman was there, I saw him, basking in the sun with his lower half all bashed up."

"Dead?"

"Yeah. He was dead."

"And Richardson?" Percy lent forward in anticipation.

"There were survivors at the wire lad, all mixed up from the waves that had gone in. Your lot, my lot, everyone mingled. I moved up and down the wire for a moment, it seemed safe there, the battle was further ahead, or behind. I couldn't see him, they hadn't seen him. Some lads were trying to get the wounded back across no-man's-land, I urged them to stop, but they wouldn't listen. Sniper got 'em when they moved out of cover."

"What about Richardson?" Percy pressed.

"While I was looking for him I found Danny, Sergeant Hope to you. Stendhurst and Cartwright had made it over with Charlie. We had to dress a wound on Danny's arm, but he was not for going back, so we rounded up who we could from the platoon. We gathered whoever we could into a coherent unit and I showed them the sap and got them into the trench. I went back out, found Shaw and Roberts in a shell hole and helped them in. None of them had seen Richardson. So, we pressed on.

Down the sap and into the trenches proper, well what was left of them. We could see helmets bobbing about down trenches, we could hear bombs going off, rifles. The artillery had moved on, to the second and third lines, we were in the clear, of sorts, but there was activity everywhere, British and German, was hard to tell.

Corporal Hamblin appeared, from down a trench to the south, he'd managed to get in with a few of the others and find their way up to us. The first waves had done a good job lad, they really did. Dead Germans everywhere, lots of ours too mind you."

Fortune paused as if reticent to proceed. He drew long and hard on his pipe once more.

"The platoon was reformed then? You had your command once more," Percy attempted to encourage his companion into revealing more.

"3 and 4-Section had done well, we'd lost Moore and the Cooksley twins to our own artillery, no surprise there. Otherwise, aye, we were doing alright. We paused to bandage anyone who needed attention. There were scrapes and what have you, naturally. They had survived. But apart from Roberts there was no sign of 1 and 2-Sections. No idea who made it or who didn't. We'll find out when this is done lad, when the final roll is called."

"So where was Richardson?"

"Alright lad, alright. He was either dead in a ditch or further on, deeper into the trenches. We could have scratched around in there for hours and not found him, so I gambled. I said I was going over the top again, dashing to the second line. I would have done it alone, but they all said they were coming with me. Their choice lad. I was desperate, I had to find him. No matter what the cost."

"And did you find him?"

"Oh aye, I found him alright."

Chapter 30 - A sacrament in savagery

1st July 1916
German 2nd Defensive Line
0945 hours
2 hours 15 minutes into the battle

Four more Germans charged around the traverse in the trench and raced at the waiting British soldiers. Fortune deflected a bayonet thrust with his own rifle, beating the enemy's weapon to one side with a powerful blow. Stepping back, the large man swept upwards with his weapon, catching the German across the face. His adversary fell to the right, his body lying motionless over another of his fallen comrades. The German behind the first assailant rushed forward, once more a bayonet was thrust towards Fortune, the blade scoring a wound upon his right thigh, leaving the battle raged sergeant enough opportunity to bring the rifle butt crashing sideways into the German's chest, winding him.

Another German pushed to get through from behind, lurching at Fortune with his rifle. Fortune parried this second aggressor with a frantic defence, while the bruised soldier, momentarily reeling before him, returned to the fray with added vigour. Fortune stepped back once more, feeling the side of the trench against his back. Like a startled animal prodded from behind, he lurched forwards forcing both men backwards with a strong shove of his rifle.

A German bayonet thrust again, catching Fortune under the armpit, the angle of its attack avoided a penetration, the blade grazing his left side, ripping his tunic. The pain incurred forced Fortune to release the grip on his weapon, which swung at first, still held by his right hand, its weight too much to support. The rifle fell to the floor of the trench. Twisting on his hips Fortune brought his huge fist to the face of the previously winded German, who fell back grasping his broken mouth. His companion, seeing the exposed Tommy without a rifle, desperately struck out with his weapon, plunging its bayonet at Fortune's stomach.

A shot rang out at close quarters and the German fell lifeless over the groaning body of his comrade. Fortune staggered to one side, his body flinching from the loud bang of Private Pocock's rifle, which had delivered the killing shot. The combat beside him in the trench raged on as Private Pocock turned to dispatch his own antagonist. Another German dashed into view and ran towards the unarmed Fortune. With a pronounced lunge the veteran grabbed at the wooden handle of a shovel, which presented itself from beneath the pile of corpses. Raising it suddenly he forced its steel head forward in a horizontal thrust, putting his entire weight behind the palm of his hand, which tightly gripped the T-shaped handle. The German fell, his head partly severed at the neck. Fortune collapsed backwards releasing the shovel, the trench was clear of danger at last. Private Pocock stepped over the bodies of his victims and finished the groaning soldier with the butt of his rifle, then turning to Fortune offered his arm to his exhausted sergeant.

Fortune took stock of his surroundings and collected his thoughts which were now returning to his mind, the fighting having relented for a moment. Private Pocock took up sentry at the traverse in front, while Privates Stendhurst and Cartwright were searching the dead for anything of value. Behind them, Private Connor stood gazing at the pile of corpses which half blocked the trench.

"Where's Danny? Corporal Hamblin? Shaw? The others?" Fortune barked.

Private Connor shook his head.

The dash across the open between the German front-line and the second line of defences had been costly. Machine gun and rifle fire from positions in the flank had taken their toll on what was left of the platoon. They had followed him over, eager to please their sergeant, who, unbeknown to them was not seeking a heroic assault rather a specific goal, 2nd Lieutenant Richardson.

"Can you see D-Company Charlie?" Fortune shouted.

"There's Tommies up along here," Private Pocock replied, "Can see 'em bombing. No clue who they are."

Fortune stood on the Germans at his feet and raised himself to full height. The parados[44] of the trench was all but collapsed here and he could peer over with ease. The German third line was visible to the east, a white chalk excavation snaking across the field. Wire defended the trench from any attack. From the helmets bobbing along in groups, indistinct shouting

---

[44] The rear-side of the trench was known as the parados. Both the parados and the parapet (the side of the trench facing the enemy) were protected by two or three feet of sandbags

and occasional rifle fire, it was clear the third line trench was strongly held. Before anymore could be gleamed from this view a bullet smashed into the earth a few yards from Fortune's face.

"Bloody hell," Fortune snapped, "Third line is still theirs, that's for sure. Got to be along here then, come on!"

The troop filed into the next bay, clambering in places over fallen soldiers from both armies. A section of the trench ahead was destroyed, they found themselves crawling to the next opening in the earth over exposed soil and shattered timber. Rifle rounds cracked over their heads periodically. Shouting some distance to the left stole their attention for a while, but nothing could be discerned from the voices. The thuds of bombs could be heard distinctively ahead of them and a machine gun rattled in controlled bursts, its deadly aspirations belonging to another trench, another fight, somewhere to the right.

They came to a dugout entrance, already smouldering from the British attack. Fortune recognised the opening all too well, it was the Mittenwald redoubt from the trench raid. A German soldier lay face down on the steps, the back of his head a pulped mass of crimson and charred flesh. Several more bodies could be seen mangled on the steps leading down into the earth. Private Cartwright had to be held back from entering its confines in search of loot.

"All repaired from when we were last in 'ere," Private Pocock gestured, "Makes you wonder what else they've repaired in short time this week."

Further on, they came across yet more corpses, this time their own countrymen lay in contorted forms about the bottom of the trench, victims of a mortar perhaps or several grenades.

"D-Company," Private Pocock exclaimed having inspected them closely.

"Come on!"

Fortune pressed onward in front of the column, he could sense Richardson was close by. The sound of fighting was soon upon them, rifles were cracking between the sudden bursting of bombs. They could hear shouts ahead, English voices. A bay they entered had partly collapsed, a wide expanse of soil piled to one side allowed a route upwards into the field. Fortune scrambled up the slope and fell prone at its summit. From here he could see the next few traverses. Three British soldiers were crouching up ahead, on the parapet, firing their rifles down into the trench. A Lewis gun spat its deadly venom into an enemy unseen. There were more Tommies within the trench, their steel helmets popping into view as they threw bombs over an obstacle. Grenades from both sides of the obstacle arched into the air with frantic regularity.

"The trench has been capped up ahead," Fortune called back at his men, "They are fighting to control it, let's give them a hand."

Looking back to watch the battle unfold, he suddenly caught sight of their officer, half in and half out of their trench, firing his revolver over the barricade.

"Richardson!" Fortune raged.

Fortune levelled his rifle, waiting for a clear shot to present itself, for a brief second his nemesis was in his sights, but with a shout of frustration he cursed himself and slid back into the trench. This was not the revenge he had been promised.

Having reached the scene of the ongoing struggle the remains of Fortune's platoon realised the situation here was bleak. A handful of men remained active in the plugged trench, feeding their bombers with grenades from the sacks of their fallen comrades. The Lewis gunner had just been wounded, dragged down into the comparative safety of the trench, his faithful weapon sat smoking on the parapet.

German stick grenades continued to twirl through the air, over the timber barricade, while a machine gun emptied into the makeshift defence from close range. Soldiers were slumped in the trench, grasping at wounds beside their dead colleagues. 2nd Lieutenant Richardson was at the front, firing his revolver or lobbing bombs around the thick tangles of barbed wire, which adorned the blockage. Another clear shot presented itself to Fortune, as Richardson endeavoured to keep the Germans at bay, completely unaware as much danger existed in the trench behind him than was trying to gain entry in front.

Private Stendhurst heaved himself up to the parapet and eagerly grabbed at the Lewis gun, removing its circular magazine, then calling down to Private Cartwright to pass a fresh one to him. Private Connor rushed to the side of a fallen man. Private Pocock looked for instruction from Fortune, who seemed paralysed on the spot, inactive and unresponsive. Private Roberts pushed by, dashed to the barricade, then taking up a bomb from his satchel he attempted to pull the pin with his teeth. His heroic act stemmed in its infancy as several of his front teeth gave way and popped from his mouth, just as bullets smashed their way through the timbers and tore into him. He fell back under the weight of his dying body, the grenade exploding in their midst. Amongst the debris and disfigured flesh sent rushing into the air, white feathers took flight for one last time, descending majestically to lie over the discarded bodies now littering the trench.

When the dust had cleared, the survivors scrambled to their feet. Private Cartwright was clutching a bleeding wound at his side. Private Connor approached, hauling the soldier back along the trench to safety. Richardson turned for the first time and surveyed the scene, he was unscathed by the detonation which had been tempered by the bodies of the wounded, who now lay dead in his trench. He glared into Fortune's eyes.

"We cannot hold any longer," Richardson announced, "Fall back!"

Fortune's men looked at him for reassurance, none came. Private Pocock grabbed at Fortune's arm unsuccessfully, the large man an unmoving rock in a turbulent tide. The 2nd Lieutenant brushed by the tall soldier and for the first time Fortune moved, he gave way as the smaller man pushed him, turning on the spot and maintaining his bewildered stare. Richardson's remaining men followed their officer, pulling with them anyone who could muster. As a cat stands poised on its haunches when its carefully stalked prey takes to the skies, Fortune watched defiantly as Richardson departed, helpless to act.

"Fortune," Private Pocock screamed, "Fortune!"

Fortune could not respond. He watched as Private Stendhurst knelt up to deliver his fiery payload to unseen Germans beyond the barricade, while Private Cartwright clawed at his friend to come down. Private Connor pulled at Private Pocock to leave the trench to which the young Irishman received a decimating frown and deliberate shove down onto his back. Germans could be heard close by, readying for their final attack.

While Private Pocock wrestled with Fortune, both Privates Stendhurst and Cartwright were set upon by Germans who clambered into the trench from above. Private Connor fired his rifle into the mass of men and a German fell forward. Leaping to his feet the young man stabbed and parried with his rifle, plunging it into the chest of another attacker. Private Cartwright sank back into the trench on all fours beneath Private Connors savage attack, while Private Stendhurst, hacking at a German with a short knife, rolled down onto the corpses below, entangled in a fierce tussle with his burly grey uniformed enemy.

Sensing all was nearly lost, Private Pocock acted swiftly. A decisive punch to Fortune's stomach collapsed the large sergeant instantly, like a can of corned beef under a heavy boot. Coughing and spluttering in the depths of the fetid trench, Fortune's rage surged through his body, tension returned to his limbs and pressure swelled in his head, bringing focus and clarity where there had been weakness and confusion.

"Get up you fuck!" his companion screamed into his ear.

"Go, go, get 'em back Charlie," Fortune groaned as he clambered to his feet.

Private Pocock grabbed Private Cartwright and with significant force, one-handedly dragged him backwards out of the melee, spinning him onto his front as they moved. Next, Private Pocock lunged at Private Stendhurst to repeat the same action. A bedraggled German, shouting angular Prussian curses from his bloodied mouth, sprang up to fill the gap made by Private Cartwright, lashing frantically with a large serrated blade, in a vain attempt to score a wound. Advancing a single, well-placed step forward, the old sailor smashed downward with Temperance, rending the German's jaw and nose into mush. The fresh corpse dropped soundly into a grisly opening between two mangled bodies at the base of the trench.

"Come get it!" Private Pocock roared.

His salivating tongue thrashed in his toothless mouth, while his sinewy limbs and heaving chest pulsed beneath his blood-soaked shredded uniform. His helmet had long since been discarded, having buckled around a stray lump of shell earlier in the day. Clumps of thin unkempt hair had been revealed, on an otherwise sun blackened bald head. Private Connor was holding off two Germans by the barricade with his rifle, their shorter trench weapons lacking the reach to engage him square-on, while shouting beyond the barricade warned reinforcements were close by, soon to be upon them.

Through all the mayhem and confusion, he could not help noticing the effigy of death closing in behind him, with his terrifying blood-stained weapons and dishevelled clothing. For a brief instant he could picture his saviour on the deck of a French ship at Trafalgar, surrounded by dead sailors as he blazed his way through all opposition at the head of a British boarding party. The tangible presence of pure violence in human form, merging so seamlessly with the heroic stories which had been repeated with regular precision at his British school, was deeply unnerving for the Irish lad.

Leaping forward from his brutal kill, Private Pocock thundered at one of the Germans who tussled with Private Connor. With rapid and ferocious attacks from Temperance and the short knife he brandished in his left hand, he presented a far more prevalent risk to the wrestling enemy. The German turned to face the wild man, bringing his arm in front of his face to protect him from the club, just as Private Pocock swiftly drove the knife upwards into his unguarded side. The German faltered, Private Pocock kept stabbing. The German slid downward and to one side, with his back against the wall of the trench, a look of pure horror on his face as his body was repeatedly holed.

His companion, now isolated and outnumbered began to have second thoughts, edging back to a possible escape route, where the side of the trench was low and in poor condition.

"Fucking kill him!" Private Pocock spat and raged.

The Irish youth plunged his unwieldy rifle and bayonet at the German, who must have been twice his age, twice his height and twice his weight. His arms regained strength as he filled with sudden determination, fuelled by desire not to let Private Pocock down in such close quarters. He struck out with his rifle catching the German in his right upper arm, the blade moving in three shuddering thrusts through the muscle, against the bone and into the barricade behind.

The German shrieked in pain, dropping his trench dagger, facing his smaller assailant with watering eyes and a sullen expression of submission. He began babbling quickly, pleading. It was momentary. Private Pocock beat the pinned soldier about his chest in two successive blows, followed by a blow to the top of the head and a blow to the nose. The German hung there limply, a fountain of gore issuing from his wounds.

Without a word, Private Pocock pushed his index finger against his left nostril and blew phlegm from the right nostril over the dead and dying Germans. With a brief but stern look at Private Connor, he rushed back to where Fortune was composing himself. Private Connor held the German in place with his foot and yanked the bayonet free, then bounded over the corpses, around Fortune and out of sight.

"Jesus Christ," thought Fortune of the spectacle, "Our savagery knows no bounds."

D.G.Baulch

Part 5 - Rapture and Recriminations

"The final hour when we cease to exist does not itself bring
death; it merely of itself completes the death-process.
We reach death at that moment,
but we have been a long time on the way."

-

Seneca (4 BC-65) Roman philosopher and playwright.

D.G.Baulch

Chapter 31 - Soul harvest

1st July 1916

German 1st Defensive Line

Mittenwald Redoubt

1125 hours

3 hours 55 minutes into the battle

Fortune hunkered down into the trench and held his Lee Enfield before him. With rapid and determined movements he cleared the breach and began to feed ammunition into the weapon, pushing individual cartridges down into the magazine, one after the other. Beside him weary men were making their own preparations. The trench was teaming with British soldiers from many battalions, all had been separated from their comrades through the death, injury and confusion of the morning. Fortune was the only sergeant present who could still hold a weapon. A corporal of the 8th York and Lancasters, who's name had not been shared, nodded at him from the opposite parapet, beyond the entrance to the dugout. The corporal gathered his men and placed them strategically along the firing step.

To his immediate left, Fortune could see Private Pocock checking the weapons of young soldiers, handing them ammunition from a canvass bag. Private Cartwright sat beside the dugout entrance resting his rifle on the body of a German. Fortune could see he had little strength left in him, nevertheless he had refused to go down into safety with the other casualties. The wound in his side continued to bleed, old bandages soaked dark crimson, in need of a fresh application. The only Medical Corp man in their number lay dying in the dugout, one of the many victims of German shellfire which had intensified throughout the morning. Private Cartwright would have to bear it.

To his right, Fortune caught sight of Privates Connor and Stendhurst, standing together against the parapet, smoking and talking. They seemed in high spirits considering the dreadful experiences of the last few hours. There was nobody else here he recognised from the platoon, save for Richardson who, deep in the dugout, was trying to command the salient of British soldiers he had gathered; his aim to hold on until relief or withdrawal that night.

The dead, both British and German, had been piled into makeshift barriers to the three trenches that entered the small redoubt. More bodies lined the area, acting as fire steps facing north, east and south. The Germans had counterattacked twice within the last hour, adding more flesh to the macabre barricades the men now manned.

"Any sign of that bombing party Charlie?" Fortune called.

"Nothing for last ten minutes. German helmets down there now though. Our lot got close, to their credit."

"Not close enough," Fortune grumbled.

He surveyed the motley crew of survivors once more. Dusty gaunt faces, wide reddened eyes, mouths hanging open like dogs waiting for their bowl. Uniforms tattered and scorched, their equipment muddied. The tools of war lay all around, discarded. Packs, belts, satchels, rifles, helmets, shovels and picks. Body parts, both large and small, interspersed with the brass and leather of kit, to form a sickening collage of man's creative engineering.

"Ammunition," Fortune blurted.

Private Pocock brought some charger clips over and pushed them into Fortune's webbing pouches.

"Thanks."

Private Pocock stared blankly at his sergeant, his polite gesture totally unexpected in such a cruel environment; giving no reply save for a grunt, he returned to his young men.

Fortune watched a soldier who was crouching alone, near the opening to one of the trenches. He was tightly crouched, his knees high and heels pulled in, rifle between his legs, both arms wrapped tightly around it. His thin dirty face rested against the rifle while he stared unblinking at the duckboards beneath his feet. The cigarette in his mouth hung limply, its curved head of ash motionless.

In stark contrast, on older man, close by, was stationed at a corpse barricade. His body twisted and jerked as he knelt there, his head constantly moving from side to side in fitful twitches, eyes wide in anticipation yet seeing nothing. Fortune recognised this lack of comfort in the man's muscles. He was a coiled spring ready to burst, the tension in his body would dissipate when the killing began again, or he would recoil into the tormented confines of his mind. His composure held together with a fine sinew of reason, like many others crouching in the redoubt.

Fortune, having appraised the motley gathering fully by now, concluded the majority of those still standing were doing well, considering what they had been through. Awake since the previous day, marched into the line, shelled and shot at all night, shelled and shot at all morning, ran up a slope while being shelled and shot at, through barbed wire and down into severe hand to hand fighting in the German trenches, where for good measure they were shelled and shot at some more. The fighting had lasted four hours, Fortune confirmed with his pocket watch. They had plenty of fight left in them yet, they just needed to stay the course.

"Why are there so many tree lined roads and leafy lanes in France?" Fortune enquired loudly to get everyone's attention.

Some of the men looked confused, others inquisitive. Private Pocock caught Private Cartwright's eyes and they both grinned.

"Germans like to march in the shade," Fortune confirmed after a reasonable pause.

It was clear the men did not really know how to react, although the sight of the large sergeant beaming at them went a long way to alleviate their frayed nerves.

"I lost my rifle, back at Loos in 15," Private Pocock responded, "The army charged me £3 and 15 shillings. That's why in the Navy, the captain goes down with the ship."

There was a murmur in the ranks of battered men. Some smiled at their comrades. Private Pocock always took particular pleasure in his own joke, his shoulders lifted accompanied with a toothless smile, the sight of which may have been counterproductive with Fortune's line of attack. The sergeant got up, weapon in hand and began to pace around the men, making sure he made eye contact with each of them.

"I came across a German, out in No-man's-land when on a patrol. Stuck fast he was in the mud at the bottom of a shell hole. I didn't shoot him, no, I felt pity for him. He'd sunk so deep only his head and pointy helmet was exposed. *Kameraden* he would holler. *Kameraden*. I tried to dig him out, but he was stuck tight. Alright mate I said, I'll get help. So, me and the lads rigged up a pulley and rope, up out of the trench, through no-man's-land and managed to get it around his upper chest. Once in place we rushed back and all started heaving and straining. He was shouting and we were shouting and heaving. After ten bloody minutes he hadn't budged an inch. I shouted over to him, sorry mate we can't shift you. He shouted back, would it help if I took my feet out of the stirrups?"

The men who had been listening attentively to the tale, hanging on Fortune's words for any wisdom they may contain, looked at each other in bemusement, but within moments several were laughing heartily and most managed a smile.

"I could go on," Fortune looked expectedly at his audience.

A resounding hurling of curses and groaning forced a willing surrender from the sergeant. He smiled at his men, nodding resolutely at Private Pocock.

The sudden shout of a rifleman in a neighbouring traverse pierced the proceedings like a sniper's bullet, "Here they come!"

"Charlie, bombs," Fortune yelled.

Riflemen standing on the makeshift fire steps began to engage bobbing helmets in the trenches close by; first the northern defences, then the south joined in the fray. What had started as pot shots at obscured helmets, built steadily into a continuous fire, the volume and frequency intensifying. The Lewis gun team guarding the northern barricade went into thunderous action, spraying their trench with controlled bursts. A dust cloud enveloped them as the gun rattled its brutal call to arms.

At the eastern corpse barricade, Fortune peered down the communication trench for any signs of attack. The men here were nervous, finding it hard to resist the temptation of looking back at what the others were up against.

"Don't you worry about the others, you keep your eyes down this fucker, I'll worry about your flanks," Fortune roared, thumping the tops of helmets to press his point.

Fortune set about establishing a full appraisal of the situation as it developed, pacing between the three points of defence. The Germans were probing, in small numbers, to test the defence and ascertain numbers. Fortune knew they were not going to push just yet; he was waiting for the sign.

A rapid onslaught of bullets crashed into the parapets, kicking more dust and debris into the air. Several men fell back shaken by close calls; wiping their eyes they struggled to refocus. The 97-round pan magazine of the Lewis gun was now empty and as the team rushed to replace it, a new sound filled the cacophonous vacuum, the whistling of shellfire.

"Find cover!" Fortune bellowed as he rushed to the dugout entrance.

With a deafening bang several shrapnel shells burst in quick succession some twenty feet above the redoubt, spewing their payload of lead balls downward into the trenches, peppering the entire area. The violent downpour ripped through everything in its path. Then came the trench mortars. Arcing high into the sky from a nearby vantage point the great lumbering devices twisted and turned as they fell towards the defenders with explosive rage. Raked by shrapnel and thrown asunder by mortar fire the scene outside of the dugout was like a hell-born charnel house.

Fortune stumbled out into smoke and dust, with an arm across his face he desperately tried to orientate himself. There were cries for help and moans of agony coming from within the battle mist, surprisingly also a fair amount of cursing and profanity directed at the Germans from unscathed Tommies. Rifles began firing again with added vigour. The vast number of corpses in the area had served to absorb the force of the shrapnel bombardment and luckily none of the mortars had found their mark precisely, falling on the parapet and roof of the dugout. A quick reckoning told Fortune they had lost four men with another six wounded.

"Cartwright, get those wounded men down into the dugout!"

Fortune quickly darted to the east.

"Connor, there's two more for your barricade, quickly man, take their ammunition!"

Fortune then clambered to the south.

"Charlie, bombs, bring the whole bag."

Fortune and Private Pocock moved north across the entrance to the dugout to the Lewis gun team.

"They'll come now lads, we've got a surprise for 'em," Fortune shouted over the din.

Sure enough the main thrust of the attack was about to fall on the redoubt from all three directions. German soldiers and their NCOs gathered in a long snaking line a few traverses away from the redoubt, trench weapons in hand, belts bristling with stick grenades, the fiercest men positioned at the front, they would lead the brutal assault. Riflemen waited behind impatiently, their NCOs behind them.

Glancing at a battered trench watch a middle-aged Prussian sergeant barked the order to attack, stirring the line of troops into movement. The bombers at the head of the line pulled on the porcelain plugs at the base of their bombs to ignite their fuses. Leaning backwards they poised to throw their deadly missiles.

Screaming around the traverse before them, at the head of a rag-tail band of British soldiers, Fortune levelled the Lewis gun and began his slaughter. A spiteful flame erupted from the wide radiator casing as the weapon clanked its rhythmic discord. Bombers fell back mortally wounded as the trench was consumed in dust. Spent brass casings chimed as they clattered to the floor. British grenades now filled the air, dropping around the traverses yet unseen ahead. Fortune released the trigger as several soldiers passed, driving themselves headlong into the battle like the head of a stampeding herd. Rifle shots rang out from both sides, German bombs exploded with their British counterparts and the skirmish descended into melee.

Private Pocock darted forwards, brandishing Temperance and a knife, one soldier had a spade, others thrust their bayonets into the clashing mass of men. The fighting was brutal and unrelenting in its ferocity. Confident that Private Pocock and his group were fully engaged, Fortune enacted the second stage of his plan, gesticulating at the soldiers who had remained with him. Helping each other they clambered out of the trench onto their bellies, then clambering to a low crouched run they dashed across the refuse and lose chalk, vaulting broken timber and pausing in shell holes. They had thirty meters to cover as quickly as they could before they would reach the eastern communication trench that wound its way to the redoubt. There they would cut off the attack from behind.

They spread themselves widely over the area, moving independently of each other. Dashing and hiding in quick succession, with no clear cadence between them, the desultory rifle fire that eventually came upon them was largely ineffective and had come too late. Fortune reached the chalk mound which denoted the trench was up ahead, quickly pushing himself tightly to its nearside slope. Glancing back, he could see his brave band ducking and diving across the dead zone between the trenches.

Fortune caught sight of the quiet lad, who had crouched so tightly into a ball of fear back at the redoubt. There he was with an expression of grim determination across his face and a fire in his eyes. Pride filled the old sergeant as he beckoned him into the relative safety of the chalk mound. The lad was smiling through gritted teeth, recognition of his own abilities flooding through is demeanour. A sniper's bullet passed through his neck silently and he fell forward out of sight into a hole.

More bullets began to impact on the chalky ground around those that had made it to the far side. There was not a moment to lose. Fortune placed the Lewis gun beside him and having shifted his weight, pulled a wine bottle from within his satchel. The rags which tightly filled the neck of the bottle were soon alight. Glancing down the line of men he could see they had all raised grenades or petrol bombs, awaiting his signal.

Fortune stood to his full height with a firm foot on the chalk mound in front of him, he could now look down into the communication trench from his lofty vantage point. Bullets cracked over his head.

The Mittenwald redoubt was a mass of smoke and dust to the right. He hoped Privates Connor and Stendhurst could hold the Germans for a few more moments while the second trap was sprung. The communication below trench was full of men and bodies from left to right, all focused on pushing forward into the withering fire coming from the redoubt, ignoring the world above them, spotting Fortune when it was too late to act. Without wasting any more time Fortune lobbed a fire-bomb down into the trench, onto the backs of unsuspecting German soldiers. His line of men followed suit, throwing death into the congested gully.

A great heat forced Fortune back a step as the fire-bombs shattered and ignited, beginning their enthusiastic maiming without prejudice within the trench. Limbs flailed as the grenades burst at soldier's feet. The dreadful wailing of dying men abruptly ceased as Fortune's team stood atop the trench, their rifles and the Lewis gun issuing their mechanical last rights over the war's latest mass grave.

Chapter 32 - Fortune's turmoil
1st July 1916
German 1st Defensive Line
Mittenwald Redoubt
1255 hours
5 hours 25 minutes into the battle

Fortune descended the concrete steps into the bowels of the dugout, two steps at a time, with long determined strides. Regimented thumps and thuds of artillery shells exploding on the surface dislodged dust from the ceiling, almost in sync with his heavy footfalls. Arriving at the final landing, the expanse of the dugout lay before him. Casualties filled the floor space, writhing and groaning in the dim candlelight. The air was thick with tobacco smoke and the ferrous smell of blood and gore. Bloody bandages and expended morphine vials lay scattered all around. His gaze was drawn to a wooden crucifix and Christ, hanging on a nail on the far wall. Fortune rested for a moment against the concrete wall, grimacing at the cries for water coming from the fallen. The instant his grubby hand pressed against the cold surface of the wall his mind withdrew.

He found his thoughts at the low stone wall at the crossing of the Tugela river once more. His hand navigated slowly over the uneven surface; the texture of the stones was so clear to him in his memory. He could hear the shouts of the men, discharging their rifles at the hill side from where the murderous Boer marksmanship was issued. His sergeant wailed and screamed into his face as he crouched there, staring down at his rifle unable to act. The soldier next to him fell back as a sharpshooter's bullet took away part of his mouth. Thousands of stone splinters leapt from the wall as small arms fire crashed into its far side. Sweat poured from beneath his helmet and incessant flies buzzed around the wounded and the dying.

The cries of the men in the dugout rang out in unison with the distraught pleading for aid in his recollection. The firing had ceased now. The battle had moved on. Dead lay along the length of the wall, the injured trying in vain to gain shelter in its shallow shadow. Fortune pushed the body of his dead sergeant away from him with his legs. Panting, his lips cracked and parched, he could not speak or raise a shout to any of the others. They wanted water. It was a long way back to camp. Fortune held tightly to his canteen. He would wait in the sun blasted valley for darkness to fall, staying quite still not to arouse suspicion.

He must have slept, somehow, a dreamless sleep derived from extreme fatigue. He awoke at dusk to find the dead sergeant covered from head to toe in flies. A dog tore at another corpse further along the wall. Those that had been pleading for aid were now silent. Then Fortune remembered a detail which had eluded him for all these years. Someone was injured, beyond the wall, unlike the others, still very much alive. The man called for water, for help, quite calmly, not like the others had. Fortune remained hidden and silent, grasping his canteen tightly to his chest, an unwilling audience to the dying man's pleading. With sunlight dwindling fast, Fortune mustered all his courage in order to leave the confines of the wall and head back across the pontoon bridge towards safety. He stood, paused, walked for a few paces and then ran, hoping the injured man would not notice him in the near darkness.

A soldier clawed hopelessly at Fortune's leg having hauled himself up two steps to the landing of the dugout stairs, bringing Fortune back to the present with a start.

"Easy lad," Fortune smiled down at the mutilated youth.

He helped the boy down to the disgusting mattress he had been placed on, unclipped his water bottle and left it with the soldier. Fortune edged further into the dugout, through a tight corridor where two soldiers, with bandages wrapped about their eyes, stood smoking. The next chamber was equally filled with casualties, every available yard of floor was the resting place for a war-ravaged Tommie. The furniture had long since been moved up to the surface to help in the construction of barricades, giving the room the appearance of a crypt. The air was stale, choked with foul smells and smoke.

"Christ," Fortune exclaimed, thinking twice about adding to the putrid atmosphere with his own cigarette.

He found 2nd Lieutenant Richardson slumped in a chair along the back wall, at a small table staring into the fetid miasma. Richardson did not acknowledge his visitor standing over him, instead refilling a dusty glass with Schnapps from a dark green bottle with his left hand.

"You're drunk," Fortune snapped.

"You're impertinent," Richardson spat.

"Good God man, is this the time? We're getting battered up there. Your place is with the men!" Fortune raged.

"And detract from your moment of glory? Your chance to redeem yourself? No Sersant. I will be quite ineffective up there I assure you. By the time I leave here I will be injured, incapacitated, yes. A greater accolade to return after a day of such bravery with an injury is it not? I look to your experience on such matters Sersant."

"Why are you doing this - sir?" Fortune growled.

"How did you feel Sersant, watching us rush the gun at Loos last year? As we raced away into glory."

Richardson met Fortune's gaze with a stern stare. Fortune ground his teeth deciding not to reply.

"Helpless. Physically unable? Certainly. An invisible force denying your limbs their faculties. A pressure, no, a cloud thwarting any rational thought."

"Is this a question or statement - sir?"

Richardson smiled briefly and finished the glass, refilling it immediately.

"I'd offer you one but - any more Kraut bottles in here?"

Richardson gesticulated wildly with the glass, spilling its contents on the tabletop and floor beneath. With slow and methodical movements Fortune reached around his belt, walking his fingers along the leather, towards his trench knife, which, glistening in the candlelight, had been unceremoniously stowed at his waist. While Richardson's attention was focused on the bottom of his glass, Fortune surveyed the room quickly. None of the poor wretches here were in any fit state to be watching the unfolding scene.

"I shot him, Sersant," Richardson sighed.

"Who?" Fortune's hand stopped, poised over the hilt of the knife.

Richardson brought his right hand up from under the table where it had been, until now, out of sight. Brandishing his revolver, he pointed it towards the dark corner of the room. Fortune's hand dropped away from the knife in an instant. Lying with his head against the wall, blood covering his tunic, was a dead German.

"What of it?" Fortune puzzled.

"He was my captive, unarmed, pleading with me to spare his life. And still I shot him."

"Of all the men in France you're the least likely to quibble over murder, what difference does a stinking Kraut make to your list hey? Private Leake, Michael, the Paddies, Bernice," Fortune barked.

"Who is Private Leake?", Richardson frowned at Fortune in confusion, "Ah, the deserter at the contraband exchange, yes."

Fortune's body tensed and every sinew wanted to lash out and stab Richardson. Sensing this immediate threat, the officer levelled his revolver with a wry smile and Fortune backed away.

"Sergeant Fitch and his men at Loos. The boy Leake, Michael, the Irish nationalists, the farm girl and indeed the countless others who followed you on your personal endeavour today. When reckoning the numbers, their unfortunate demise was by your hands, either directly or indirectly. How many did you lose to reach me? A list superior in size to mine Sersant, no? A trail of misery, you have carved for yourself, there is no denying it.

People have a habit of ending up dead when you are around Sersant. You must understand that you and I, in many ways, are not that dissimilar. It should go without saying that your breeding is inferior, likewise your station and education are not the subject of my comparison I draw for you here. But, your journey of self-discovery shall we call it, shares such similarities, familiar paths along the same river of blood.

We enjoy the same passions it would seem, morally questionable, naturally. Why else would I seek to protect you for all this time? Others would have cast you out after your cowardice at Loos, brawling in Amiens, your audacious yet unforgivable actions on the practice march, or your insubordination on the raid, not to mention the attempted murder as we escaped. The York and Lancs were left unaided when you decided to flaunt your orders this morning, your petty feud with your officer, the only one here who understands who you really are, the only one who has shown willingness to aid you on your journey. All these things have put countless lives at risk."

Fortune took a further step back, bewildered. A pallid nervousness overcoming him as Richardson's account reached its end. Richardson stood, his previous gloom passing all too quickly, his facial features betraying a vaunted arrogance and guile which Fortune had been subjected to far too often.

"What is this? Another ruse or one of your flamboyant points of order?" Fortune spat, "We're nothing alike each other. Michael was a petty crook, not deserving of what you did. Leake was innocent as was the girl. The men followed me today out of loyalty, something you are yet to understand. My actions have a purpose while your motives are selfish and vile and only serve to amuse you in some perverted fashion."

"Self-righteous conceited nonsense and you know it," Richardson snarled, "The only difference between you and I is that you languish in regret. Remorse clouds your judgement and reveals itself in your cowardice. We live in a world so desensitised to murder that we find ourselves arguing the semantics of who's killings are justified and who has committed a crime. You tear yourself apart with this continual, cyclical argument, don't you? It's folly, Sersant. There is no separation here, only men that kill and men that would be killed."

Fortune's chin dropped to his chest with a sigh, his eyes tightly shut in grim contemplation. With a deep breath he suddenly reached with a fist towards the ceiling.

"You've made your point Mary, well done, now show yourself," Fortune raged.

"Ah yes, Private Merry, another name for the memorials of sacrifice which are etched into your soul," Richardson sneered.

As if related to the utterance of his name, a tremendous crash directly above was followed by a biblical thunder, shaking the room and its contents violently as a shell exploded on the surface. The ceiling splintered and groaned, dust falling throughout the chamber, snuffing the candles and plunging the dugout into darkness.

Fortune launched himself at Richardson, grabbing with both hands the wrist of the officer's pistol arm, forcing it backwards and skyward. The two men came together with a jolt, slamming against each other, both men jostled against their opponent's strength. A shot rang out, sending cement cascading over injured men while deafening the antagonist's hearing with a shrill ringing. The bright flash from the muzzle momentarily illuminated the grappling figures.

Fortune carried the momentum of his assault forward, smashing Richardson towards the table, which without resistance crumbled to fragments. Richardson let out a grunt as his back hit the wall. Fortune towered above him, still holding a tight grip on the pistol arm, thus exposing his right side. Identifying the weakness, Richardson jabbed with his left fist, pummelling Fortune's side with several well-placed strikes.

Fortune recoiled somewhat, spinning the tangled men on their axis. Another shot from the revolver reverberated around the chamber in a blinding flash. Fortune brought his forehead down onto Richardson's face in a brutal butting which left the officer bloodied and disorientated. Fortune could feel the grip on the revolver loosening, he mustered more strength to continue the hold above their heads. Richardson recovered and jabbed at Fortune with his free hand followed by a knee seeking out Fortune's groin. Lighters and then candles began to illuminate the room.

The tall sergeant delivered another devastating blow to Richardson's nose with his forehead and the South African went down, sliding to the floor, releasing the revolver which clattered to Fortune's feet. Blood streamed from Richardson's broken nose as he panted in a submissive posture, electing not to press the attack further. Fortune crouched, knees wide, seeking the revolver in the semi-darkness. It was shortly discovered and stashed securely in his belt behind him.

"I've had long to ponder the means of your death, you pompous prick," Fortune whispered at close quarters, "I am not known for my indecisions, but this, well I have been unusually hesitant."

Richardson spat blood over Fortune's boots.

"Ha! You sound like a pup but fight like a dog, I'll give you that - sir."

"Here's what I have planned for us. You'll carry me from this place Sersant," the officer demanded through his pain, "Your final actions as my pawn, I'll surely receive the Military Cross, it goes without saying I'll put you up for the MM for your trouble."

"No bribes can dissuade me, your poisoned plots are over. You'll die here," Fortune growled, reaching for his knife.

"Not if you want to know who killed the girl," Richardson grinned while meeting Fortune's fierce and vengeful stare in the shadowy gloom.

A short and sharp jab at Richardson's chin with the back of Fortune's forearm sent his eyes spinning into the back of his head, his limp body collapsing into Fortune's shaking arms.

Fortune emerged from the dugout into a scene of confusion and mayhem. Smoke billowed around the redoubt from a fire at the dugout's entrance. Dust from the renewed bombardment swirled amongst the corpses. Sporadic rifle fire and shouting disclosed the presence of soldiers close by. A stray bullet ricocheted off the timber frame beside Fortune's head, forcing the tall sergeant to crouch, protecting his trophy, which lay unconscious across his shoulders.

"Charlie! Charlie!"

Bounding out of the gloom the toothless wild man appeared. His uniform was crimson, collar to waist, a grim acknowledgement to the redcoats of previous wars.

"I'm leaving Charlie, with him. My business with him is my own, elsewhere."

"What? Are you fucking mad? We're holding 'ere for fuck's sake," Private Pocock fumed.

"Listen Charlie, if I don't do this now it will haunt me for the rest of my days."

"Stick him now, nobody will see nothing. Here use mine, she's all warmed up."

"No Charlie, listen to me, I'll slip up and over, along the wire, it'll give me the time I need with him, I'll find somewhere."

"Jesus fucking Christ, a bike a baker and a virgin!" exclaimed Private Pocock.

"What?!"

"Long story for another time," Private Pocock dismissed his exclamation with a grunt, "I'm coming with you."

"No you aren't! You're needed here, hold on or get 'em to safety."

"You're needed here, fuck sake, you get us to safety, the lads need you. You've lost your mind you selfish fucker, they died for you out there today. Ditch this useless piss pot and get back on it - you're running again ain't ya? That's what this is."

Charlie's words struck deep, pinpointing the old soldier's gnarled heart and slicing it in two with a single blow. Fortune froze, releasing his grip on Richardson who fell to the floor beneath the battered timber framed entrance. The battle mist swirled behind Private Pocock and for a moment Fortune thought he could see Private Merry, his bloodied arm hanging limply at his side, his face covered with dirt and grime, uniform smouldering. The grey-white fog framed the apparition as it stood there, unblinking and malevolent. Fortune squinted and rubbed his eyes, the smoke cloud billowed with a change in the breeze and any sign of the spectral casualty was gone.

Richardson and Charlie were right, Fortune realised with the sudden situational sobriety which flushed his mind in times of battlefield stress. His boiling personal vendetta had claimed lives and would earn him yet more tortured souls before the day was out if he did not change tact. The trench raid was repeating itself on a grander scale. Private Merry was the first but not the last to succumb to Fortune's turmoil. Between Richardson and himself they had notched up more death than a German flamethrower, spilling their incendiary machismo upon anyone in their unholy path. Two fiercely proud and stubborn men wreaking havoc around them over their selfish squabbles, against a backdrop of mass slaughter waged by equally overbearing and irreconcilable nations.

"Very well. Round up anyone who can still move Charlie, we're leaving."

"Alright, alright," Private Pocock nodded enthusiastically, "How will we get through?"

"We'll carve our way out. We're all moving on."

Chapter 33 - Final parting
No-Man's-Land

Fortune breathed a sudden sigh of relief, rubbing his hands together briskly as a builder celebrates the final brick of a newly constructed wall. His attention turned to the discarded cigarette packets around him, turning them out in quick succession only to be tossed unceremoniously into the lower confines of the shell hole. His hand reached carefully, deep into his tunic pocket where Bernice's last cigarette had waited patiently for an appropriate time to be of use. Lifting it reverently to his lips Fortune paused, leaving it hanging perilously in his dry mouth, unable yet to apply flame and condemn the artefact to its glorious death throws. A ship without a tide, it would have to wait patiently.

There had been no interruption from the boy for some time, which was curious considering his impetuous nature throughout the retelling of the story. With his nicotine focused fumbling at an end, Fortune's gaze fell back on the young lad who sat solemnly on the opposite side of the hole.

"Well?" Fortune probed, "No scriptures to quote? No logic to apply? Questions and procrastinating have ceased? Didn't expect that lad to be honest. The floor is yours, we await your wisdom, yet you are, for once, quiet."

"That's not the end, you know how this ends already," Percy announced finally, "Must you prolong this further Fortune? You're quite enjoying this aren't you?"

"Humour me boy, this may be the last time I get to tell my tale. I've grown accustomed to it, it's been with me for so long, my only comfort."

"No, the expression on your face betrays your true motive. Where there was scorn and resentment at the world there is excitement, almost joy. Life once more flickers in those piercing eyes. You are prolonging the hunt, yet, the end is close. The cigarette you have been toying with all this time is finally in the open, therefore, your final words are close and this pause is purely dramatic, serving no other purpose than a fleeting enjoyment."

"Very good, son. You've not lost your touch yet. So, how do we proceed? May I suggest, *The avenger of blood shall himself put the murderer to death; when he meets him, he shall put him to death.*[45]"

"Your knowledge of the scriptures surpasses your own admission on the subject."

"I may have had help over time, from those more highly educated."

Percy lent forward, clasping his knees within his arms as he perched on the incline of the hole.

"What happened next?"

"I kept to my word. I led them out of there, anyone who could. Those that couldn't we left behind. We followed the same route out that you and I took going in. Down the sap, crawling up and out over the bodies, through the wire, into the grass and here to the hole. We said our farewells, wished each other luck and they all slipped away into the grass to meet their own fate. Three lads remained with me, one of them injured, he'd been carried this far. Needed attention."

"Richardson?"

Fortune patted the head of the officer who lay next to him, the contorted corpse carrying an expression of revulsion at Fortune's disrespectful handling.

"Quite alive at the time I assure you."

"Did you kill him Fortune? Did you go through with it?"

"I had no reason to lad, he was right. My path was no more righteous than his. Pure selfish folly. Navigating this horror in the only way we know how, unjust, unconventional, immoral, selfish folly."

"But Bernice, you specifically sought revenge for Bernice."

"Aye, but he didn't do it, did he."

"How can you be sure he wasn't evading you?" Percy snapped impatiently.

"He made no effort to deny the others, Michael, the paddies. I could tell the inclusion of Bernice on his list of victims was not a welcome entry, out of place almost, unbecoming, like a tankard in a tea service. This is a man of principle not one of passion."

"After everything you have told me, you found a sudden desire to exercise forgiveness? I find this hard to believe, such concepts are lost on you, no, never had to be lost, I would say."

"I didn't forgive him, don't get me wrong, he was an almighty prick. The world would not weep to see the back of him, but neither would tears flow at my passing. He was a brave soldier, a clever officer. He had, in

---

[45] Numbers, Chapter 35, Verse 19, (NIV)

hindsight, given me more benefit of the doubt as anyone has ever bestowed. Yet the red haze of vengeance had blinded me to it, I'd have had an ally not an enemy if I'd ever reached out to take it. Now, let it be understood, with profound frequency when I found myself at this juncture in the story, I'd resolve it all by ending his life. But, after living through all of this, so many times, each traversal manipulates the story's ending, in some finite way. You'll understand eventually."

"If you didn't kill him, how did he end up in this repose?"

"Oh. We were shelled, soon after we'd all slipped out of the line. No heroics, no final clash, no biblical engagement between good and evil. Just shells raining down causing a nuisance. I pulled him over me as one exploded, right above us, used him as a professionally tailored sandbag. Those wretches down there bought it in the blast while patching that lad up and Richardson was torn up badly to boot.

That's how these things end, no punch line, no sunsets, no great speeches denouncing adversity. Just four men randomly torn apart by white hot metal, fired here by another man, miles away, who will never know who or how many he has killed. He'll sleep well all the same. No remorse. It's like you said lad, when you're on the right side, doing the right thing, its glorious work. There's no shame in it, it's proud work for most of us. But when you fall from that grace and your path is shadowed by questionable motives, you're just a murderer with a gnawing conscience."

"We're back here?"

"Yes we are! Damn well we are," Fortune growled, "This is what it's always been about. This choreographed yarn, my own form of scripture to force a point of order. War is war, vengeance is murder. Percy Trevis, Vicar's son. Son to the man I left to the birds in South Africa."

"How long have you known?" Percy slumped back onto the incline.

"I think I knew who you were from the start, the likeness is not surprising, just took me some time to piece it together, well, alright an eternity. The face glaring at me from the line of Tommies at the farm, such hatred in those young eyes. There's not much in life that will fuel such rage, a loved one, family, had to be someone close. That's where you saw her isn't it? That's the moment your heart was set on retribution.

And here, employing your scriptures, the words of others not your own, the words of your father, filling my boots with guilt, remorse at my cowardice, when all along it was you, your vengeance not mine, that was the centre of this hell I have lived through. Besides, there was honour in him to the last, he whispered it to me, his final breath. Vicar's son. Same two words on the tormented lips of Berner-Potts this morning."

Percy sat forward once more, moisture lining his eyes, his expression was stoic and his gaze distant.

"He made it home, he didn't die where you abandoned him. But, he was not the same man that set out with God's love in his heart. I was too young to really know him before his war, but I do remember a warmth, safety, just a distant feeling like recalling the rays from a previous summer's sun. His faith was in tatters in the years I do remember with painful alacrity. He would sob after Sunday sermons, guilt I would surmise, for portraying himself falsely with his parishioners. There was violence, on occasion. Behind closed doors of course. I was not scathed, he assumed I was asleep when mother would reluctantly soak up his rage as it was spilt. He killed himself Fortune," Percy began to cry silently, "Can you imagine the shame? A vicar none-the-less, committing the ultimate sin in the house of Christ."

"I've known many do the same lad, once they've come out. Sometimes a soldier needs to stand down, the sins we must observe too heavy a burden to keep resisting. There is no shame in sacrifice. Many of us wish to die here upon the field, as we know what lies ahead out there is worse still. Those brief glimpses of life beyond the army, away from here, when on leave, fill me with more dread than an exploding shell."

"I'm not sorry for what I did," Percy blurted, "I'd do it again if given the chance. To sit here and hear your pain at her passing. The pain you passed to me I give back."

"Aye, I know. I know that feeling too well. Plenty of eyes and teeth around here to pluck out before there's fair reckoning, I'd say. Burn for burn, wound for wound, bruise for bruise. It will eat you up lad, consume you and spit you out before you are ready to move on, but I'm guessing, your journey towards that distant light has been greatly accelerated today. My part in it though, is more than complete."

Fortune retrieved the embossed lighter from his pocket and lit the cigarette that had been eternally patient. Percy looked somewhat stunned at the premature gesture.

"That's it?" Percy spat.

"Aye, that's it. Let me smoke now."

"We're not finished."

"I am. I'll not dissuade you from the rage you still embrace boy. How could I? I'll not fuel the fire for you, it's got some time to burn I'll wager. Our time here, our story, someday you'll come to terms with, as I have. Your folly will consume you until you do. What's done is done. My own turmoil is settled, paid up in full, but my journey's an old one, yours is just beginning, now fucking shut up and let me enjoy her."

Percy's expression changed suddenly as a thought exploded through his mind.

"The lighter, you gave it to her that night."

Fortune replied only with a grim smile, ignoring the boy's plea for further dialogue, instead projecting his voice out of the shell hole, "I'm ready."

"I believe you are, old friend," came a familiar voice from above.

Although Fortune could not perceive Private Merry standing atop the crater rim, his striking form filling the surroundings with a soft radiance, the memories of him being there were now real, although their source could not be pinpointed in the mind of the old man who stood beside him. The old man gazed into the hole in wonder, had he seen Private Merry as a younger man, he thought he may have, but the memories now prevalent were, he concluded, figments of his present rather than of his past. Like the image in a fairground hall of mirrors his mind stretched out across time warping the truth as he searched for answers.

"Which memory came first? Him or me? And, how many times have you brought me here, dear friend?"

Without responding Private Merry assisted the old man on his steep descent into the muddy cavity, frail and uncertain of his footing, but with the aid of the soldier safely escorted to a clear patch of earth onto which he slowly seated, distant sensory memories returning to him of the fetid, earthen cavity.

"What will happen to him Mary?" the old man asked, pointing at the lifeless body of Percy which had slumped awkwardly to one side.

"Would you prefer an answer if I told you you'll not remember it?" the soldier enquired quietly.

"Perhaps not. How do I normally answer?"

"We don't have long enough to answer you respectfully," Private Merry chortled.

"Hmmm. I've helped many this way, haven't I?" the old man chose his next question carefully.

"Many are worth saving, are they not old friend? And there are many to save."

"Without doubt they must be, with what we went through back then. I must say this to you though, and I'll not deny them the chance, goodness knows I need my penance but," the old man lingered on his words.

"I have not forgotten your request."

"So, how many times must I serve you until I can see them?"

"I have not forgotten your request, as you ask it of me every time. And every time old friend, it is granted. Look, do you remember? Darkness falls and you leave the shell hole."

"Yes, of course."

"There, you see the bargain is honoured. Fate would have you dashed apart with the others, when the shell explodes, another casualty on that insidious day. Instead, you return from death and your son you will see.

Our arrangement is concrete old man and always shall be. You have already claimed your reward, many times over."

The old man sat in silence now, a single tear navigating the deep ravines of his weathered face, watching Fortune gathering his precious items into a soldier's pack. A Very light raced across the dusk drawn sky, bursting into brilliance as desultory rifle fire cracked over the wheezing valley. Life, or rather the vibrancy of death, had returned to the world outside of the shell hole. Men called out for help, for water, for their mothers and sweethearts. Most would not receive a satisfactory response that night to any of their demands.

Fortune, unscathed and determined to live, grabbed the ostentatious German pipe and clambered out of the crater, into the grass and darkness beyond.

Epilogue

Chapter 34 - The Watchers' gathering
20th May 1926
St Andrews Church, Church Hill
Clevedon, Somerset

Fortune emerged from the simple arched doorway and stood for a while before the entrance. He pulled his tattered great coat around him as he stood looking up at the church tower, ignoring the warming rays of the sun over-head. A chill raced through his bones; the thick coat could not abate the gelid sensation spreading from the traveller's heart. In his hand he clutched at a book, its cover worn and spine bruised. A solitary seagull soared above the cemetery calling with a baleful wail. Fortune's attention was dissuaded from the steady lines of the tower as the bird flew effortlessly overhead on the coastal breeze. His gaze fell upon the stones of the church yard as he began his slow amble up the path between the graves. Passing between the motley collection of Victorian headstones, his eye was drawn to a grave by its beautifully uniform headstone, its white stone surface gleaming triumphantly in the midday light. He walked slowly towards it, as he had for so many in the recent years, coming to a stop a few yards from its exquisitely carved face.

Fortune sighed and removed a cigarette. He searched with his right hand into the deep pocket of his coat, retrieving a disk-shaped lighter from within. Once lit he produced a short bottle from inside his left pocket, still wrapped in brown paper, its label obscured from view. His shame would be hidden from the seagulls and the dead this day. He frantically imbibed a significant quantity of its contents before shuddering and coughing uncontrollably. Having doubled up to release the inner demon, he took a final long drag on the still young cigarette, stubbing it out with his foot and cursing to himself as his lungs heaved once more to rid him of their dark burden. He walked on by the grave, resting his hand momentarily on its peak.

Beyond the cemetery, Fortune climbed a short rise to the edge of the path and stopped at the summit to look out over the Bristol channel. Visibility was perfect, the Welsh coast was clear to his view. Several coal ships fought against the powerful tide while two small, white sailed, pleasure boats wound their way up towards the river Avon, tacking into the wind much to the enjoyment of their leisurely occupants.

Fortune's head twitched to one side, instinctively recognising movement to his right. In an instant his chest pounded into action; his senses became focused. A dog and its owner crested the top of the hill fort which presided above the church and its grounds. Fortune stiffened as the pair approached, the dog walker raised his cap in greeting as he went by, Fortune's instincts again took president, avoiding the walker's eyes by looking away nervously.

Fortune descended the slope, keeping the cliff to his left, no barrier existed to keep him from falling to the seaweed covered rocks below. A barrier would have been no worthy prevention to Fortune's desires should he have wished to answer the call of death which lay heavily in his soul. Further on, Fortune came to a high stone wall which bisected his passage with an arched wooden doorway, set into its length beside a castellated tower, built on the very edge of the cliff. The short tower sported large arched windows which looked out over Salthouse Bay and the channel beyond. Passing through the wooden door he continued his descent towards the sea front at Clevedon, around the headland and into full view of the town. He stood and scrutinised the settlement with eyes full of distrust and anxiety at what he might discover here.

Georgian houses lined the hill side, the skyline punctuated by trees as if the town itself had grown from within a forest, set beside this ancient shore. In the distance a lone motor car trundled along Elton Road, passing in front of Clevedon Court. He could see people, walking in groups, couples, making their way slowly along the promenade. A cricket match was in play on a large expanse of grass where the salt flats had once been. The breeze carried with it the sounds of a brass band, a spectre of a time now passed, Fortune assumed, a time of joy and happiness buried so deep in the unrelenting egress of time. The breeze shifted and the music was gone.

Fortune moved quietly through the trees above the Salthouse Hotel and peered down through the vegetation at the scene below. He could hear voices, muffled by the distance, their threat once more enraging his senses. Several men were below him, of unknown intention. He decided to wait for them to leave, until his passage into the town was safe. Fortune sat nursing the short bottle and smoking his cigarettes. He occasionally turned to his small book for comfort, but every time he opened its pages the words would not come to him. Frustrated he closed its cover and returned to the aid of his injury's efficacious crutches. Fortune waited patiently as a hunter watches his prey. The revellers below spent the next hour and several pints of cider thwarting his progress.

Once the group of drinkers had departed, Fortune stood, without rubbing the dirt from his coat, he proceeded down towards the path which would take him along the sea front. Emerging from the trees he squinted in the sun light, turned and entered the wood once more, only to re-emerge moments later with a deep frown upon his face. Once more he stopped, fists clenched in his pockets. He turned part way back towards the safety of the woods but stopped himself from moving any further. Closing his eyes tightly Fortune prayed for courage, which he found in the remaining liquid he carried in his left pocket. The walk ahead was arduous.

He passed couples and families, dog walkers and cyclists. Each group was a potential threat and he scrutinised their approach carefully. As they drew near, he stepped away from the path to allow them plenty of room, all the while his jackknife was poised to act in his tightly gripped hand within a coat pocket. The kind folk of Clevedon paid him little attention, the occasional prolonged glance or bark from a dog being the only interjection on his journey, yet the journey was fraught with anxiety for Fortune. He was, however, soon walking through Littleharp bay and Green Beach where the bandstand was a source of mesmerising entertainment for tourists and locals alike.

People sat with parasols and blankets enjoying the band while children chased their toys beneath the wind warped trees which lined this part of the front. The band struck out their tones dressed proudly in blue uniforms, some of the members wearing medals upon their chests. The band master, with his large sweeping grey moustache, twitched and swept his sticks through the air with full gusto, as if his very life depended on his abilities. Yet Fortune felt no joy here, only desperation and loathing and soon moved on, giving the civilians a wide berth by negotiating the obstruction beneath some shadowy trees beside the road.

Fortune used the road to keep him from most of the people who were enjoying the summer's day, progressing further along Elton road to where the beach road dissected it. At the junction he stared in wonder at how the scene had changed since his last visit in 1914. The old auction house on the corner was now "Alonzo Dawes and Son Estate Agents" and where horses and carts had once trotted in procession, blissfully ignoring the scenery on their way to the rail head or factory, motor cars now parked, facing out to sea, in a uniform line as if waiting for inspection for a parish prize. People were everywhere, with no apparent purpose or calling other than to worship their own social liberation.

Fortune crossed the road and took time to reflect at the South African war memorial which stood there. A proud column of purple marble topped with a sphere and bearing the names of local men who had perished in that forgotten and overshadowed conflict. Escaping the bustle of the sea front Fortune progressed at a greater pace down Seavale road, a quieter, more cramped thoroughfare devoid of humans. Safety, however, was not a guarantee in such surroundings. Fortune looked at each window, each doorway as if a threat were to appear from them without warning. Behind every lace window drape lurked a hidden sniper, behind every door and wooden gate a machine gun crew readied their weapon. Fortune's grip on his jackknife became painful as he moved down the street.

He looked all about him, over his shoulder, spinning and searching for the elusive enemy. He stumbled near the gate to a three-story dwelling, his clumsy feet knocking milk bottles into the street with a high-pitched clatter. His mind fixated on a bottle, rolling slowly across the road, rolling on and on, time slowing to a crawl as the device lost momentum, turning over, for one, last, time. Fortune doubled up instinctively, grabbing the back of his head, his arms contorted over his face. He pressed his body against the brick pillar of the gate, it was too late to seek cover. The milk bottle stopped by the far curb but did not explode.

Fortune wept. He sat leaning against the pillar with his knees drawn up against his chest, his head in his hands. Shaking fingers retrieved a cigarette from his pocket, stopping short of administering his treatment. There he sat, holding the disk-shaped lighter, turning it over in his hand, inspecting its surface with both eyes and thumb. The regimental badge of the Somerset Light Infantry was rubbed clean of grime and tarnish, its surface smooth and shining, a stark contrast to the dull brass lighter it was affixed to. He had come so far, the end of his journey was in sight, however, there he sat, without the fortitude to continue.

"I didn't know you came," confessed Private Merry solemnly, while perched on the edge of the old man's bed, "Why didn't you make yourself known?"

"I couldn't. Easier to watch from a far. Watching the 'Watchers'. I saw you there, standing in the front garden observing your mother as they left for the church. I could not approach; it didn't feel appropriate. You looked smart, in your parade ground best, buttons gleaming, boots polished. A grand show," the old man smiled in encouragement, "Once they were out of sight you turned and were gone."

"Every year I watched over her on that day. Until. Less of a fuss made before long, you know, when the other war came. She would still walk up to the memorial, but always alone by then. I stopped going, I forget why."

Private Merry looked up at the old man.

"Why did it take you ten years?" he scowled.

The old man sighed and relented any attempt to make excuses.

"What happened? After they had gone?" Private Merry demanded.

"The poem you had handed me that day, as you lay dying, I had kept it in a book, safe, for when the time came. I posted it through her door."

"Cowardly," Private Merry snapped.

The light bulb above flickered impatiently.

"Yes," the old man relented.

"And the lighter?"

"I had always planned to return it Mary, you must believe me I did. But standing there at the door, rubbing it between my fingers, I realised it was now a part of who I was. It was my cross to bear, my crown of thorns, my nine-inch nail. Not a day went by when it failed to remind me of what had happened."

"Do you have anything more to say old man? It's time. I will be leaving now. There are others who need our help," Private Merry responded solemnly.

"Wait just a while Mary, one last story before you go," pleaded the old man.

Fortune made his way down the hill towards the sea front once more. The streetlamps were now blazing their soft illumination over nocturnal charges below. Approaching the road which ran along the beach to Clevedon Pier, Fortune could hear laughter, voices and strange upbeat music issuing from a public house on the corner. Taxis trundled along the thoroughfare and a bus laden with visitors prepared for the steep climb out of the town to the north.

Crossing the road quickly, Fortune made his way onto the promenade. The last rays of light were struggling against the Sun's decent into the deep waters of the estuary, the final essence of the day sucked beneath the horizon like doomed sailors dragged down by their stricken ship. Having stared in wonder at the sunset, Fortune made his way down onto the pebble beach where a causeway struck out from civilisation down into the cold waters of the Bristol Channel. Lights, visible on the far side of the estuary, flickered like stars in the evening gloom. Fortune clambered down from the esplanade and made his way across the rocks to the base of the pier. While the gas lamps dazzled and sparkled along the length of the structure, carrying its occupants safely through the darkness to the pavilion at its furthest extremity, another fire burned beneath their feet. The dancing flame of a campfire, within the iron cage of struts and supports, drew Fortune closer.

He approached with caution, out of respect for what he knew lay ahead. Figures, motionless at first, slowly began to rise to their feet and turn to face him. Acknowledging their glances, he joined the congregation, sitting precariously on a large rock. The men passed a bottle between the group. Each in turn taking a gulp of its harsh content.

"To Mary," a dishevelled, bearded man announced in a croaky voice.

"Private Merry," said another, raising the bottle to the sky.

"Mary," Fortune took his communion and passed the bottle to the next veteran.

Once the ritual was complete Fortune brought out his small book and in the orange light of the campfire read verse from its pages.

> "*Old Yew, which graspest at the stones*
> *That name the under-lying dead,*
> *Thy fibres net the dreamless head,*
> *Thy roots are wrapt about the bones.*
>
> *The seasons bring the flower again,*
> *And bring the firstling to the flock;*
> *And in the dusk of thee, the clock*
> *Beats out the little lives of men.*
>
> *O, not for thee the glow, the bloom,*
> *Who changest not in any gale,*
> *Nor branding summer suns avail*
> *To touch thy thousand years of gloom:*
>
> *And gazing on thee, sullen tree,*
> *Sick for thy stubborn hardihood,*
> *I seem to fail from out my blood*
> *And grow incorporate into thee.*[46]"

Private Merry sat once more, staring intently at the old man, the bulb above dimming itself to a soft light.

"You met there, every year?" Private Merry enquired softly.

"Yes, until nobody was left."

"Who?"

"Cartwright, Connor, Stendhurst, Shaw."

"Tell me about them, please."

---

[46] In Memoriam A.H.H. OBIIT MDCCCXXXIII:2 by Alfred Lord Tennyson, 1849

"Cartwright would sit there with his potato peels, his old large army pack full of them. Spent most of the day wondering the streets, going through bins, collecting the peels and other kitchen rubbish. He'd been a prisoner, in Germany. Right at the end of the war, taken when they came over in the March of eighteen. There wasn't any food for prisoners you see, their people were starving, there was nothing to share. Affected him, you know?

He couldn't stand to see anything go to waste. Was just skin and bones even then, he never fully regained it. Wasn't much for conversation at that time, so we left him to his thoughts and his potato peels. But he'd made the trip down from Birmingham or wherever it was he called home. Walked the whole God damned way too. Didn't see him after 1930, 1931, something like that. Heard he had passed away, drowned in a canal up there."

"Go on."

"Stendhurst, the bearded one, terrible state of a human being, but that was his choice, not fortune's luck," explained the old man, "Word had it he inherited quite a tidy sum of money, house, grounds, car you name it. A wealthy uncle, industrialist or something. Had made a packet at the start of the war stockpiling equipment to sell back to the War Office. But, Stendhurst never even saw the place, wasn't interested. Roamed the country, working farms as labour, until his limbs gave out. Sold his medals rather than take any of the family money. It all passed to his niece when he went. Not long after I recall, the same year. The gas got him see, he had this terrible cough, he couldn't shake it."

The old man paused but the private said nothing, waiting for the natural flow of the old man's story to proceed.

"Shaw, well you didn't know him, did you? He would always come, he felt guilty see, was one of the last ones through the wire the night of the trench raid and always said it was his fault for not coming back when he heard the bomb that killed you. Always said he could have done something, daft of course, but when a man gets something in his head, well you know. He'd been with Corporal Hamblin when he went down, on the dash across the lines on 1st July. He stayed with Henry while he died, in a shell hole. Was making his way back that night when a shell caught him. He had a family, they came to terms with his injury, amazing what the doctors did with those chaps, rebuilding them. He was an usher in a cinema, you know in the dark so nobody could see his face."

"And Richard Connor, tell me what happened to Richard, he was kind to me."

"Connor bought it in seventeen, up at Ypres, the big show there, drowned in the mud they said trying to pull another chap out of the mire. But he used to come along none-the-less, every year without fail."

Chapter 35 - Dusk
1st July 1996
Blighty Valley Cemetery
Authuille Wood
Somme

The coach drew up on the roadside verge and decanted its precious cargo to the freshly cut grass path which would take them down to Blighty Valley Cemetery. Old soldiers, many helped by relatives or officials, proceeded slowly towards the iron gate of the Commonwealth War Graves cemetery. Looking about them the veterans imagined the valley when they had last seen it, devoid of trees, scarred with craters and littered with discarded equipment and damaged vehicles. One old soldier pointed to the middle of the field which buffeted against the beautifully presented pathway, indicating with his frail hands where the light railway used to run, beside the dressing station. Others chose not to speak at all.

Passing through the low stone gateposts the party spread out into the rectangular cemetery, seeking gravestones of specific importance to the visitors. The rows of white stone grave markers gleamed proudly in the sunlight.

The old man quietly surveyed the visitors as they shuffled through the stones. He caught the eye of another Watcher and smiled in acknowledgement. Children ran between the plots, laughing and playing, their innocent excitement bringing life and joy to the seldom visited spot. The tall trees above swayed their branches in positive affirmation. But the other Watcher, beyond the groups, stood with clenched fists at his side, his expression having changed to one of disgust and anger, the invasion of this sanctuary an objectionable act.

The old man chose to ignore his distant incorporeal companion and instead moved amongst the visitors. He peered inquisitively over the shoulders of sobbing relatives to read the inscriptions they had placed on wooden crosses or to inspect the photographs they had brought with them of men in sepia uniforms from a time long ago. He felt the joy of the fallen surge through the earth as their families knelt to place wreaths onto graves in sombre remembrance.

Birds tweeted and chirped in the branches of the old trees which flanked the cemetery. The old man listened to their song for a while, allowing the warm sun to heat his cold face. The site was tranquil and at peace, colourful arrangements of blooming flowers filled every gap between the stones yet, beneath the vibrant reds and yellows of the roses there were thorns, hidden but dangerous. The old man could sense the others who watched, those who had chosen to remain unseen. This was the moment for the righteous, it was theirs to command, while the cold places of the cemetery, of which there were several, bore no visitors to them.

The coach pulled slowly away, its passengers aboard once more. The old man stood on the verge and stared longingly at the vehicle until it disappeared from view. He chose not to linger, for the evening was drawing in. He moved silently down the long turf path, through the iron gates and into the cemetery once more. With slow but determined steps he paced the stones arriving at his favourite. With a wrinkled hand he comforted the surface of the white shrine.

263878 PRIVATE
G. MERRY
SOMERSET LIGHT INFANTRY
20TH MAY 1916 AGED 19

At the base of the stone several words were obscured by plants. The old man slowly crouched, steadying himself against the gravestone. With gentle movements he cleared the plants away, revealing the epitaph beneath.

DEATH OPENS UNKNOWN DOORS

As a chilled breeze whipped up around the cemetery, the old man rose, his essence vanishing into the treetops, swirling with the leaves of the steadfast canopy, as the sun receded behind a blood-red horizon. The silent vigil continued below, the rows of stones standing proudly to attention as the final light of the day cast great shadows before them. Atop Private Merry's stone, a circular object glinted in the last precious moments of dusk.

About the author

Writer, historian, family history researcher, battlefield tour guide, wargamer, husband, father and home office hermit, Daveran Baulch lives in North Somerset surrounded by books, paintings, artefacts, uniforms and weapons from the First World War period. Daveran spent his childhood years in Street, Somerset, attending Millfield School where a passion for writing was cultivated. Dusty boxes in the attic still contain half-finished short stories, printed on a dot matrix printer, using fledgling word processing software in the days of the ZX Spectrum and BBC Model B computers.

Daveran left Somerset in 1993, attending Nottingham University, where he met his wife Vicky. They settled in the city, both embarking on a successful career within the pharmaceutical industry, raising two daughters, Mia and Poppy. In their youth the clubs and bars of Nottingham were a significant draw, the green fields and relaxed pace of Somerset life a distant memory for Daveran amongst the bustle of traffic, incinerator chimneys and brickwork terraces.

Returning to Somerset in 2014, near the town of Clevedon, the subtleties and pleasures of rural living in the South West, ignored and unappreciated in his youth, at a time when bright lights and noise were a significant lure to a country boy, were once again prevalent and cherished.

Flat feet and asthma had denied him the honour of following his ancestors into service, however, Daveran chose to repay a perceived debt, by researching soldiers of the Great War, at first exploring his own family history in which both great grandfathers and 16 other relatives served during the conflict. Having gained experience in the field of research, absorbing as much knowledge as possible from a formidable collection of reference books on the subject, the natural progression was to offer research and education as a service for those who yearned to know more about the lives and deaths of their relatives. Daveran's passion had begun to carve a path into the world of WW1 history and remembrance thereof.

In 2013 Daveran hosted history talks and a research group at work, culminating in a tour of the battlefields of Belgium and France, uniting relatives with the stories and graves of great uncles and great-grandfathers. As interest surged during 2014-2018, Daveran conducted battlefield tours throughout 2015 then changed focus from singular research to concentrate on the Battle of the Sambre, 1918, organising and hosting a large commemorative event, gathering relatives of the dead in the village of Locquignol, France on 4th November 2018.

Having absorbed so much from the stories of the fallen, a work of fiction on the subject became a reality in 2016 when the "sergeant in a shell hole" concept was born. The early stages of the novel came in fits of activity, delimited by long periods of sluggishness, exhaustive work within the pharmaceutical industry often depleting any energy or motivation to continue with the novel. However, annual leave and the occasional weekend alone at home enabled the book to develop. For the Easter week of 2019, Daveran journeyed to the Somme battlefields once more, armed with laptop, cheese and enough red wine to sink the Lusitania. It was here, in the idyllic setting of Le Clos du Clocher, Gueudecourt, that Fortune's Turmoil entered its final draft.

Email: dgbaulch.author@gmail.com
Facebook: www.facebook.com/daveran.baulchauthor
LinkedIn: linkedin.com/in/daveran-baulch

Fortune will return.

Printed in Great Britain
by Amazon

50171138R00173